Thomas Wentworth Higginson

English History for Americans

Thomas Wentworth Higginson

English History for Americans

ISBN/EAN: 9783741186875

Manufactured in Europe, USA, Canada, Australia, Japa

Cover: Foto ©ninafisch / pixelio.de

Manufactured and distributed by brebook publishing software (www.brebook.com)

Thomas Wentworth Higginson

English History for Americans

FOR

AMERICANS

BY

THOMAS WENTWORTH HIGGINSON

AUTHOR OF "YOUNG FOLKS' HISTORY OF THE UNITED STATES," ETC.

AND

EDWARD CHANNING

ASSISTANT PROFESSOR OF HISTORY IN HARVARD UNIVERSITY

NEW YORK
LONGMANS, GREEN, AND CO.
15 EAST SIXTEENTH STREET
1894

Copyright, 1893,
BY LONGMANS, GREEN, AND CO.

University Press:
JOHN WILSON AND SON, CAMBRIDGE, U. S. A.

PREFACE.

THE name "English History for Americans," which suggests the key-note of this book, is based on the simple fact that it is not the practice of American readers, old or young, to give to English history more than a very limited portion of their hours of study. However much we may regret this fact, it is undeniable. This being the case, it seems clear that such readers will use their time to the best advantage if they devote it mainly to those events in English annals which have had the most direct influence on the history and institutions of our own land. For instance, an English reader might regard the acquisition of the Indian Empire as an event rivalling in importance the rise and growth of Puritanism in the English Church; but there can be no comparison in the relative importance of these two events to an American. Every American sees in the rise of Puritanism an essential factor in the creation of the thirteen colonies, while the Indian Empire is simply a matter of curiosity or wonder. The authors of this book have therefore boldly ventured to modify in their narrative the accustomed scale of proportion; while it has been their wish, in the treatment of every detail, to accept the best result of modern English investigation, and especially to avoid all unfair or one-sided judgments. The career of England is too important in the history of the human race to be handled in any petty or partisan spirit.

THE AUTHORS.

A LIST OF SOME USEFUL BOOKS FOR CONSULTATION.

Books suitable for young students are marked with an asterisk.

BIBLIOGRAPHIES.

This list is in no sense a complete list of authorities. For such information, reference should be made to the following: —

ALLEN, WM. F. *The Reader's Guide to English History.*

GARDINER AND MULLINGER. *English History for Students.* — Contains an historical sketch by Gardiner, and a comprehensive bibliography by Mullinger.

Lists may also be found prefixed to the first three volumes of Bright's *English History*, and in Gardiner's *Student's History*, pp. 100, 172, 288, 359, 480, 577, 648, 744, 818, 890, 972.

GENERAL WORKS.

ACLAND AND RANSOME. *Handbook in Outline of the Political History of England.* — Arranged in three parallel columns, with topical summaries at the end. The most useful book of its kind for teachers and readers.

LONGMANS' *Summary of English History.*

GARDINER, S. R. *A Student's History of England.* 1023 pages. — The best single-volume history of England, profusely illustrated, but without maps. The latter are provided in the following volume: —

GARDINER, S. R. *Atlas of English History.* — Contains 88 maps or plans.

BREWER, J. S., Editor. *The Student's Hume.*

GREEN, J. R. *A Short History of the English People.* 1 vol.
— Also printed in parts, and in a profusely illustrated edition in three volumes.

MACAULAY, LORD. *History of England.* — The introductory matter in vol. i. is especially valuable.

MAHAN, A. T. *The Influence of Sea Power on History.*

GREEN, JOHN RICHARD, Editor. *Readings from English History.*

WHEELER, A. M., Editor. *Sketches from English History.*

Among the longer works may be mentioned, —

BRIGHT, G. F. *A History of England.* 4 vols. I., 449-1485 (pp. 354); II., 1485-1688 (pp. 449); III., 1689-1837 (pp. 666); IV., 1837-1880 (pp. 577). — Well supplied with maps and tables.

GREEN, J. R. *A History of the English People.* 4 vols.

KNIGHT, CHARLES. *Popular History of England.* — Profusely illustrated.

POWELL, F. YORK } *History of England, for the Use of Schools.*
TOUT, T. F.

In Three Parts. With Maps and Plans.

    Part I. *From the Earliest Times to the Death of Henry VII.* By F. YORK POWELL.

    Part III. *William and Mary to the Present Time.* By T. F. TOUT.

POWELL, F. YORK, Editor. *English History from Contemporary Writers;* especially

    ASHLEY, W. J. *Edward III.*

    HUTTON, W. H. *Misrule of Henry III.*

    HUTTON, W. H. *Simon of Montfort.*

    HUTTON, W. H. *S. Thomas of Canterbury.*

HENDERSON, E. F. *Select Historical Documents from the Middle Ages.* — The first 165 pp. contain documents illustrating English history before 1349.

GARDINER, S. R. *Documents illustrating the Puritan Rebellion.*

Among the books designed for children the following may be mentioned, —

* CREIGHTON, LOUISE. *A First History of England.* Illustrated.

* GARDINER, S. R. *English History for Young Folks.*

* YONGE, CHARLOTTE M. *Young Folks' History of England.*

*FISHER, Mrs. ARABELLA B. [BUCKLEY]. *History of England for Beginners.*
*CREIGHTON, MANDELL, Editor. *Epochs of English History.* 1 vol.

Also printed separately in eight small cloth-covered volumes with the following titles:—

POWELL, F. YORK. *Early England to the Norman Conquest.*
CREIGHTON, Mrs. MANDELL. *England a Continental Power, from the Conquest to the Great Charter.*
ROWLEY, JAMES. *The Rise of the People, and the Growth of Parliament.*
CREIGHTON, MANDELL. *The Tudors and the Reformation.*
GARDINER, Mrs. S. R. *The Struggle against Absolute Monarchy.*
ROWLEY, JAMES. *The Settlement of the Constitution.*
TANCOCK, Rev. O. W. *England during the American and European Wars.*
BROWNING, OSCAR. *Modern England.*

SPECIAL WORKS.

Arranged chronologically according to contents.

FREEMAN, E. A. *Old English History.*
HUGHES, THOMAS. *Life of King Alfred.*
FREEMAN, E. A. *William the Conqueror* (Twelve English Statesmen).
*FREEMAN, E. A. *A Short History of the Norman Conquest.*
STUBBS, W. *Early Plantagenets* (Epochs of History).
GREEN, Mrs. J. R. *Henry II.* (Twelve English Statesmen).
MAURICE, C. E. *Stephen Langton* (English Popular Leaders Series).
LONGMAN, W. *Edward III.*
OMAN, C. W. C. *The Art of War in the Middle Ages.*
ASHLEY, W. J. *An Introduction to English Economic History.*
SELIGMAN, E. R. A. *Two Chapters in the History of the Mediæval Guilds of England.*
PALGRAVE, Sir F. *The Merchant and the Friar.*
SEEBOHM, F. *The Oxford Reformers* (Colet, Erasmus. More).

A LIST OF SOME USEFUL BOOKS

CREIGHTON, MANDELL. *Cardinal Wolsey* (Twelve English Statesmen).
CREIGHTON, MANDELL. *The Age of Elizabeth* (Epochs of History).
BEESLEY, E. S. *Queen Elizabeth* (Twelve English Statesmen).
PAYNE. *Elizabethan Seamen.*
CORDERY, B. M. (Mrs. S. R. Gardiner) AND PHILLPOTTS. *The King and Commonwealth.*
GARDINER, S. R. *The Puritan Revolution* (Epochs of History).
SMITH, GOLDWIN. *Three English Statesmen* (John Pym, Oliver Cromwell, William Pitt).
BOYLE, G. D. *Selections from Clarendon's History of the [Puritan] Rebellion.*
GUIZOT, F. *Oliver Cromwell.*
HARRISON, FREDERIC. *Oliver Cromwell* (Twelve English Statesmen).
CARLYLE, THOMAS. *Letters and Speeches of Oliver Cromwell.*
HANNAY, D. *Admiral Blake.*
TRAILL, H. D. *William III.* (Twelve English Statesmen).
LECKY, W. E. H. *History of England in the Eighteenth Century.* 8 vols. — A new and convenient edition has been published, in which the portions dealing more particularly with Ireland are printed separately.
MORRIS, E. E. *The Age of Anne* (Epochs of History).
MORLEY, JOHN. *Sir Robert Walpole* (Twelve English Statesmen).
TREVELYAN, G. O. *Early History of Charles James Fox.*
ROSEBERY, LORD. *William Pitt* (Twelve English Statesmen).
RUSSELL, W. CLARK. *Lord Nelson.*
MARTINEAU, HARRIET. *History of England during the Thirty Years' Peace* (1816-46).
WALPOLE, SPENCER. *A History of England from the Conclusion of the Great War in 1815* (to 1857).
MCCARTHY, J. *Epoch of Reform* (Epochs of History).
MCCARTHY, J. *A History of our Own Times.*
THURSFIELD. *Robert Peel.*
MORLEY, JOHN. *Richard Cobden.*
FROUDE, J. A. *Lord Beaconsfield.*

CONSTITUTIONAL WORKS.

AMOS, SHELDON. *A Primer of the English Constitution and Government.*
MONTAGUE, F. C. *The Elements of English Constitutional History.*
* CREIGHTON, LOUISE. *The Government of England.*
* FONBLANQUE, A. DE. *How we are governed.*
RANSOME, C. *Rise of Constitutional Government in England.*
CREASY, E. *The English Constitution.*
TAYLOR, HANNIS. *Origin and Growth of the English Constitution.*
TASWELL-LANGMEAD, T. P. *English Constitutional History, from the Teutonic Conquest to the Present Time.*

The following three works form together a comprehensive treatment of the subject:—

STUBBS, W. *Constitutional History of England in its Origin and Development.* 3 vols.
HALLAM, H. *Constitutional History of England from the Accession of Henry VII. to the death of George II.* 3 vols.; American edition in 2 vols.
MAY, T. E. *Constitutional History of England*, 1760–1860. 3 vols.

MINOR WORKS.

* CREIGHTON, LOUISE. *Stories from English History.*
CREIGHTON, LOUISE. *Social History of England.*
* YONGE, CHARLOTTE M. *Cameos from English History.*
* JONES, M. *Stories of the Olden Time,* from De Joinville and Froissart.
* LANIER, SIDNEY, Editor. *The Boy's Froissart.*
* EDGAR, JOHN G. *The Wars of the Roses.*
* GILMAN, ARTHUR, Editor. *Magna Charta Stories.*
* KINGSLEY, ROSE G. *The Children of Westminster Abbey.*
EWALD. *Stories from the State Papers.*

A LIST OF SOME USEFUL BOOKS.

* DICKENS, CHARLES. *A Child's History of England.*
* RIDEING, WILLIAM H. *Young Folks' History of London.*
* BROWN, CORNELIUS. *True Stories of the Reign of Victoria.*
* VALENTINE, Mrs. R. *Sea Fights and Land Battles.*
* BISHOP, COLEMAN E., Editor. *Pictures from English History.*
* SCOTT, Sir WALTER. *Tales of a Grandfather.*
* STRICKLAND, AGNES. *Tales from English History, for Children.*

CHRONOLOGICAL TABLE OF CONTENTS.

CHAPTER I.

EARLY BRITAIN.

DATE.		PAGE
	Continuity of English and American History	1
	Early British Races	2
	The Gaels	3
	The Britons	4
	Mode of Life	4
	Religion	5
	Stonehenge	5
B. C. 55– A. D. 84	Roman Conquest of Britain	7
	Roman Walls and Roads	7–8
A. D. 410	Roman Army withdrawn	9

CHAPTER II.

HOW BRITAIN BECAME ENGLAND (449–827 A.D.).

449	Coming of the Jutes	10
	The Saxons	11
	The English	12
	Religion of the English	13
	Institutions: the Township, Hundred, and County	14
	The Land System	14
	The Meeting of the Wise Men	15
	Conversion of the English to Christianity	15
827	England united by Egbert of Wessex	16

CHAPTER III.

THE NORTHMEN IN ENGLAND (827-1042).

DATE.		PAGE
	The Vikings	17
879	Treaty of Wedmore	18
871-901	King Alfred of Wessex	18
	St. Dunstan	19
1017-35	Cnut the Dane, King of England	19
	The Earldoms	22

CHAPTER IV.

THE NORMAN CONQUEST (1042-1087).

1066	Harold, Son of Godwin, chosen King	23
1066	Battle of Senlac, or Hastings	24
1066-87	William the Conqueror	25
	His Claim to the English Throne	25
	Effect of the Conquest	26
	Continuity of English History	26
1086	Domesday Book	27
1086	Oath of Salisbury Plain	27
	Influence of the Catholic Church on England	28
	The New Forest	28
	London Tower and Westminster Hall	29
1087	William's Death	29

CHAPTER V.

THE NORMAN KINGS (1087-1154).

1087-1100	William II., the Red	30
	His Extravagance	30
	His Death	31
1100-35	Henry I.	31
	Conquers Normandy	32
	The White Ship	32
	Geoffrey of Anjou marries Maud	33
1135-54	Stephen	33
	Civil War	34

CHAPTER VI.

THE FIRST TWO PLANTAGENETS (1154-1199).

DATE.		PAGE
1154-89	Henry II.	35
	His Reforms	35
	Shield-money	36
1164	Constitutions of Clarendon	36
	Conquest of Ireland	37
	Henry's sons	37
1189-99	Richard I.	39
	Richard's Death	39
	His Place in England's History	40

CHAPTER VII.

KING JOHN AND MAGNA CHARTA (1199-1216).

	Prince Arthur	41
	Philip of France seizes Normandy and Anjou	41
	The Interdict	42
	John submits to the Pope	42
1215	Magna Charta	43
	John's Death	44

CHAPTER VIII.

HENRY III. (1216-1272).

	Earl Simon of Montfort	47
1265	Earl Simon's Parliament	48
1265	Battle of Evesham	48

CHAPTER IX.

THE FIRST TWO EDWARDS (1272-1327).

1272-1307	Edward I.	50
1276-1284	Conquers Wales	50
	Prince of Wales	50
	The Welsh Bards	51

DATE.		PAGE
	Balliol and Bruce	51
1296	Conquest of Scotland	52
	Sir William Wallace	52
1298	Battle of Falkirk	52
	Robert Bruce	52
1295	The First Perfect Parliament	53
	Its Composition	53
1297	Confirmation of the Charters	54
1307-27	Edward II.	54
1307-12	Piers Gaveston	54
	Bruce in Scotland	55
1314	Battle of Bannockburn	55
	The Irish	55
	The Despensers	55
1327	Murder of the King	56

CHAPTER X.

EDWARD III. (1327-1377).

1327-30	Supremacy of Mortimer	57
1333	Battle of Halidon Hill	57
	Cause of the Wars with France	59
1340	Sea-fight at Sluys	60
1346	Battle of Cressy	60
1346-47	Siege of Calais	62
1348-50	The "Black Death"	62
1356	Battle of Poitiers	63
1360	Peace of Bretigny	63
1333	Parliament separates into two Houses	65
1353	Statute of Præmunire	66
	John Wycliffe and the Lollards	66
	Copyhold Tenure	67
1349	Statute of Laborers	67

CHAPTER XI.

RICHARD II. (1377-1399).

1381	The Peasants' Revolt	68
1399	Abdication of Richard	70
	Henry of Lancaster's Claims to the Crown	72

CHAPTER XII.

ENGLAND IN THE FOURTEENTH CENTURY.

DATE.		PAGE
	Trade	73
	Financial Policy	74
	Clothes	74
	Commerce	74
	The Guilds	75
	Rise of the English Language	76

CHAPTER XIII.

THE FIRST TWO LANCASTRIAN KINGS (1399-1422).

1399-1413	Henry IV.	77
	Rise of the Commoners	77
	Maintenance	78
1413-22	Henry V.	78
	Renewal of the War with France	79
1415	Battle of Agincourt	80
1420	Treaty of Troyes	80

CHAPTER XIV.

HENRY VI. (1422-1460).

	Regency of Bedford and Gloucester	82
1428-53	Loss of France	82
1450	Jack Cade's Rebellion	83
1460	Richard of York claims the Throne	83
1455	The Wars of the Roses begin	84
1461	Edward I. of York crowned King	84
	Forty-shilling Freeholders	85

CHAPTER XV.

THE YORKIST KINGS (1461-1485).

1461-83	Edward IV.	86
1475	Invasion of France	87
1478	Murder of the Duke of Clarence	87

Date.		Page
1483	Edward V.	88
1483-85	Richard III.	88
	The Tudors and their Claims	88
1485	Battle of Bosworth	90

CHAPTER XVI.

SOCIAL CHANGES DURING THE FIFTEENTH CENTURY.

End of the Middle Ages	91
Printing	91
Abolition of Villeinage	92
Loss of Power by Parliament	93
Money Bills	94

CHAPTER XVII.

HENRY VII. (1485-1509).

Henry's Home Policy	95
The Pretenders, Simnel and Warbeck	95-96
Henry's Foreign Policy	96
Court of Star Chamber	96

CHAPTER XVIII.

HENRY VIII. (1509-1547).

	The Spanish Marriage	98
1513	War with France and Scotland	100
	Battle of Flodden	100
	Cardinal Wolsey	101
	The Divorce from Katherine	102
	Henry's Personal Rule	103
1533	The Statute against Appeals to Rome	104
	Destruction of the Monasteries	106
	Effect of this Destruction	107

CHRONOLOGICAL TABLE OF CONTENTS.   xix

DATE		PAGE
1536	Execution of Anne Boleyn	108
1539	The Act of the Six Articles	108
1540	Fall of Cromwell	109
	Last Years of Henry VIII.	109

CHAPTER XIX.

EDWARD VI. (1547-1553).

	Protector Somerset	111
1547	The Scottish War	111
1551	Fall of Somerset	112
	Lady Jane Grey	112

CHAPTER XX.

MARY THE CATHOLIC (1553-1558).

	Mary's Policy	114
1554	Marriage with Philip of Spain	114
1554	Risings in England	116
	The Martyrs	116

CHAPTER XXI.

ELIZABETH (1558-1603).

	Character of the Reign	119
	William Cecil, Lord Burleigh	121
	The Church of England	123
	The Puritans	124
	The Roman Catholics	125
	Mary, Queen of Scots	126
	Foreign Policy	128
1569-86	Roman Catholic Plots	129
	Court of High Commission	130
1587	Execution of Mary, Queen of Scots	131
1588	The Invincible Armada	132
	The English in Ireland	135
	Elizabethan Settlement of Ireland	135
	Elizabeth's Last Years	137

CHAPTER XXII.

STATE OF SOCIETY.

DATE.		PAGE
	Commerce	140
	Architecture	140
	The Poor Law	142
	Literature	142

CHAPTER XXIII.

JAMES I. (1603-1625).

	His Character	144
	Sir Walter Raleigh	146
1605	The Gunpowder Plot	146
	The Puritans	149
	"The Spanish Marriage"	151
	The "Divine Right of Kings"	151
1621	Impeachment of Bacon	151
1621	The Great Protestation	152

CHAPTER XXIV.

CHARLES I. (1625-1649).

	The French Marriage, and War with France	153
1627	The Attempt to relieve La Rochelle	154
1628	The Petition of Right	154
1629	Sir John Eliot's Resolutions	157
1629-40	Personal Government of the King	158
	Archbishop Laud and the Puritans	159
	Ship-money	160
1637	Hampden's Case	160
	The Scottish Church	163
1639	The First Bishops' War	164
1640	The Short Parliament	165
1640	The Second Bishops' War	165
1640-60	The Long Parliament	165
1641	Execution of Strafford	166
	Constitutional Reforms	167

CHRONOLOGICAL TABLE OF CONTENTS.

DATE.		PAGE
1641	The Patriots disagree about Religion	168
1641	The Irish Rebellion	168
1641	The Grand Remonstrance	168
1642	The Attempt to arrest the Five Members	168
1642	Civil War begins	170

CHAPTER XXV.

THE CIVIL WARS (1642-1649).

1643	Death of John Hampden and of John Pym	172
	Oliver Cromwell	173
	Cromwell's Ironsides	173
1644	Battle of Marston Moor	175
1645	The Self-denying Ordinance	176
1645	"The New Model" Army, and Battle of Naseby	176
	Charles flees to the Scots	177
	The Independents	177
	The Army seizes the King	178
1648	The Scots invade England	179
1648	Battle of Preston	179
1648	"Pride's Purge"	179
1649	Execution of the King	180
1649	Cromwell in Ireland	181

CHAPTER XXVI.

THE COMMONWEALTH (1649-1653).

	Charles II. in Scotland	182
1650	Battle of Dunbar	183
1651	Battle of Worcester	183
1653	The "Rump" expelled	186
	Barebone's Parliament	186
1653	The Instrument of Government	186

CHAPTER XXVII.

The Protectorate (1653-1659).

Date.		Page
	Oliver, Lord Protector	188
1655	The Major-Generals	189
	War with the Dutch	189
1657	The Petition and Advice	190
1658	Death of Cromwell	192
1660	The Restoration	193
	Puritan Ideas	194

CHAPTER XXVIII.

The Restored Stuarts (1660-1688).

1660-85	Charles II.	196
1660	Act of Indemnity and Oblivion	198
	The Regicides	198
1661-79	The Cavalier Parliament	199
1661	Corporation Act	199
1665	The Plague	200
	The Dissenters	200
1666	The Great Fire	201
1666-67	War with the Dutch	202
1670	The Secret Treaty of Dover	203
1672	Declaration of Indulgence	204
1673	The Test Act	204
1678	Popish Plot	205
1679	Habeas Corpus Act	206
1680-81	Exclusion Bills	207
1683	Rye-House Plot	207
1685-88	James II.	208
1685	Monmouth's Rebellion	208

CHAPTER XXIX.

The "Glorious Revolution" of 1688-1689.

The Case of Sir Edward Hales	210
Revocation of the Edict of Nantes	210

CHRONOLOGICAL TABLE OF CONTENTS.   xxiii

Date.		Page
1688	Declaration of Indulgence	211
	Birth of the Old Pretender	212
1688	The Seven Bishops acquitted	212
	The Invitation to William of Orange	213
Nov. 5, 1688	William lands at Torbay	213
	Flight of James	214
	The Jacobites	214
	The Convention	215
1689	Declaration of Right	215

CHAPTER XXX.

The First Constitutional Monarchs.

1689-1702	William and Mary	216
	The Mutiny Bill	216
	The Nonjurors	217
1689	Siege of Londonderry	218
1690	Battle of the Boyne	219
1690	Battle off Beachy Head	220
1692	Battle of La Hogue	221
1694	Bank of England established	221
1695	Liberty of the Press	222
1692	Massacre of Glencoe	222
1702-14	Queen Anne	224
1704	Battle of Blenheim	224
1704	Seizure of Gibraltar	226
1707	Union with Scotland	227

CHAPTER XXXI.

George I. (1714-1727).

1701	Act of Succession, or Settlement	229
1715	Jacobite Plot	230
1715	Riot Act	230
1716	Septennial Act	230
1720	South-Sea Bubble	230
1721-42	Sir Robert Walpole, Prime Minister	232
	Walpole's Policy	233

CHAPTER XXXII.

GEORGE II. (1727-1760).

Date		Page
	Queen Caroline	234
	The Methodists	234
1739	War with Spain	234
	War with Prussia and France	236
1744-54	Pelham Ministry	236
1745	Stuart Rising	236
1746	Battle of Culloden	238
1751	New Style adopted	239
1754-63	Causes of the French and Indian War in America	240
1756-63	The Seven Years' War in Europe	240
	William Pitt	242

CHAPTER XXXIII.

GEORGE III. (1760-1820): PART I. (1760-1783).

Date		Page
	Character of the New King	244
1763	Peace of Paris	245
	John Wilkes	246
	The North American Colonies	248
1765	The Stamp Act	249
1765	The Regency Question	249
1766	Stamp Act repealed	250
	"The King's Friends"	251
1768	Wilkes and the Middlesex Election	251
1773	The Boston Tea Party	253
1774	The Boston Port Act and other Oppressive Measures	254
1775	Lexington and Concord	254
1776	The Declaration of Independence	255
1776	The Surprise at Trenton	255
1777	Burgoyne's Surrender	256
1778	The French Alliance	257
	Lord North's Plan of Reconciliation	257
	Economical Reform	258
1780	Lord George Gordon Riots	258
	The Southern Campaigns	259
1780	Arnold's Treason	260

CHRONOLOGICAL TABLE OF CONTENTS. xxv

Date.		Page
1781	Capture of Yorktown	261
1782	End of the North Ministry	261
1782	The Second Rockingham Ministry	262
1782	Independence of the United States acknowledged	264
1783	Conclusion of the War	265

CHAPTER XXXIV.

George III. Part II. (1783–1820).

1783	The "Coalition"	266
1783	Fox's India Bill	266
1783–1801	William Pitt, Prime Minister	267
1784	Pitt's India Bill	268
	Pitt's financial policy	269
1788	Trial of Warren Hastings begins	269
1788	The Regency Struggle	269
1789	The French Revolution	271
1793	France declares War against England	271
	Pitt's Policy	272
1797	Mutinies in the Fleet	272
1798	French invasion of Egypt	272
1798	Battle of the Nile	273
	Ireland in the Eighteenth Century	273
1779	The "Volunteers"	273
1791	The "United Irishmen"	274
1796–98	Rebellion in Ireland	274
1801	The Union	275
1803	Emmett's Rebellion	275
1801–4	The Addington Ministry	275
1802	Peace of Amiens	276
1803	War renewed	276
1805	Battle off Trafalgar	276
1803–6	Pitt's Second Ministry	277
1806–7	Ministry of "All the Talents"	277
1807–27	The Tory Ministry	277
	The Spanish Resistance to Napoleon	279
1809–14	The Peninsular War	279
	Napoleon's Downfall	281
	War of 1812 with the United States	281
1815	Battle of Waterloo	282
	Agricultural Distress	283

CHRONOLOGICAL TABLE OF CONTENTS.

Date.		Page
	Corn Law of 1816	283
	Commercial Depression	283
	The Luddites	283
1819	The Manchester Massacre	284
1819	The Six Acts	285
1810–20	The Regency	286

CHAPTER XXXV.

George IV. (1820–1830).

	Queen Caroline	286
	George Canning and the Monroe Doctrine	287
1828–30	Wellington-Peel Ministry	287
	Daniel O'Connell	288
1829	Catholic Emancipation	289

CHAPTER XXXVI.

William IV. (1830–1837).

	Character of the new King	291
	Causes of Discontent	291
1830–34	The Grey Ministry	293
1830–32	The Struggle for Reform	293
1832	The First Reform Act	294
1833	Emancipation of Slaves	295
1833	The Factory Act	295
1834	Reform of the Poor Law	296
1834–35	Peel-Wellington Ministry	296
1835–41	Second Melbourne Ministry	296

CHAPTER XXXVII.

Victoria (1837–   ).

	Difficulties of the Ministry	297
1840	The Canada Act	299
1839	The Bedchamber Question	300
1841–46	Sir Robert Peel's Ministry	300
	Overthrow of the Protective Policy	301

CHRONOLOGICAL TABLE OF CONTENTS. xxvii

Date		Page
	The Anti-Corn-Law League	302
1844–49	The Irish Famine	303
1846	Repeal of the Corn Laws	303
1846–52	Lord John Russell's Ministry	305
	"Young Ireland"	306
	The "Clearances"	306
	The Chartists	306
1851	Dismissal of Lord Palmerston	307
1852	The First Derby Ministry	308
1852–55	The Aberdeen Ministry	308
1854–56	The Crimean War	308
1855–58	First Palmerston Ministry	309
1857–58	The Sepoy Mutiny	309
1858–59	Second Derby-Disraeli Ministry	311
1858	Jews admitted to Parliament	311
1859	The "Fancy Franchises"	311
1859–65	Second Palmerston Ministry	312
	Gladstone's Financial Policy	313
	The Cotton Famine	313
	England's Policy during the Civil War	314
	The "Alabama"	314
1865–68	Derby-Disraeli Ministry	315
1868	The Second Reform Act	315
1868	Compulsory Church Rates abolished	315
1868–74	First Gladstone Ministry	316
1869	Disestablishment of the Irish Church	316
	The System of Landholding in Ireland	316
1870	The Irish Land Act of 1870	319
	The "Bright Clauses"	320
1881	Irish Land Act of 1881	320
1871	National Education	320
1871	Reorganization of the Army	320
1872	The Ballot Act	321
1884	Third Reform Act	321
1874–80	The Disraeli Ministry	322
	Disraeli's Imperial Policy	322
1876	Congress of Berlin	324
1880	Mr. Gladstone's Second Ministry begins	324
	The British Empire	325
	Conclusion	325

INDEX 327

GENEALOGIES.

	PAGE
The Norman Kings	31
The Earlier Plantagenets	49
Succession to the Scottish Throne in 1290	51
Succession to the French Crown in 1328	59
The Later Plantagenets	71
Claims of York and Lancaster	81
Lancasters and Tudors	89
The Howards	102
The Tudors	110
The Stuarts	143
The House of Hanover	242

MAPS.

At the beginning:

1. Britain before the Norman Conquest.
2. The Dominions of Henry II.

At the end:

3. England at the beginning of the Puritan Rebellion.
4. England since the Restoration.

Folding Maps, after the Index.

5. The World, 1772, } showing growth of the British Empire.
6. The World, 1892. }

IMPORTANT DATES.

	YEAR
Cæsar in Britain	B.C. 55
Coming of the Jutes	A.D. 449
Egbert of Wessex, Overlord of all England	827
Treaty of Wedmore	878
Battle of Senlac	1066
Murder of Becket	1170
Magna Charta	1215
Simon of Montfort's Parliament	1264
Confirmation of the Charters	1297
Battle of Bannockburn	1314
Battle of Cressy	1346
Peace of Bretigny	1360
Battle of Agincourt	1415
Battle of Bosworth	1485
First Act of Supremacy	1534
Defeat of the Spanish Armada	1588
Petition of Right	1628
Battle of Naseby	1645
Battle of Worcester	1651
The Restoration	1660
Bill of Rights	1689
Act of Settlement	1701
Union with Scotland	1707
Battle of Blenheim	1704
Peace of Paris	1763
Declaration of American Independence	1776
Union with Ireland	1801
Battle of Trafalgar	1805
Battle of Waterloo	1815
Catholic Emancipation	1829
First Reform Act	1832
Overthrow of Protection	1845-46
Second Reform Act	1868
Disestablishment of the Irish Church	1869
First Irish Land Act	1870
Elementary Education Act	1870
Ballot Act	1872
Second Irish Land Act	1881
Third Reform Act	1884

LANDMARKS IN CONSTITUTIONAL HISTORY.

[For supplementary reading on this topic, see p. xi.]

DATE		PAGE
	Character of the English Conquest of Britain	12
	Institutions of the English	14
827	Union of the Kingdoms under Egbert of Wessex	16
1066	The Norman Conquest	26
1086	Domesday Book and the Oath of Salisbury Plain	27
1154–89	Reforms of Henry II. in the Administration of Justice and in Finance	35
1164	The Constitutions of Clarendon	36
1215	Magna Charta	43
1265	Earl of Simon of Montfort's Parliament	47
1295	The First Perfect Parliament	53
1297	Confirmation of the Charters	54
1327	Edward II. deposed by Parliament	55
1332	Separation of Parliament into Two Houses	65
1353	Statute of Praemunire	65
1399	Abdication of Richard II.	71
1407	The Commons obtain the Right to Originate Money-Bills	77
1430	Restriction of the Franchise	85
1461	The Practice of Passing Statutes begins	94
1487	Court of Star Chamber established	96
1494	Poynings' Law	135
1534	First Act of Supremacy	106
1583	High Commission Court	130
1601	The Poor Law of Elizabeth	142
	The "Divine Right of Kings"	151
1621	The Great Protestation	152

LANDMARKS IN CONSTITUTIONAL HISTORY.

Date		Page
1628	The Petition of Right	154
1629	Sir John Eliot's Resolutions	157
1634–36	Ship-Money	160
1640	Meeting of the Long Parliament	165
1641	Constitutional Reforms	167
1641	The Grand Remonstrance	168
1649	Establishment of the Commonwealth	180
1653	The Instrument of Government	186
1657	The Petition and Advice	190
1660	The Restoration	193
1660	Act of Indemnity and Oblivion	198
1661 / 1665	The Corporation Act, Act of Uniformity, Conventicle Act, and Five Mile Act	199
1673	The Test Act	204
1679	Habeas Corpus Act	206
1688	Declaration of Indulgence	211
1688–89	The "Glorious Revolution"	213
1689	The Declaration of Rights	215
1689	The Mutiny Bill	216
1689	The Toleration Act	217
1695	Liberty of the Press	222
1701	Act of Settlement	229
1707	Union with Scotland	227
1715	Riot Act	230
1716	Septennial Act	230
1721	Rise of Cabinet Government	232
	Character of the Whig Administrations	233
1763	Wilkes and General Warrants	246
	Constitutional Relations of the Colonies to Great Britain	249
1765	The Stamp Act	249
1766	The Declaratory Act	250
	"The King's Friends"	251
1768	The Middlesex Election	251
	Economical Reform	258
1783	The "Coalition" dismissed	266
1788	The Regency Struggle	269
1801	The Union with Ireland	275
1819	The Six Acts	285
1829	Catholic Emancipation	289
1832	The First Reform Act	294

DATE		PAGE
1839	The Bedchamber Question	300
	The Chartists	306
1858	Jews admitted to Parliament	311
1868	Second Reform Act	315
1868	Compulsory Church Rates abolished	315
1869	Disestablishment of the Irish Church	316
1870	The Irish Land Act	319
1872	The Ballot Act	321
1884	Third Reform Act	321

LIST OF ILLUSTRATIONS.

	PAGE
View of Stonehenge	5
Views of Parts of the Roman Wall	8, 9
Saxon Horsemen	16
Rural Life (Eleventh Century)	20, 21
An English Vessel	22
Silver Penny (time of William I.)	29
Seal, showing Mounted Armed Figure (time of Henry I.)	34
Effigies of Henry II. and Queen Eleanor	38
Silver Penny (time of John)	40
Royal Arms of England (Richard I. to Edward III.)	45
Effigy of a Knight, showing Armor worn between 1190-1225	47
Seal, showing Mounted Knight in Mail Armor (about 1265)	48
Armed Knights (about 1300)	56
State Carriage (Fourteenth Century)	58
Contemporary View of a Walled Town (Fourteenth Century)	61
Tomb of Edward III. in Westminster Abbey	64
Rural Life (Fourteenth Century)	69, 70
Gold Noble (time of Edward III.): *from the Luttrell Psalter*, "Vetusta Monumenta"	72
Geoffrey Chaucer (*from* Harl. MS. 4866)	76
Effigy of Knight in Plate-armor (about 1460)	79
Royal Arms (1408-1603)	85
A Fifteenth-Century Ship	90
Tudor Rose	97
Henry VIII.	99
Sir Thomas More	105
Angel of Henry VIII. (1543)	113
Queen Mary Tudor	115
Mounted Soldier (1596)	118
Queen Elizabeth (1588)	120
William Shakspere	122
Mary, Queen of Scots	127
Sir Francis Drake	133
William Cecil, Lord Burleigh	138

LIST OF ILLUSTRATIONS.

	PAGE
Coaches in the Reign of Elizabeth	141
Sir Walter Raleigh	145
James I.	150
Charles I.	155
The "Sovereign of the Seas" (1637)	161
Coach (Seventeenth Century)	169
Military Equipment (Seventeenth Century)	171
Oliver Cromwell	174
John Milton	185
Wagon (Seventeenth Century)	187
Charles II.	197
Yeomen of the Guard (Seventeenth Century)	209
William III.	218
Mary II.	219
Queen Anne	225
Royal Arms (1603-1714)	228
George I.	231
Costumes and Sedan Chair (about 1720)	233
Sir Robert Walpole	235
George II.	237
William Pitt (afterwards Earl of Chatham)	241
Coach (about 1700)	243
George III. (in 1767)	245
The House of Commons in 1741-42	247
Costumes of Persons of Quality (about 1783)	260
Edmund Burke	263
Royal Arms (1801-1816)	265
William Pitt	268
Headdress of a Lady (about 1778)	270
Lord Nelson	278
The Duke of Wellington	280
George III. in old age	284
George Canning	288
Royal Arms (1816-1837)	290
Old Sarum	292
Queen Victoria	298
Sir Robert Peel	304
Lord John Russell	312
Mr. Gladstone	318
Lord Beaconsfield	323

ENGLISH HISTORY

FOR

AMERICANS.

———•———

CHAPTER I.

EARLY BRITAIN.

OFF the western coast of Europe there are two large islands. One of these is a little larger than are the States of Ohio and Pennsylvania united, and the other is almost as large as the State of Indiana. Two thousand years ago these islands were mentioned by an old Greek author, Polybius, as "the two Britannic islands of Albion and Ierne;" and they are now known to us as Great Britain and Ireland. Small as they are, their history is of more importance to Americans than that of all Europe besides; for the ancestors of the majority of Americans came from these islands, and thence came many, if not all, of our most important institutions. Indeed, the history of these islands until within two centuries and a half is a part of American history; without it we cannot understand our own institutions, or trace the history of our ancestors.

Who were the earliest inhabitants of these islands? How did they live? What did they eat and drink,

Continuity of English and American history.

and what kind of clothes did they wear? These questions cannot be answered with certainty, for the very first inhabitants of Albion and Ierne lived before the period of written history. Let us begin at the beginning, and see what is really known about them.

Early inhabitants.

In many parts of the larger of these two islands there are still to be seen a great many small, roundish hills, commonly called barrows. They were made by human hands, and graves have been found in the middle of some of them. When these graves were first opened, they were found to contain bones, not only of men, but of animals. Tools of stone and bronze were found in them, and also in the earth around them. In other cases everything but the stone graves had crumbled away and disappeared; and when the graves are thus empty and uncovered, they are usually called cromlechs. Until lately the cromlechs were supposed to be altars, on which human beings were sacrificed; but they are now known to be only graves.

Barrows.

The human bones found in these graves were evidently those of the early residents of Britain; so they have been carefully measured and examined. It is found that they belonged to two different races, who can only be known apart as being the people with long, narrow heads, and those with short, round heads. The long-headed people appear to have been the older race, and the more ignorant. They were a good deal like the Eskimo, or Esquimaux, of the present day. They lived in caves, and in villages built over shallow water. They used stone tools, and ate the flesh of wild beasts;

Early British races.

Long-headed people.

but they had tame animals also, for the bones of the ox, the horse, and even the goose, have been found in the graves. It is not known who these long-headed people were; but they have been thought to belong to a race called Iberian, or perhaps Ivernian, who were the early occupants of the peninsula of Spain, and also of Ireland, or Ierne.

The people with the round heads came at a later day, although long before the time of written history. They were larger, stronger, and less barbarous than the race just described. This is shown by the fact that they used bronze tools; for bronze is a mixture of copper and tin, and it cannot be made without some skill. They made earthen pots also, wove a rough kind of cloth, and built their villages over deeper waters than the others. They were perhaps of the Finnish race, which still occupies the northernmost part of Europe, although some regard them as Celts, or Kelts. Round-headed people

At any rate, we know that men of Celtic, or Keltic, blood lived in Britain at the beginning of written history, and they are the first British men of whom we know much. Men of the same race still live in France, especially in Brittany, in Spain, and in Northern Italy. Of those who came to Britain, the tribes of whom we know most were the Goidels, or Gaels, and the Brythons, or Britons. The Goidels came first, and then passed over into Ireland, where the western Irish are probably their descendants. Some of them passed over into Scotland, where the Scottish Highlanders are supposed to be sprung from them, and still speak a language called Gaelic. On the other hand, the Brythons came to the southern part of

Great Britain, and the Welsh are their particular descendants. Their old neighbors on the continent of Europe gave them this name of Brythons, meaning either clothed men or painted men; but they called themselves Cymry, and their descendants, the Welsh, call themselves by that name to this day.

We know more about these early Britons than about any of the other early races, because the Romans, who afterwards conquered them, have told us a great deal about them in their books. They lived in huts shaped like beehives, made of planks, and covered with basket-work and mud. The only ornaments of these huts were the heads of the owner's enemies; and this shows what a savage race they were. The heads that were thought most valuable were kept in boxes, and were brought forth only on great occasions. In this they were no better than the wild tribes called head-hunters, who are still to be found in the island of Borneo. The Britons were a tall and well-formed race. They were dressed in skins and in woven cloth, this last being dyed in gaudy colors. The men allowed their moustaches to grow so long that they strained what they drank through them as through a sieve. They were good farmers, and raised large crops of grain. Cattle and sheep abounded among them, and they had little horses, or ponies, which, when too old to labor, were killed and eaten like other animals. The Britons were brave, and fought chiefly from chariots drawn by three horses. When going to war, a soldier colored his hair bright red, and painted streaks of blue and green on his face and legs, like the American Indian. When the Romans afterwards conquered Britain, the

The Britons.

Their mode of life.

race which they overcame was really not much more civilized than the Mandans or Choctaws or Apaches of America.

The religion of these early Britons was called Druidism, and their priests were called Druids. They wor-

VIEW OF STONEHENGE. (FROM A PHOTOGRAPH.)

shipped several deities, and offered human sacrifices to them. They held oak groves sacred, and particularly the mistletoe that hung from the boughs. *Religion.*
There are in England several great buildings, or structures of stone resembling buildings, which are *Stonehenge.* supposed to have been built in the time of the Druids, though no one can fix the date. As the traveller goes out from the city of Salisbury over a bare undulating plain, like one of the rolling prairies of the

West, he sees at a distance a vast gray structure made of huge stones now fallen apart. This is called Stonehenge. The largest upright stones are nearly thirty feet long, and hold up cross-pieces that are sixteen feet long and weigh eleven tons. How these great stones were brought or shaped and raised to such a height with the imperfect tools and machinery of a barbarous age, is very puzzling; but there is no way of learning exactly when Stonehenge was built, or another structure of the same kind at Abury. But we have every reason to believe that the people who built them were ancestors of our own; for the island of Albion, or Great Britain, has been conquered so many times that there is a great mixture of race in all English-speaking people. Iberian and Finn, Gael and Briton, all mingle their blood in our veins; and so do other races yet to be mentioned, such as Angle and Saxon, Dane and Norman. But it is a curious thing that our institutions and laws are mainly based on those of the Angles and Saxons.

At a time when Britain was in an almost barbarous condition, the southern portions of Europe were much more civilized, and we know something of the early state of Britain through the writings and traditions of these more advanced races. For instance, an early Greek explorer named Pytheas is supposed to have visited the island, and the Phœnicians at Carthage used tin that probably came from British mines, and they knew something about the Britons. Yet the route of Pytheas is not easy to make out, and the Phœnicians may, after all, have obtained their tin and their information from Gaul or Spain. But as to the Roman knowledge of Britain, we are on surer ground.

Early visitors.

THE ROMAN CONQUEST.

We know that, fifty-five years before the birth of Jesus Christ, the great Roman general, Julius Cæsar, crossed over to Britain, he being then governor of Gaul. The next year he came again, and marched over part of the southeastern portion of the island. He did not stay long; but his coming was of great importance, for he made the island known to the Romans, who were then the great conquering race of Europe. A century later these mighty conquerors came again and subdued Britain itself, making it a province of the Roman Empire. This took place under the Emperor Claudius (43 A. D.). The Britons were brave and warlike, but they were no match for the disciplined Roman soldiers. The chief who made the bravest resistance was Caradoc, or Caractacus; and he was at last captured and sent to Rome, where the emperor was so pleased with his frank and open manner that he set him free. But the Romans in Britain were not so kind as was this emperor. They oppressed the Britons terribly, and even tortured them to obtain money from them. At last this could be borne no longer, and there was a rebellion under a brave chief named Boadicea, a woman. The Britons took and plundered the Roman town of Londinium (London); but they were defeated at last, and Boadicea is said to have taken her own life in her despair.

After this the Romans went on from one conquest to another. In the time of the Governor Agricola (A. D. 78-84), all Britain, as far north as the Clyde and the Firth of Forth, was in their hands. At that point the island is very narrow, and Agricola caused a wall to be built across it, to aid in keeping back the wild Highland tribes called Scots and Picts, who made constant raids upon the country. Fifty years later these bold mountaineers pressed the Romans so hard that the Emperor Hadrian caused another wall to be built, much farther south, between the Tyne and Solway Firth. Later still, the Emperor

VIEW OF PART OF THE ROMAN WALL.

Severus rebuilt this wall, and a part of it is still standing, although much has been taken away to mend the roads. While the Scots and Picts thus troubled the Romans by land, the sea-fighters, or vikings, also attacked them by water; and to meet these the Romans built great roads, so that soldiers could be hurried from one part of the island to another. Some of these roads can still be traced; and all over England there yet remain ruined walls and fragments of tiled floors to show where the towns and camps of the Roman conquerors of Britain were built.

The Romans, having become Christian, introduced Christianity into Britain, and in this way the Britons became Christians. But soon the Roman power declined. In A.D. 410, Rome was taken by the West Goths under their chief, Alaric, and in the same year the Roman legions were withdrawn from Britain. This strong arm being gone, the Britons had to defend themselves from Scots and Picts and other invaders,—a task in which they succeeded very ill.

PART OF THE ROMAN WALL AT LEICESTER.

CHAPTER II.

HOW BRITAIN BECAME ENGLAND.

A. D. 449–827.

BY the seaside, in winter, we may sometimes see a floating log or plank on which a little flock of sea-fowl has perched. Then comes another flock, and another, all ready to alight, and each flock must either make room for the next, or be driven away. The early history of the island of Britain is very much like this. One flock of invaders after another settled upon it, each having a name of its own, but all belonging in general to the great Germanic, or Teutonic, race, which spread all over northern Europe. The modern Germans, Dutch, and Danes all belong to this race, and so did the successive flocks of invaders who came to Britain.

There were the Jutes, for instance, from whom the peninsula of Jutland is still named. They landed about 449 on the southeast coast of Britain, and soon overran all that part of the island. It used to be said that they were led by two brothers, named Hengist and Horsa, whom a British chief, named Vortigern, had asked to help him against his enemies. But it is now thought that this whole story may be false, and that Hengist and Horsa mean only horse and mare. Yet it is certain that the Jutes themselves came, and brought with them their families,

Coming of the Jutes (449).

slaves, and cattle. The Romans had called the southeastern part of Britain Cantium, and the Jutes changed the name to Kent, — a name it still bears. They called themselves Kentsmen, and named their chief town Kentsmen's borough, or Canterbury, as it is now spelled. This is interesting to Americans, because a large part of those who first settled this continent came from this county of Kent, and kept up its way of speaking and its institutions.

The next flock of invaders, also belonging to the great Teutonic race, were of the Saxon tribe, and settled upon the land south and west of Kent, calling this region Sussex, or the land of the South Saxons, — a name it holds to this day. *The Saxons.* Then another band of Saxons settled to the west of Sussex, and called that region Wessex. They are said to have fought many battles with the British king Arthur, about whom there are so many legends and poems, — he that founded the Round Table of famous knights, who went in search of the Holy Grail. The poet Tennyson, in our own time, has written much about King Arthur, but it is now believed that he existed only in poetry, as none of the early historical writers even mention his name. But the leader of these Saxons of Wessex was a real person, named Cedric, who was the ancestor of most of the later sovereigns of England, including the present queen. Cedric's settlement of Wessex was the most important Saxon colony. Other Saxons settled in the eastern part of England, calling their part of the country Essex, while others settled between these tribes and called that region Middlesex. These two names yet belong to English counties, though the name of Wessex is lost.

Then other Teutonic invaders settled in the central and northern parts of Britain. These were called Angles, or English, so that we now see whence came the words "English" and "Anglo-Saxon." They settled north of Essex, and gradually got to the borders of Wales. The old English word for border is "march;" so these English were called "marchmen," and their country was called "Mercia." Other Angles also settled north of the river Humber, and were finally united in a large kingdom, called Northumbria. They gradually spread yet farther north, and founded a city named Edwin's-borough, or Edinburgh, after a King Edwin of Northumbria, who lived in the seventh century. Thus the Angles, or English, gradually got possession of the greater part of the island, and it came to be called Angleland, or England.

The English.

What became of the early British tribes we do not know, although it is very likely that the present inhabitants of Wales and Cornwall are mainly descended from them. Some writers, too, think that the presence of so many dark-haired Englishmen shows that the slaughter of the Britons was not so complete as many historians have thought. For the English, Danes, and Normans belonged to the Teutonic race, and had light hair, while we know that the early Britons had dark hair. At any rate, there are hardly any British words in our present language, but there are many Latin words, and some of these may have come from the Britons, who probably spoke a dialect of Latin after the Romans conquered them. And our customs, like our language, came mainly from the Teutonic tribes, who, one after another, possessed England, and whom we must now call English.

Treatment of the Britons.

But we must not forget that these old tribes, from whom most of us are descended, were not only almost savages, but they were pagans; that is, worshippers of many gods. What little of Christianity had been planted in the island by the Romans had disappeared, and the new tenants of England worshipped various gods, the chief of whom was Wodin, or Odin. Next to him was Thor, or Thunder. To this god the horse was sacred, and the English held feasts of horseflesh in his honor. After they had been converted to Christianity they gave up these feasts altogether; and this change of habits has been thought to be the reason why we do not eat horseflesh, as is done by some races. To this day we keep the names of Wodin and Thor in our Wednesday and Thursday; and this is why our Puritan ancestors in England and America refused to use these names, which they thought heathen, and why they preferred to name the days of the week by simple numbers, — First Day, Second Day, and so on, — as the Quakers, or Friends, now do. But as all these early English kings claimed to be descended from Wodin, they thought it very proper to call one day in the week by his name.

Religion of the English.

All these English tribes kept up the customs of their Teutonic forefathers; and it is thus that those customs have been handed down to Americans. To begin with, each tribe, as it settled down on its part of the conquered territory, divided most of the arable land among its members according to the old Teutonic method, — a portion to each family. Several families living near together formed a township, and the affairs of the township were arranged at a meeting of the male freeholders, or freemen, of the

English institutions.

township. After Christianity was introduced, this "town-moot," or "town-meeting," took charge of the religious affairs too, and did this under the name of "parish." The English parish-meeting, or "vestry," of our own time is the survival of this organization; and so, probably, is the town-meeting of the New England States.

<small>The township.</small>

Several townships, enough to furnish a hundred or so of warriors, formed what was called "The Hundred." The hundred had its own meeting, at which the town priest and reeve, with four more men from each township, were present. This organization of the hundred is still preserved in some States of the American Union. Then, as time went on, and there came to be but one king in all England, the little kingdoms of former days became shires, or counties. The affairs of a county were conducted at an assembly over which an officer called the ealdorman (alderman) presided.

<small>The hundred.</small>

<small>The county.</small>

The land was not all divided among separate owners. According to some writers a part of it was always reserved, to be given by the lords at some future time to those who deserved it, or to be let to those who had no right to a portion of free land, and who had to put themselves under the protection of some strong man. According to other writers, most of the land was owned by the community in common. Moreover, many of the people were thralls, or slaves, some of these having sold themselves into slavery because they were poor, or having been fined for some offence, and having been unable to pay the fine. All who have read Scott's novel of "Ivanhoe" will remember Gurth and Wamba, who were slaves, and actually wore collars

<small>The land.</small>

around their necks; although Scott must not be too closely followed, as it is said that there is some historical error in almost every page of "Ivanhoe."

Besides these various classes of freemen, dependants, and slaves, there were the fighting men, or thanes, who followed the fortunes of their chief, or king, and were often rewarded by a gift of land or by a title of nobility. Where these thanes, or nobles, were powerful, the poorer and weaker were glad to come under their authority and have their protection; and thus the simple early Teutonic institutions went through a change, and became more like what was called "feudalism" in the rest of Europe. This change was seen, for instance, in the growth of the Witenagemot, or meeting of the Wise Men (Witan). This was a body of great power, and took in some degree the place of a legislature or congress. It elected the king, sometimes passing over the older heir, and choosing some other member of the ruling family. It also appointed the officers of state, and decided questions of peace and war. At first the freemen had the right to attend its meetings; but the attendance was gradually composed of the leading officials and nobles. *The thanes.* *The meeting of the Wise Men.*

For many years the English still remained pagan, worshipping the old Saxon gods; but just before the end of the sixth century Augustine, a monk, visited England. Fortunately for him, the king of Kent, named Ethelbert, had married a Christian wife, daughter of the king of the Franks, so Augustine was allowed to land. Between his wife's persuasions and those of this monk, Ethelbert became a Christian, and allowed Augustine to live at *Conversion to Christianity.*

Canterbury, where the head of the Church of England has ever since had a palace, his title being that of Archbishop of Canterbury. Then Edwin, king of Northumbria, the most powerful of the various English kings, married a daughter of Ethelbert, and was also converted; and by degrees all the other kings and their people became Christian. And what was almost as important, before long the English Church became a portion of the Roman Catholic Church, to which the leading nations of western Europe also belonged. In this way England was brought again under the influences of civilization.

During all this time no English king succeeded in really uniting all England, though by 827 Egbert of Wessex was recognized by all Englishmen living south of Edinburgh and the Firth of Forth as their ruler, or "over-lord."

<small>England united (827).</small>

SAXON HORSEMEN (HARL. MS. 603).

CHAPTER III.

THE NORTHMEN IN ENGLAND.

827-1042.

IN those days there were certain sea-rovers, called vikings, who used to land upon the coasts of England and France, and often took possession of the land and held it. The word "vikings" does not mean that they were kings, but that they dwelt on a *vik*, or bay. They came in long boats with high prows, often bearing the head of a dragon or some other animal. There were sometimes fifty rowers, whose shields were hung over the sides of the boat; and when the boat was upset in a sea-fight, the men would escape their enemies by swimming, with their heads under their floating shields. These sea-rovers were called Northmen, or Norsemen, so that when they took possession of a part of the coast of France it was named Normandy, and has held that name ever since. Some of these same Northmen afterwards made their way to Iceland, and thence, it is believed, to America. But the sea-rovers who invaded England were from Denmark, and came from the same part of Europe as the Jutes, who had landed in England before. They spoke a Teutonic dialect, probably not differing much from that spoken in England at the time.

The Danish sea-rovers landed first in Ireland, where the people had been converted to Christianity before

Margin note: The vikings.

the English, but were still far from being civilized. The native tribes retreated before the warlike Danes into the forests and wilds of the interior. Then the Danes crossed to England, and overran Northumbria and Mercia; but when they came to Wessex they met with some resistance from young king Alfred, Egbert's grandson. But he had to retreat to the forest, and is said to have taken refuge with a cowherd, whose wife did not know he was a king, and set him to tending the cakes that she was baking before the fire. Coming in, she found that they were burning; and she said to him, according to an old ballad: —

The Danes and King Alfred.

> "There, don't you see the cakes on fire?
> Then wherefore turn them not?
> You're glad enough to eat them
> When they are piping hot."

At last he gathered men enough about him to leave his retreat and attack the Danes. They were taken wholly by surprise, and he drove them out of his kingdom of Wessex; but he could not drive them out of England, and he had to let them remain, on condition of acknowledging him as their superior, or "over-lord." They thus ruled over the northern part of England; but we cannot trace many of our institutions to them, although the names of many English towns are Danish, as those of Whitby and Derby.

Treaty of Wedmore (878).

Although Alfred could not get rid of the Danes, he was the best and greatest of these early English chiefs, or kings. He brought together the laws and customs of the nation into a kind of code. He encouraged learning by translating books from other

Alfred's government.

languages into English, and above all he built a navy, and brought England more into connection with the outer world. Under his son, Edward the Elder, and his successors, the work of Alfred was completed; so that, by the middle of the tenth century, the Danes were conquered, and even the Scots and Welsh acknowledged the authority of the English king.

Edward died in 925, and the next fifty years were years of comparative peace and quiet. The ablest man of the period was Dunstan, a monk, afterwards known as Saint Dunstan, who became Archbishop of Canterbury. Under his wise guidance the Danes put away their wild habits, and became like Englishmen, and the Scottish king became a subject of the king of England, taking some of the northern part of England for his own, and having the old English town of Edinburgh for his seat of government. Dunstan died in 988. Even before his death another horde of Danes came, this time determined to conquer England and rule it themselves. The English king, Ethelred "the Unready," or "Without Counsel," foolishly gave the Danes money to go away. Of course they came back the next year in still greater numbers. Their leader was their king, Swend, or Swegen, Forkbeard, who became king of England; and when he died, his son Cnut, or Canute, was king after him, although Edmund Ironside, the brave son of Ethelred the Unready, divided England with Cnut for a time.

Saint Dunstan.

Cnut, the Dane, king of England.

Cnut was a man of much force and energy. He succeeded to all Ethelred's possessions, and at last even married his widow; so that he no longer seemed a stranger to the people. He was not only king of

Rural Life in the Eleventh Century. — January to June (Cott. MS, *Julius A.*, vi.).

RURAL LIFE IN THE ELEVENTH CENTURY.   21

RURAL LIFE IN THE ELEVENTH CENTURY, — JULY TO DECEMBER (Cott. MS., *Julius A.*, vi.)

England, but of Denmark, of a part of Sweden, and at last of Norway. He divided England into four earldoms, giving each to an earl, of whom the ablest was Earl Godwin of Wessex. The best remembered story of Cnut is that of his ordering the sea to obey him; and it is told by an old monk named Henry of Huntingdon. One day, as the story goes, Cnut sat down in a chair upon the beach below high-water mark, and bade the tide stop rising. "O sea, I am thy lord. My ships sail over thee whither I will, and this land against which thou breakest is mine. Stay thou thy waves, and dare not to wet the feet of thy lord and master." But the tide kept on, and wet the royal feet before they could get out of the way; and it is said that he was so humbled as never to wear his crown again. In fact, his children did not wear it long either. His sons died without children, and the "Wise Men" gave the crown to Ethelred's son, Edward.

AN ENGLISH VESSEL (HARL. MS. 603).

CHAPTER IV.

THE NORMAN CONQUEST.

1042-1087.

THE new king's early years had been spent in Normandy, and he was more Norman than English in his feelings. He liked to have his Norman friends around him, and gave them important offices, even making one of them Archbishop of Canterbury. This was bitterly opposed by a large party of the English, headed by Earl Godwin. This led to constant quarrels, and when the great earl died, and his son Harold succeeded him as Earl of Wessex, Harold really became more powerful than the king. Then the king himself died, and his influence became greater after his death than in his lifetime. Remembering his mild rule, so different from the oppressions that came later, men called him "Edward the Confessor," or "Saint." He was buried in the great Church or West Minster, which was completed before his death, and which is now called by the same name, Westminster Abbey, although of Edward's original building only the bases of a few columns remain.

Edward the Confessor was the last of the direct descendants of Cedric the Saxon; and the day after his death the "Wise Men" met and chose his young rival, Harold, to be king of England, Edward himself having recommended this. But the

Harold chosen king.

new king had little peace. William, Duke of Normandy, had hoped for the crown of England, and was furious when he heard of the "Wise Men's" choice; for he claimed that Harold had promised in the most solemn way to help him to become king of England. Indeed, it seems certain that Harold had promised to do something William wished, though probably only to marry William's daughter. Then another Harold, surnamed Hardrada, or "stern of counsel," resolved to invade England, and did so; but his namesake defeated him utterly, Sept. 25, 1066. A few days later, while the English Harold was celebrating this victory, some one entered the room and said that Duke William of Normandy had landed, and had taken up his position near Hastings. Harold knew that the time for a decisive battle had come, and with all speed gathered his men, and marching southward, took up a strong position on the heights of Senlac, as the battle-field was afterwards called, seven miles from William's camp.

Early the next morning the Normans prepared to storm the English fortification on the hill. It is said that William, as he was putting on his hauberk, or body armor, turned it the wrong way. His men were alarmed, thinking it a bad omen; but William, with ready wit, claimed it as a good omen, for that day, he said, was to change a Norman duke into an English king. The fight was long and doubtful, Harold's position being very difficult of attack. At last William pretended to retreat. This drew a part of the English out of their stronghold, and the Normans turned upon them, defeated them, and again attacked the fort. They fought with bows and arrows, and an arrow pierced Harold to the brain.

Battle of Senlac, or Hastings. (Oct. 14, 1066).

He fell mortally wounded, and William of Normandy became master of southern England.

Who was this William of Normandy, and what right had he to claim the throne of England? Long before, while King Alfred was fighting the Danes in England, another northern tribe under Rollo, or Rolf, was besieging Paris in France; and the French king, to get rid of Rolf, gave him the city of Rouen, and some land along the sea-coast, on condition that he should become a Christian, and should render service to the French king in time of war. The region first given to him was called the Northmen's land; but as years went on, and the Northmen grew civilized, and adopted the French language, they called themselves Normans, and their land Normandy. Now, William, the Conqueror of England, was the descendant and successor of this Rolf, who had invaded France. *William the Conqueror (1066–1087).*

As to his right to the throne of England, William always said that Edward the Confessor had promised it to him; but it was not Edward's to promise, and the "Wise Men" had, at any rate, chosen Harold. William, however, referred the matter to the Pope of Rome, and by promising to bring the English Church into closer union with the Roman Catholic Church, he won the Pope's consent to his invasion. At Senlac he broke the strength of England; and though it took five years more to complete the conquest, yet the date of this battle is perhaps the most important in English history. To fix the memory of the event, the Conqueror built an abbey on the spot where Harold fell, and inscribed in it the names of the Norman knights who fought there. Only the foundation of the building now remains; but Americans and Englishmen still like to trace their "Norman blood" to those whose names are on the roll of Battle Abbey.

Effect of the Conquest. The Norman Conquest was unlike any other conquest of England, because it gave only a new set of rulers, and left the laws and political institutions to a large extent unchanged. Yet there was a great change in the ownership of the land, and it came about in this way. In the first place, William claimed that ever since Edward's death he had been the only lawful king in England. If this was true, then it followed that Harold had not been king at all; and from this it followed again that every one who had supported Harold, or had failed to support William, was a traitor. Now, it was the English law that the lands of traitors should be taken from them, and become the property of the king. Therefore, as nearly all Englishmen had been on Harold's side, or had opposed William's claim in some way, nearly all lost their lands, which the king gave to his favorites; and this, it must be remembered, not by mere right of conquest, but under the regular forms of English law. In other ways, too, the same thing took place; that is, the old forms were kept up, but were in the hands of different men. The English "Meeting of the Wise Men," for instance, was still continued, but only Normans came to it. However, within less than a hundred years the Normans themselves changed very much, becoming English in looks and manners, *Continuity of English history.* so that it was really hard to tell from which stock a man was descended. Thus the old English institutions were again carried on by Englishmen. This continuity of English history is a very important fact. To it we owe much that is best in our laws and institutions, and to it we owe the best and strongest part of our speech.

After a time a great many Englishmen were able to buy back part of their land from their Norman rulers. Now, all landowners, whether English or Norman, owed certain duties, called "services," in person or in money to the king, as their "overlord." To find out exactly what was due him, the Conqueror sent men to all parts of England to look into the titles of estates and estimate their value. The results were most carefully written down in a great book, called the "Domesday Book," which was then kept at Winchester. It can still be seen at London, and is so valuable that every page has been photographed and reprinted exactly as it was first written. *Domesday Book.*

It took about a year to make this Great Survey. When it was done, William ordered all but the smallest landowners to meet him on Salisbury Plain. Sixty thousand came. They took a most solemn oath to support William as king, even against their own lords. This made the English for the first time one nation. It was also a most important modification of the feudal system, for it made all landowners directly subject to the king. Then, too, William did away with the old earldoms, and his foresight in these regards prevented his nobles or barons from becoming the equals of their king, as was the case in France and Germany. Thus England, in a great measure, escaped the petty wars which for centuries disturbed the rest of western Europe. *The oath of Salisbury (1086).*

In many other ways, too, the Norman Conquest affected England. For example, before long all the best places in the Church were filled with foreigners. But most of the new bishops and abbots were far superior in morals and education to the Englishmen whom they succeeded. They were also devoted to the Pope of Rome, and soon made the English National Church a part of the Roman Catholic Church. But William, while willing to bow to the Pope as his chief in religious matters, refused to give way to him in things which concerned only this world. No former English king had done that, he knew, and no more would he. This union with the Roman Catholic Church was of the greatest benefit to England, as it brought her once more into connection with the educated men of Europe. Indeed, Lanfranc, the Conqueror's Archbishop of Canterbury, was one of the best and wisest men of his day.

Influence of the Roman Catholic Church on England.

In character the first William was stern to those who disobeyed him. "So harsh and cruel was he that none dared withstand him," says an old chronicle. But it must be remembered that it took a man of very strong will to rule England at that time. Next to war, William's greatest passion was for hunting. "He loved the tall deer as though he had been their father." To provide a home for them he ordered a large tract in Hampshire to be turned into a forest. And still better to preserve them, he made a law that any one who should kill a deer without leave should lose both his eyes. The very name of this New Forest, therefore, was hateful to his subjects, and two of his sons and one grandson lost their lives within its limits.

The New Forest.

The Normans were great builders. The White Tower — the oldest part of the Tower of London —

was built by the Conqueror as a fortress to hold the Londoners in check. The old Westminster Hall was the work of his son William, the Red King, while all over England some of the grandest cathedral churches were planned and built by the early Norman bishops.

<small>London Tower and Westminster Hall.</small>

The Conqueror's last years were very unhappy. His oldest son, Robert, rebelled, and the French king did his utmost to annoy him. At last, in answer to one of this king's insults, William ordered the little town of Mantes to be burned. While he was riding through the town to see that his orders were carried out, his horse stepped on a burning coal. The king's fat body was thrown against the high point of his saddle, and in three weeks he died. Normandy passed under the rule of his eldest son, Robert. The second son, William, received his ring and a letter to Lanfranc desiring the archbishop to crown him as king of England, if it were right. To Henry, the youngest son, he gave only a sum of money. As soon as the Conqueror was dead his sons hastened away to take possession of their inheritances. So stern had he been to his servants that they refused to touch his body; and it was with difficulty that even a piece of land was bought for a grave.

<small>William's death (1087).</small>

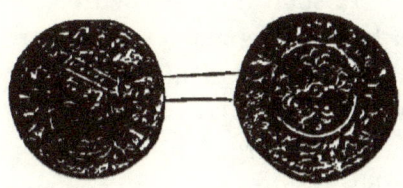

A SILVER PENNY OF WILLIAM THE CONQUEROR.

CHAPTER V.

THE NORMAN KINGS.

1087-1154.

THE younger William had a big red face, and people called him Rufus, or the Red. Many of the great barons of England, owning large estates in Normandy, would have preferred to have but one ruler for both countries. But Robert was absent, and as William Rufus promised Lanfranc to govern well, the archbishop crowned him king without delay. William was a good soldier and hunter, and he kept the nobles in order; but there was nothing else that was good about him.

William II., the Red (1087-1100).

Above all, he was fond of extravagance and show. One day his servants brought him a pair of new boots. "How much did they cost?" demanded the king. "Three shillings," the man replied. In a rage the Red King threw them from him, demanding boots that cost three times as much. The servant was a sharp man. He soon returned with a pair of cheaper boots, though he told his master they were very expensive. "Ay," exclaimed Rufus, as he pulled them on, "these are suited to royal majesty." After this his servants always charged him twice as much as his food and clothes really cost. They grew rich very fast. But the English people, who had to pay for all this waste, were not very sorry when the Red King was

His extravagance.

found one afternoon in the New Forest with an arrow in his shoulder. No one knows who killed him. An intimate companion named Wat Tyrrel, who was with him at the time, rode away as fast as he could. It is thought that perhaps Wat Tyrrel killed him by accident. Others say his servants shot him. At any rate, no sooner was the breath out of his body than his servants deserted him. If a poor charcoal man had not found the body, and carried it to Winchester in his cart, William Rufus might never have been buried.

His death.

It chanced that the Conqueror's youngest son Henry was riding in the New Forest at the time. The instant he knew of his brother's death he put spurs to his horse and galloped to Winchester, where the royal treasure was then kept. After he had once made sure of that, his election was certain, and

Henry I. (1100-1135).

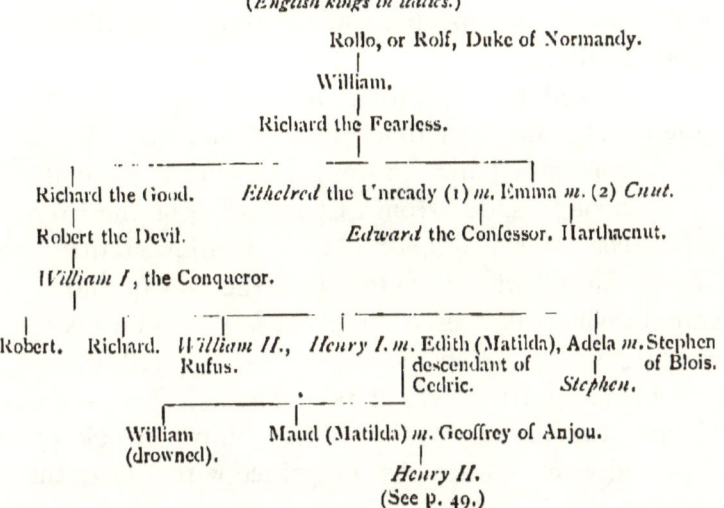

three days later he was crowned at Westminster. Still there were many barons who would have preferred the elder brother Robert, Duke of Normandy, for king; so Henry was obliged to fall back on the native English for support. To please them he married Edith, or Matilda, daughter of the king of Scots. She was descended, through her mother, from the old English line, and in this way a descendant of Cedric again came to rule in England. This marriage bound the English to Henry, and they stood by him in all his quarrels and wars.

Indeed, he soon found himself so strong in England that he crossed over to Normandy, took his brother Duke Robert prisoner, and shut him up for the rest of his life. What was more important still, he conquered a large part of Wales and joined it to England. In England itself he governed so well that an old writer declared: "No man durst ill-treat another in his days. Peace he made for man and beast." He had a good education, too, for a soldier of his time, and people called him "Beauclerc,"—good-scholar.

Conquers Normandy.

Henry had two children, William and Matilda, or Maud. He was very fond of them, and they often accompanied him in his journeyings. One afternoon he sailed from a little harbor on the French coast for England. His son followed in "The White Ship," whose captain was the son of the very captain who had steered the great William on his conquering voyage. The young people delayed, dancing and drinking till it was dark. Then, just as she was leaving the harbor, "The White Ship" struck on a rock and went down. As the prince with a few others

The White Ship.

was rowing away in a little boat, he heard his fair cousin, the Countess of Perche, calling after him. He went back. The drowning men crowded into the boat. It sank, and when morning dawned one only, a butcher of Rouen, was saved. When Henry heard of his son's sad end he dropped senseless to the floor, and is said never to have smiled again. One of Mrs. Hemans's best-known poems is founded on this event, and also a poem by Rossetti, "The White Ship."

But Henry did not give up all idea of founding a line of kings. He made the barons swear to be true to his daughter Maud, and then married her to Geoffrey Plantagenet, Count of Anjou, one of the greatest nobles in France. No sooner was Henry dead, however, than his barons broke their oaths, and made his nephew, Stephen, king of England.

_{Geoffrey of Anjou marries Maud.}

This Stephen was a handsome, good-natured, popular man, and at first everything went well with him. He even defeated Maud's uncle, David, king of Scots, in battle. But when he had given to the barons much of the land and money belonging to the Crown, they deserted him, and took the part of Maud. She came to England, and at first was so successful that Stephen was captured and put in prison, and she was recognized as queen, or rather "lady," of the English; for they used this last phrase commonly in those old days. Maud even went to London to be crowned. But she was so haughty and proud that the Londoners turned her out before her coronation-day. Stephen, too, gained his freedom, and in the end Maud had to flee from England.

_{Stephen (1135–1154).}

This civil war lasted fourteen years. It was a terrible time for the English people. The great barons would sometimes come forth from their castles and plunder whole towns. The roads were so unsafe, it is said, that a lonely traveller, if he saw another man in the distance, would leave the road and try to conceal himself until danger was over. But everything has an end, and in 1153 the bishops contrived to make an agreement by which Stephen was to be king for the rest of his life, with the understanding that at his death the throne should go to Maud's son, Henry Plantagenet. The next year Stephen died.

Civil war.

SEAL OF MILO OF GLOUCESTER, SHOWING MOUNTED ARMED FIGURE IN THE REIGN OF HENRY I.

CHAPTER VI.

THE FIRST TWO PLANTAGENETS.

1154-1199.

HENRY the Second was only twenty-one years old when he became king of England. But he already was a very powerful man, as he ruled over more than one-third of France. He was called Plantagenet, from a bit of broom plant (*plante-de-genêt*) which he and his father were accustomed to wear in their helmets to distinguish them from other knights. Henry II. (1154-1189).

Henry was a very great king. He made many changes in the laws and customs of England, the effects of which we still feel. He divided England into circuits, and appointed persons, on whom he could rely, to travel round in these circuits, and see that all men, nobles and commons alike, obeyed the laws. The English judges still travel through England, as do many American judges through our country. When these judges came together in London, they sat as the King's Court, and were then called justices. When hearing cases in which the revenue was concerned, they sat around a great table with a top divided like a chequer-board. They were thence called barons of the exchequer,— a word which is still used as the name of one of the departments of the English government. His reforms.

All these good things Henry was able to do because he had the support of the great mass of the people. *Shield-money.* He trusted them, and instead of disarming them, ordered every freeman to keep arms suitable to his social position. In addition to this national militia, Henry had a feudal army. It must be remembered that since the time of the great William nearly all English land was held on what was called a feudal tenure. That is, instead of paying rent for their pieces of land, or feuds, the great landholders promised to serve the king in time of war with their followers for forty days every year at their own expense. Henry made a law that all who were legally obliged to follow him, and yet wished to stay at home, could do so if they would pay "shield-money," or "scutage," instead. A very great many preferred to stay at home; and with this money Henry hired a large army of foreigners. The result was that the barons grew less and less warlike, and, on the other hand, the Crown was much strengthened.

There was one thing, however, that proved even stronger than Henry Plantagenet; that was the Church. *The Constitutions of Clarendon (1164).* The king wished to have the clergy, whenever they committed criminal acts, tried by his judges, like other people. He summoned the bishops and the great barons to Clarendon, and by the "Constitutions" formed at that place they all agreed to do as he wished. The Pope did not approve this, and, following him, the Archbishop of Canterbury withdrew his consent. Henry could not reach the Pope, but he revenged himself on the archbishop. This was Thomas Becket, the son of a Norman citizen of London. In earlier days he and Henry had been great friends; but no sooner had Thomas become archbishop than he did all he could to strengthen the Church, whether the king liked it or not. Becket fled to France; but in 1170 he and Henry became reconciled. He had hardly reached Canterbury, however, before he suspended the Archbishop of York, who had done Henry a service. When Henry heard this he flew into a passion, exclaiming: "What cowards have I brought up in my court! Not one will rid me of this low-born priest." Reginald Fitzurse and three other knights took this as an order. They hurried to Canterbury, pursued Thomas Becket even to the altar in the cathedral, and killed him. It was a dreadful deed, and Henry was very sorry that he had lost his temper. Indeed, all his good fortune seemed to desert him from that time, until he knelt before Becket's tomb and bade the monks beat his bare shoulders.

It was in Henry's reign that Richard of Clare, Maurice Fitz-Gerald, and other Norman knights went over to Ireland and put Dermot, king of Leinster, back on his throne again. After Dermot's death, Richard of Clare married his daughter, and ruled over Leinster; but he was afraid of Henry's jealousy, and gave up his conquests to him. Henry crossed over to Ireland, and was recognized as the sovereign of the island. But he never really conquered it, and for hundreds of years Ireland remained the scene of strife between the descendants of the Normans on the one side, and their Irish neighbors on the other. *Conquest of Ireland.*

Henry's last years were even more unhappy than those of the Conqueror. His sons rebelled, and were so ably assisted by King Philip Augustus *Henry's sons.*

EFFIGIES OF HENRY THE SECOND AND QUEEN ELEANOR.

of France that he had to submit to their demands. He asked to see the list of those joined against him. It was headed by the name of his favorite son, John. The old king's heart was broken. "Now let things go as they will," he said; "I care no more for myself or the world." In a few weeks he was dead.

But John did not at once become king, for Richard, his elder brother, was in the way. Richard came over to London, was crowned, and then, as soon as he had scraped together all the money he could, set out with his friend King Philip to conquer the Holy Land. They quarrelled almost as soon as they reached that land, and Philip returned home to seize all of Richard's French possessions that he could reach. In England, too, John rose to the head of affairs, although Richard had left a friend of his own to govern in his absence. Richard did not lay siege to Jerusalem, but set off on his return to England. He was wrecked on the shores of the Adriatic, and while trying to get through Austria unseen, was arrested by Duke Leopold, whom he had insulted in the Holy Land. Duke Leopold handed him over to the Emperor, who kept him close prisoner until the English people paid a large ransom. It is said that John even tried to bribe the Emperor to keep him still longer.

Richard I. (1189-1199).

At any rate, when he got back to England, Richard did not punish John very severely for his disloyalty. As soon as he got together an army, however, Richard crossed over to France to take vengeance on Philip Augustus. He accomplished little, and while trying to capture a castle in his own dominions, where he said there was some treasure that belonged to him, he was mortally wounded by an arrow. The castle

Richard's death.

surrendered before he died, and he ordered all within it to be hanged, except the boy who had shot him. "What have I done that you should take my life?" said the king. "You have killed my father and two brothers," was the reply. King Richard commanded that the brave boy be set free; but after the king's death he was hanged, with cruel tortures.

Richard Cœur de Lion was in England for but eight months during his whole reign. He cared nothing for England or for Englishmen, except as they supplied him with money to carry on his costly wars. Nevertheless, he soon came to be looked upon as the nation's hero, and he is described as such in Scott's novel, "Ivanhoe." Traditions gathered about his name all over Europe, and it is said that for hundreds of years the tired Arab mothers were wont to terrify their crying babes into silence with, "Hush ye! here comes King Richard."

_{His place in England's history.}

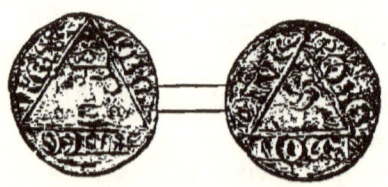

A SILVER PENNY OF JOHN, STRUCK AT DUBLIN.

CHAPTER VII.

KING JOHN AND MAGNA CHARTA.

1199–1216.

RICHARD'S younger brother John was crowned king in England. But in France there were many nobles who wished to have John's nephew, Prince Arthur, for their duke. Philip Augustus took the young prince's side. John captured the boy, and ordered Hubert de Burgh to put out his eyes. "For," thought he, "the Normans will never want a blind man to be their duke." But the poor boy begged so hard that Hubert did not have the heart to carry out his orders. There was no mercy in John, however, and after he got possession of Prince Arthur the boy was never seen again. Men said that John had stabbed him to death; but no one really knows how he died. *Prince Arthur.*

Now, John, as Duke of Normandy and Count of Anjou, was a vassal of the king of France. So Philip summoned him to Paris to clear himself of this charge of murder. John, who knew better than to trust himself within Philip's power, refused to appear, and so Philip seized his French dominions. Aquitaine and the Channel Islands alone remained to the English Crown. Aquitaine has long since been lost; but the Channel Islands (Jersey, Guernsey, Alderney, and Sark) still belong to the *Philip of France seizes Normandy and Anjou.*

English sovereign, — the only remnant of the Norman possessions of William the Conqueror. In this way John was forced to become a real English king.

His next quarrel was with the Pope. It was about the election of a new Archbishop of Canterbury. The Pope declared that an Englishman, Stephen Langton by name, was the duly elected archbishop. John refused to recognize him. Then the Pope ordered all religious services to cease in England. This was called an interdict. If we remember that the Roman Catholic faith was then the only religion practised in England, we can see how serious a thing this interdict was. It lasted six years, and for six years almost no one was married with regular religious services in all England. Still John did not yield. So the Pope cast him out of the Church, or excommunicated him. And as this did not bring him to terms, the Pope deposed him, or declared him to be no king at all, and ordered Philip Augustus to carry out the sentence.

The interdict.

Now, if John had been a good king, he might perhaps have been strong enough at home to care very little for the Pope and the French king put together. But unfortunately he was a very bad ruler, and all his people hated him. So he soon found that his barons were actually conspiring with the French Philip against him. This so alarmed him that he not only recognized Langton as archbishop, but he put himself and his kingdom under the protection of the Pope, actually agreeing to pay rent for it.

John submits to the Pope.

Philip never came over, but John kept on governing as badly as ever. The barons determined to stop it. With their armed followers they marched to London.

THE GREAT CHARTER.

Nearly every one deserted John. He met the barons on a little island in the Thames not far from Windsor and near the meadow of Runneymead. There, on the 15th of June, 1215, he assented to the Magna Charta, or Great Charter, which his barons presented to him. This can still be seen, carefully preserved, in the British Museum, and it is the most important document in English history.

<small>Magna Charta (1215).</small>

In England there is no written frame of government like the American constitution. The English government is based on the laws and customs of the kingdom, and especially on three great documents, — this Great Charter of rights of the thirteenth century, and the Petition of Right and Bill of Rights of the Stuart time. These documents are so important that Lord Chatham once called them "The Bible of the English constitution." The Great Charter is in reality a treaty between the king and the people of England. To it we, in common with English-speaking people the world over, owe many of the rights which distinguish us from all other nations.

<small>The provisions.</small>

The most important clause of this Great Charter was that relating to taxation. Richard, and after him John, had wrung tax after tax from the barons and people. The barons now determined to put an end to this. It was provided, therefore, in the charter that thenceforth no tax (other than a few taxes specified in the charter itself) should be laid by the king without the consent of the nation, given through a national council. It was further provided that all the greater barons should be summoned to this council by a royal summons directed to each one of them, while the lesser landholders were to be summoned in a less formal way, by a writ directed to the sheriff of their shire. This provision never went into actual operation, and was omitted from the later issues of the charter. Yet its importance can hardly be over-estimated. It was the basis for the summoning of Simon of Montfort's Parliament, and of the first regular Parliament in the great Edward's time.

The more famous sentences of the Great Charter are the following, which have been thus translated from the original Latin: "No free man shall be taken, or imprisoned, or disseised [dispossessed], or outlawed, or exiled, or any ways destroyed. Nor will we go upon him, nor send upon him, unless by the lawful judgment of his peers [equals], or by the law of the land." "To none will we sell, to none will we deny or delay right or justice." It is on these sentences that the right to a speedy trial by jury is based, "the most effectual security against oppression which the wisdom of man has hitherto been able to devise."

Twenty-five barons were chosen to see that King John obeyed the Charter. In truth, he had no idea of doing what he had promised. It is said that he was so angry at having been compelled to sign it that he rolled on the floor in rage, and gnawed a stick. The Pope soon declared that the charter had no force, as the king had been compelled to sign it; and John hired some French soldiers to help him put down his barons. But Stephen Langton, the archbishop, took their side, and they resolved to have a new king. So they called Prince Louis of France to be their ruler. As soon as he appeared, John's French soldiers refused to fight. The Scots and Welsh turned against their king; and there is every

John's death.

reason to believe that he would have been the last of his race to rule in England, had not the vexation of spirit at his losses thrown him into a fever, from which he died. It may be that too many peaches and too much ale hastened his end, and there is a story that he was poisoned by a monk. In whatever manner he died, the English people were not sorry to have him out of the way.

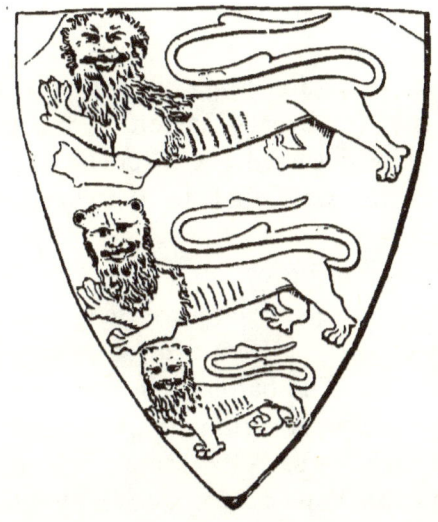

ROYAL ARMS OF ENGLAND FROM RICHARD I. TO EDWARD III.

CHAPTER VIII.

HENRY III.

1216-1272.

A FEW barons had stood by John to the end, and one of them, William Marshall, Earl of Pembroke, proclaimed John's son as king, under the title of Henry III. As the new king was only nine years old, Pembroke ruled for him. The first thing he did was to re-issue the Great Charter. This pleased the barons, and they deserted the French prince in such numbers that he was glad to get back to France alive.

But in time Henry grew up, and began to govern as badly as his father had ever governed. Above all, he made the barons pay a great deal of money to support his foreign wars. The barons rebelled, and compelled Henry to place the government of England in their hands. Then they quarrelled among themselves, and as Henry had the Pope on his side, he tried to get his power back again.

Even in those old days young men came from all parts of England, Scotland, and Wales to the colleges at Oxford to pursue their education. They thought on political subjects very much as their fathers thought; and having no responsibility in the matter, expressed their feelings more openly than did their fathers. In fact, their fights in the streets of

Oxford.

Oxford so often showed the position which their fathers were about to take that it became a common saying:

> "When Oxford draws the knife,
> England's soon at strife."

They now showed the approach of civil war by driving the Pope's legate, or lieutenant, out of Oxford.

The head of the national party was Simon of Montfort. He was by birth a Frenchman; but he had inherited an English earldom, and had become a thorough Englishman. He collected an army, and meeting the king at Lewes, captured him and his whole family. He then summoned a Great Council, to which not only the barons and large land-owners were admitted, but also representatives from the

Earl Simon of Montfort.

EFFIGY OF A KNIGHT IN THE TEMPLE CHURCH, LONDON, SHOWING ARMOR WORN BETWEEN 1190 AND 1225.

great towns, or boroughs. For some time the Great Council had been called a Parliament, from the French word *parler*, "to speak," because affairs were spoken about, or debated, there. This Great Council was therefore called Earl Simon's Parliament. It was really the beginning of the present form of government in England.

Earl Simon's Parliament (1265).

It happened one day that as the king's eldest son, Prince Edward, was out riding, he escaped from his jailers. Gathering an army, he came upon Earl Simon at Evesham, and overthrew him. The great earl was killed during the battle, but his work did not perish with him, for Prince Edward, who ruled

Evesham.

SEAL OF ROBERT FITZWALTER, SHOWING A MOUNTED KNIGHT IN COMPLETE MAIL ARMOR. DATE, ABOUT 1265.

for his father, was a wise man, and governed well. In fact, so quiet did the barons become that the prince left England and went on a crusade. Before his return King Henry died. As his body was lying in Westminster Abbey, Gilbert, Earl of Gloucester, placing his hand on the dead king, swore allegiance to King Edward the First, and the king was proclaimed.

It was in the Third Henry's time that Roger Bacon, a great scholar and a friar, put forth many famous books (*Opus Majus*), applying to the natural sciences what was afterwards called the inductive method of reasoning; that is, reasoning from observation and experience. It is said that the clergy were so afraid that the new ideas would destroy their hold on the minds of men that they put Bacon into prison. It was in Henry's time, too, that the old Norman way of building with round arches gave place to the lighter style of pointed arches. When, in its turn, this latter mode went out of fashion, men called it, after the barbarous Goths, the Gothic style. Salisbury Cathedral is one of the most splendid examples of this mode of architecture.

THE EARLIER PLANTAGENETS.

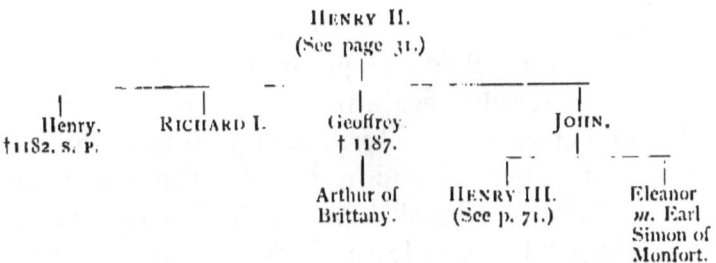

CHAPTER IX.

THE FIRST TWO EDWARDS.

1272-1327.

AS the new king was the first of his name to rule in England since the Norman Conquest, he was called Edward the First. He was a very great and wise man, and did many important things. The first Edward I., "Long-shanks" (1272-1307). was the conquest of Wales; and this was how it happened. The Welsh chieftains had been vassals of the English king for many years. But Llewelyn, who was prince of all Wales when Edward became king, thought that it would be a good time to make himself an independent prince. He was Conquers Wales (1284). betrothed to a daughter of Earl Simon, and it may be that he was really the head of a conspiracy to dethrone Edward. Now the king, who had defeated Simon of Montfort at Evesham, was no ordinary soldier, and in a short time he conquered Wales, and compelled the prince to submit. A few years later Llewelyn again rebelled. He himself was killed in a chance encounter, but his brother, the real leader, was captured and executed. From that day Prince of Wales. Edward governed Wales as if it were a part of England. To please the Welsh, he made his eldest son Prince of Wales, and the title has been borne by the eldest son of the king of England ever since. There is a story that Edward promised to give them a native prince, who could not speak one word of

English, and that he then showed them the young Edward, who had just been born in the Welsh castle of Caernarvon. But it is not certain that this is really true. Another story is that Edward, seeing the Welsh bards, or minstrels, kept alive the spirit of liberty, ordered them all to be killed. No historian now believes this, but it forms the basis of a poem called "The Bard," by the poet Gray.

<small>The Bards.</small>

It so happened that at this time there were many claimants to the crown of Scotland. They referred their claims to Edward, who decided that John Balliol ought to be king. Balliol and his rival, Robert Bruce, were of Norman descent on their father's side. They inherited their claims

<small>Balliol and Bruce.</small>

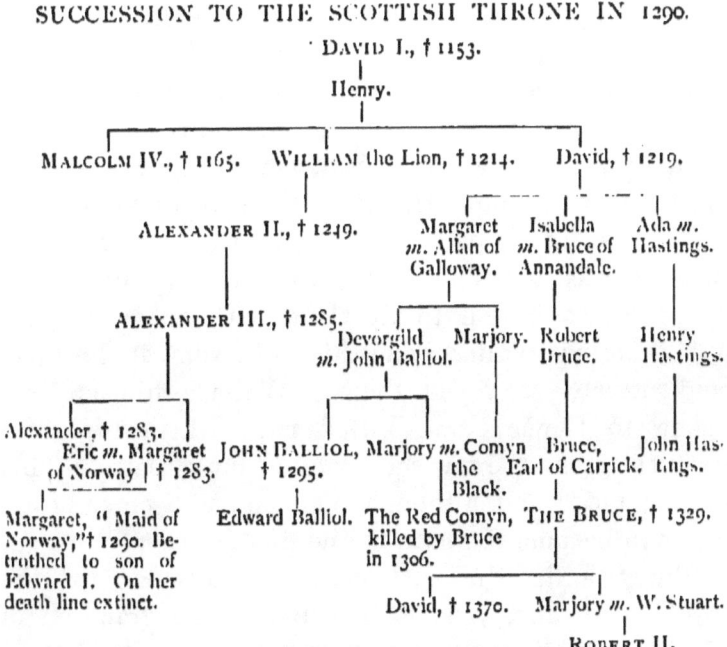

to the Scottish throne through their mothers. Balliol agreed to hold his kingdom as a gift from the English king. But this made him and his son unpopular in Scotland, and so, after his father's death, the younger Balliol made an alliance with the French king. He soon found himself a prisoner in London Tower.

Edward now determined to govern Scotland as if it were his own kingdom. To show his right to that throne, he carried to London the Stone of Scone, on which the Scottish kings had been crowned. There he had a chair built around it, and upon it every king of England has been crowned from that day to this.

<small>Stone of Scone.</small>

Now, the Scots did not at all like losing their independence. As soon as Edward got into trouble with France, they rebelled. Their leader was an outlawed knight called Sir William Wallace. He was so very cruel to the English who came in his way that the great Scottish writer, Sir Walter Scott, wrote of him, "He left nothing behind but blood and ashes" in his path along the English border. His success was but short-lived, for the very next year Edward went to Scotland with an army. He found Wallace and his followers at Falkirk, and utterly destroyed them. Wallace himself was taken to London, and killed with all the dreadful cruelties that the law then visited on outlaws. This was in 1305; and, although Wallace had been so cruel, he soon became the national hero of Scotland.

<small>Sir William Wallace.</small>

<small>Falkirk (1298).</small>

But troubles did not cease in Scotland; for the very next year Robert Bruce, the grandson of Balliol's rival, met Comyn, who was after Balliol

<small>Bruce murders Comyn.</small>

the next heir to the Scottish crown, in a little church in Dumfries, and stabbed him to the heart. Bruce then declared himself the true king of Scotland. King Edward was greatly enraged at this foul murder. His soldiers hunted Bruce from place to place, but they could not seize him; and while journeying north to take command of his army, Edward died, within sight of the Scottish border. *Edward dies (1307).*

These wars, however, were the least important events of Edward's reign. The most important thing was that it took a great deal of money to carry them on; and this money the king could not get without agreeing to certain laws which have influenced the history of England ever since. *The first perfect Parliament (1295).* It was in 1295, just before the invasion of Scotland, that Edward held his first parliament. As he needed the support of all his subjects, he took Simon of Montfort's Parliament for a model. The assembly of 1295 was the first legal Parliament in which the people of England were really represented, and therefore the great historian of the English people, John Richard Green, has called its assembling "the most important event in English history." Let us stop a moment and see who came to it.

In the first place, there were the great barons and churchmen. They were the king's greater feudal vassals, and came in person. There were too many smaller landowners to admit of their coming in person, so the sheriff of each county held an election for two knights to represent all the landowners of that county. They were called knights of the shire. Next came two citizens from each city, and two burghers, or burgesses, from each burgh, *Its composition.*

borough, or large town. These last two classes represented the merchants and mechanics of the cities and boroughs.

But the greatest law of all was the Confirmation of the Charters, which Roger Bigod, Earl of Norfolk, and Humphrey Bohun, Earl of Hereford, extorted from the king. It seems that Edward was afraid of the power of these two men, and he ordered them to lead an army into southern France. They refused. In a rage the king exclaimed to Bigod, "Sir Earl, you shall either go or hang!" "Sir King," the Earl Marshal replied, "I will neither go nor hang." The king then laid a tax upon wool, and sailed for Flanders. The two earls forbade the collection of the tax. The Londoners, and even the churchmen, joined them. The king was helpless. At Ghent he confirmed the charters, with the additional promise that he would not lay a new tax without the common consent of the nation.

Confirmation of the Charters (1297).

Edward of Caernarvon, known as Edward II., was the first Prince of Wales to become king of England. He was also the first king to date his reign from the day of his father's death. This may seem to be a very small thing in itself, but it showed that the old custom of waiting to elect a new king was being forgotten. Yet even at the present time the form of election is kept up at the coronation. The new Edward was very unlike his father. For one thing, he was too fond of foreigners. Especially was this true of a certain Piers, or Pierce, Gaveston, who had a very bad influence upon him. For one thing, Gaveston was all the time making fun of the barons, and calling them nicknames; and this trick led at last

Edward II. (1307–1327).

to his death. Headed by the Earl of Lancaster, the
king's uncle, the barons captured Gaveston and executed him. The execution, however, was due <small>Gaveston
mainly to the Earl of Warwick, whom Gaveston hanged
had called "The Black Dog." (1312).</small>

While all this was going on in England, Bruce was
not idle in Scotland. On the contrary, he overran the
greater part of that country. In 1314 Edward <small>Bruce in
marched to the relief of Stirling Castle. He Scotland.</small>
had with him nearly one hundred thousand men; but
Bruce, with scarcely thirty thousand, met him on the
banks of a little brook, or burn, the Bannockburn,
not far from Stirling Castle, and defeated him <small>Bannock-
utterly. It was with the greatest difficulty that burn
Edward escaped, and from this time Scotland (1314).</small>
was lost to the English.

The Irish, too, thought that this would be a good
time to assert their independence. But the Norman-
English nobles living in Ireland were too strong <small>The
for their wild Irish neighbors, and the rebellion Irish.</small>
ended in nothing but increased suffering for the
conquered Irish.

One would have thought that the fate of Gaveston
would have been a warning to the king. But it was
not long before he had more favorites. This <small>The De-
time they were named Despenser, or Spenser, spensers.</small>
father and son. The barons again rebelled. But
this time they did not have it all their own way, and
the Earl of Lancaster was taken by the king and
hanged. It happened that the queen, who was a
Frenchwoman, cared more for an earl named Mortimer
than she did for the king. So she hired some soldiers
in France, and brought them over to England. The

56   THE FIRST TWO EDWARDS.   [1327.

king and his favorite tried to run away, but they
fell into the barons' hands. The Despensers
were hanged, and Edward, after being deposed
by Parliament, was cruelly beaten to death, at
the order, it is supposed, of Mortimer.

<small>The king murdered (1327).</small>

GROUP OF ARMED KNIGHTS, ABOUT 1300.

CHAPTER X.

EDWARD III.

1327-1377.

KING Edward the Third was only fourteen years old at this time, and a council of regency was appointed to rule in his name. But Mortimer and the queen really possessed all the power, and they used it very ill. Suddenly, in 1330, the young king arrested Mortimer, and took the control of affairs into his own hands. Not long after, Mortimer was hanged, and the queen was kept a close prisoner for the rest of her life. *Mortimer hanged.*

Of course during these disturbances the Scots had not been idle. They had actually invaded England, and had returned to Scotland only when Bruce was acknowledged as the rightful king of Scotland by the English Government. But the peace thus bought did not last long, and in 1333 the Scottish army was totally overthrown at the battle of Halidon Hill. Nothing was really decided by this battle, for the Scots were far from being subdued. But the victory put new heart into Englishmen, and gave them more confidence in themselves. And they were soon to need all the confidence such a victory could inspire. *Halidon Hill.*

During all this time the English had retained possession of a few domains in southwestern France, and this had been a constant source of dispute between

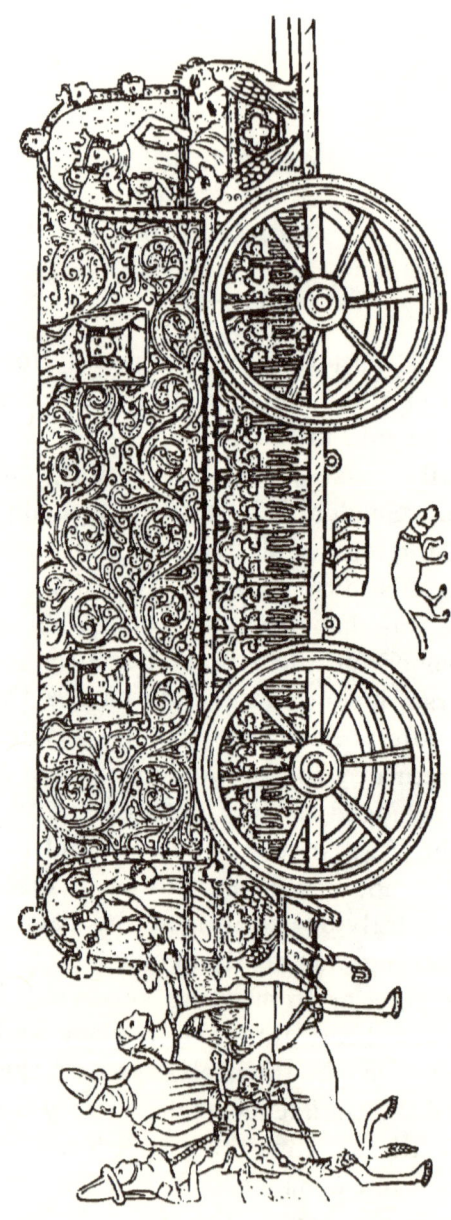

STATE CARRIAGE OF THE FOURTEENTH CENTURY. FROM THE LUTTRELL PSALTER.

the kings of England and France. It seemed to the French king at this time that he might compel Edward to do what he wished by interfering in Scotland. Edward, of course, resented this, and Philip of France seized some of the English possessions in France. To make his cause seem more just, Edward laid claim to the French throne in right of his mother. There was a law in France, called the Salic law, which prevented a woman from either ruling herself or transmitting any rights to the crown to her descendants. Now, the descent of the French crown was regulated by French law, and Edward's claim was very weak in other ways. Edward probably never regarded it as good for much; but he thought that Frenchmen, being discontented with the ruling king, would be more likely to fight on his side if he called himself king of France, and in this he was right. The motto which he adopted at this time, — "Dieu et mon droit," — is still retained, though the title of king of France was dropped nearly a hundred years ago by the English kings.

Cause of the wars with France.

At first it was very hard to get money to pay the soldiers; but after a while, as one victory after another

---

SUCCESSION TO THE FRENCH CROWN, 1328.

[The dates are those of the kings' deaths.]

PHILIP III., 1270.

PHILIP IV., 1285.   Charles of Valois.

Louis X., 1314.   PHILIP V., 1316.   Charles IV., 1322.   Isabella *m.* Edward II. of England.   PHILIP VI., 1328.

Joan of Navarre.   Edward III. of England.

was won, the war became self-supporting. The first great success was on the water. In the year 1340, Edward and his English sailors defeated a French fleet in the harbor of Sluys. So great was the slaughter that no one seemed willing to tell King Philip of France of the disaster. Finally, the court jester, or fool, cried out: "What cowards those English are! They had not the courage all to jump overboard, as the French did." This victory broke the naval power of France, and for a whole generation the English could sail up and down the Channel without fear of attack.

<small>Sea-fight at Sluys (1340).</small>

For five years there was no serious fighting; but in 1345 the war began again. The English in southern France were soon hard pressed. Edward thought he could best relieve them by invading Normandy. So he landed with an army at La Hogue, and attempted to march across the country to Flanders. The bridges over the Seine were broken, and it was some time before he could get across. Finally, however, he outwitted the French, and crossed the river not far from Paris. Then, passing the Somme, near its mouth, when the tide was low, he drew up his men on the hill of Cressy, or Crécy. The French army was several times larger than that of the English; but Edward had with him only trained soldiers, whose sole business was to fight, while Philip's force, on the contrary, was a feudal army of the old pattern, being composed of knights and gentlemen, clad in suits of heavy iron armor, and a mass of poorly armed and entirely untrained peasants. It was a mob rather than an army. When the two armies came together, the English bowmen shot their arrows so accurately and well that the

<small>Cressy (1346).</small>

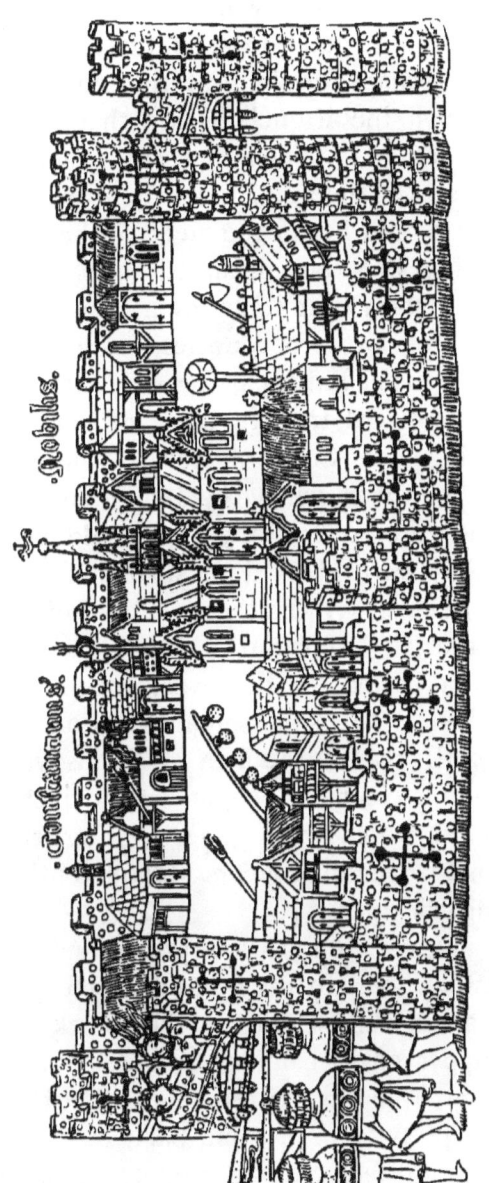

CONTEMPORARY VIEW OF A FOURTEENTH-CENTURY WALLED TOWN.

French knights and cross-bowmen were thrown into utter disorder; and to add to the confusion some cannon, then used perhaps for the first time in European wars, so frightened the French horses that there was no controlling them. When the sun went down, Edward was master of the field, and soon after marched in peace to Calais, and began the siege of that town.

While the king was thus occupied in France, the Scots were doing their best to annoy him in England. But the men of the northern counties, inspired by the brave words of Queen Philippa, turned back this invasion, and left Edward free to carry on the French war. The siege of Calais lasted a whole year.

Siege of Calais. At last, however, when the inhabitants of the town had eaten everything that could be eaten in the town, they were obliged to surrender. Six of the principal citizens, with halters around their necks, marched into the English camp. Edward, when they came before him, called for the executioner. But it is said he winked at the same moment to one of his courtiers. At all events, the men of Calais were not killed, though the common people were driven from their city homes, which were given to English emigrants, and for two hundred years Calais continued a flourishing English town.

The next few years were years of peace, due in part to a truce between the two kings, but more especially

The Black Death (1349). to a fearful disease called the Black Death, which appeared in England in 1349. It is supposed that from one-third to one-half of the population was swept away. In some parts of the island whole districts were left without people. One half of the priests of Yorkshire died at this time, and the

Archbishops of Canterbury and York were killed by this scourge. A similar disease attacked the cattle; and this, with the scarcity of farm laborers, threatened a famine. At such a time war was hardly possible.

Indeed, it was not until 1355 that the war was begun again in earnest. The next year Edward's eldest son, the Black Prince, as people called him, from the color of the armor which he had worn at Cressy, marched into the heart of southern France. At length the French closed in upon him; but he posted his men with such skill among the vineyards of Poitiers that the French were beaten off with terrible slaughter. Even King John of France was captured and taken to London, where he found King David of Scotland, who had been captured years before at Nevil's Cross.

_{Poitiers (1356).}

The war dragged on a few years longer, but in 1360 a treaty was made at Bretigny. By this treaty Edward was to keep the southern provinces as an independent king. On his part he was to give up his claim to the French throne, and to release King John on payment of a large ransom. Now, it is often much easier to make a treaty than to carry out its provisions, and so it proved in this case. Edward never gave up his title of King of France, and many of the barons in southern France refused to become his subjects. So the war broke out again, and dragged on for many years. In the end the English lost nearly all their French conquests, owing mainly to the cruelty and bad policy of the Black Prince. He never lived to be king, as he died in 1376, one year before his father's death.

_{Peace of Bretigny (1360).}

We must now turn to England itself, and see what had been accomplished during all these years in the

TOMB OF EDWARD III. IN WESTMINSTER ABBEY.

way of better government. Arbitrary as Edward was, he had been led into many reforms by the necessity of raising large sums of money, and of securing and keeping the good-will of the English aristocracy and the wealthier classes. For this reason we find the power of Parliament increase step by step. About 1332 the knights of the shire (as the representatives of the lesser landowners were called) and the burgesses (as those who were elected by the people of the towns and boroughs were termed) separated themselves from the great lords and bishops, and sat apart as the House of Commons; the others forming the upper house, or House of Peers. This division into two houses without any sharp dividing line between them, and with two classes of men sitting in each house, is of great importance in English history. In the first place the king was never able to play off one class against another, as would have been easy if the four orders had sat each by itself, or if they had all sat and voted together. In the next place, as time went on, it became common for members of the great baronial families to sit in the lower house side by side with the representatives of the merchants of the towns. In this way they became accustomed to the ideas of the middle class, and never formed such an exclusive caste as the nobles did in the countries of the Continent.

Now, at this time the popes did not live at Rome, for since the early part of the century they had resided at Avignon, in southern France. The Pope thus came completely under the control of the French king, and was therefore regarded with suspicion and dislike by the English people, as being a kind of Frenchman, and therefore their enemy. So strong did this feeling become that Parliament passed two laws, forbidding any one from taking a church office from the Pope, and bringing suits in his court. This latter was called

Parliament separates into two houses.

the Statute of Præmunire, from words in the writ by which it was enforced. The penalty for disobeying this statute, or law, was forfeiture of property and imprisonment during the pleasure of the king. Another thing which showed the growing dislike to the Pope was the rise of the people called Lollards.

Statute of Præmunire.

Exactly what "Lollard" means is not clear; but it probably signified an idle babbler. These Lollards thought that the bishops and the clergy generally lived too easy and luxurious lives, and gave too little attention to their real work, which should be the care of men's souls and deeds of charity. The leader and the founder of this sect was John Wycliffe, one of the great scholars and teachers of his time. Wycliffe gathered around him a band of earnest men, who went through the country preaching to the poor, and by their example teaching men to live upright and pure lives. Before this time the Bible was only to be found in Latin or some other learned language. Copies of it were quite rare, and only the upper clergy could read it. Wycliffe thought that the Bible should be the common property of all Englishmen, and he translated the New Testament into simple English. Of course it was still a rare book, as printing had not then been introduced into England.

The Lollards.

John Wycliffe.

The dreadful Black Death, too, had caused great discontent, and had some serious consequences. The king had allowed the great barons to pay him a sum of money instead of doing the personal service which the feudal system required, and in the same way the landowners had allowed their serfs, or villeins, to pay a small sum of money instead of performing the personal service (such as two or three days' work every week on the lord's farm) which their obligations required. The conditions of this money payment were written down on the records of the estate, a copy being given to the serf. Thus he became a "copyholder," and his holding, or farm, became a "copyhold;" and this form of tenure went by the name of "copyhold tenure." Now, the Black Death, by killing so many laborers, made it very difficult for the lord to hire men to do his work. And so he tried to make his serfs perform their work in person, as they formerly had done, instead of paying money. Of course this caused great opposition. The Parliament, too, as it was mainly in the hands of the land-owners, tried to keep wages down by passing a law called the Statute of Laborers. This law forbade laborers to receive higher wages than they had earned before the Black Death. As the prices of bread and all the necessaries of life had risen, this resulted in great hardships, the outcome of which we shall soon see.

Copyhold tenure.

Statute of Laborers.

CHAPTER XI.

RICHARD II.

1377-1387.

THE Black Prince's son Richard, a lad of eleven years, succeeded to his grandfather's throne, the government being carried on by some one else, called a regent. It was a bad time for such an experiment, for on every side there was discontent. There were large debts remaining from Edward's time, and these were soon increased by the expense of stopping a threatened French invasion. Parliament tried to raise money in various ways. Finally, it hit upon a scheme called a poll-tax. It was called a poll-tax because it was a tax of so much per head, or poll. A poll-tax is not bad in itself, but it was arranged at that time so as to fall most heavily on the poorer classes. It could not be collected. Finally, a man was found who promised to collect it if the judges should be ordered to help him. This was done, and collectors went through the country compelling people to pay, under the most fearful threats in case they refused. At last one of these collectors insulted a daughter of a Kentish blacksmith named Walter, and called from his trade Wat the Tyler, or simply Wat Tyler. Before the collector could escape, Wat the Tyler dashed his brains out with his hammer; and then,

[marginal note: The Peasants' Revolt (1381).]

putting himself at the head of the peasants of Kent, marched towards London. Men flocked to his standard from all sides. Among the rest there was a priest who called himself Jack Straw, and who led the men of

PLOUGHING.

Essex. Then, too, another priest, named John Ball, went with them, preaching from the text, —

> "When Adam delved, and Eve span,
> Who was then the gentleman?"

Sixty thousand strong, they reached London, killed the archbishop and all the lawyers they could find, and

HARROWING. A BOY SLINGING STONES.

burned the houses of those whom they hated. At last Wat the Tyler was himself killed; and, deprived

of their leader, the rebels dispersed. While he was in their power the king had made great promises to these people, all of which he now broke. And the Parliament, too, passed laws tending to keep the lower classes forever in the condition of serfs; but they were never carried out, as no one feared another peasant revolt more than did these same landowners. Indeed, it is from this time that the rise

REAPING.

of the class of independent farmers called "yeomen" dates.

The remainder of Richard's reign was taken up with disputes between his favorites and the nobles who were out of power. In 1387 the parliamentary party, led by Richard's uncle, the Duke of Gloucester, gained the upper hand, and turned the favorites out, even executing many of them. But before long the king again got control. For a time he governed well; but as soon as he felt himself strong enough, he revenged himself on his enemies. The Duke of Gloucester disappeared, and every one thought he was murdered, though it is now believed that he died from natural causes. Soon after this the Duke of Hereford, Henry of Bolingbroke, son of John of

Abdication of Richard.

Gaunt, Duke of Lancaster, was exiled to France on a most frivolous charge. John of Gaunt felt his son's disgrace very keenly, and presently died. Richard, in defiance of a solemn promise, seized his estates. The king then went to Ireland to try to restore the waning fortunes of the English in that island. This was the young Duke of Lancaster's opportunity. Crossing over to England, he was everywhere most gladly received by the people. Richard, returning in haste from Ireland, was captured and forced to abdicate. Years before, he had been warned that the time might come when the English people would rise and depose him, and Parliament now did this very thing, on the ground of misgovernment. Then Henry of Lancaster, rising in his place in the House of Lords,

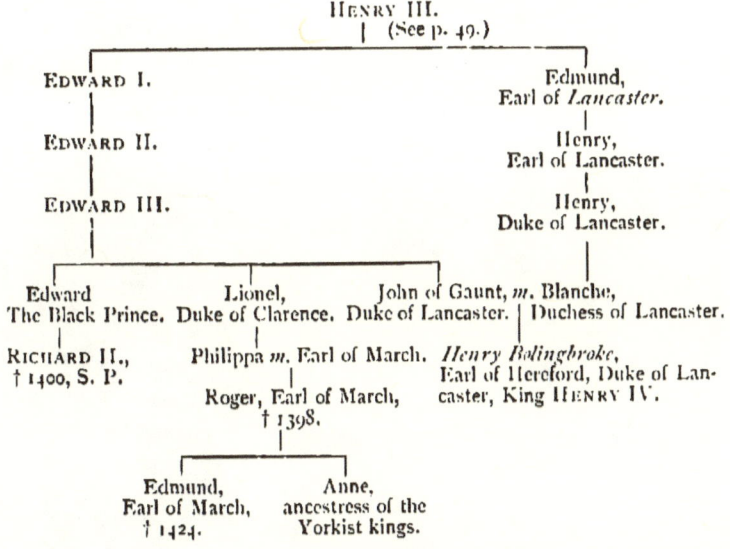

THE LATER PLANTAGENETS.

claimed the crown as the descendant of Henry III. It was said that his ancestor was the elder brother of the first Edward, and had been passed over on account of his humpback. Probably this was not true. At all events, Henry was elected king by Parliament, and took the title of Henry IV.

A GOLD NOBLE OF EDWARD III., STRUCK BETWEEN 1360 AND 1369.

CHAPTER XII.

ENGLAND IN THE FOURTEENTH CENTURY.

IN many ways the fourteenth century marked an epoch in the history of the English people. Let us stop a moment and see why this is so. In the first place, the fact that Richard was deposed proved to be of the very greatest importance. It was then established that the nation might depose the king if it wished. Years after, when this question again came up, in the time of James II., statesmen, turning back to find a precedent, relied on this one. In the next place, the English common people were every day acquiring more power and influence in the state. We have seen how the Commons began to sit by themselves, and we have seen how, in the rise of copyholders, the serfs began to free themselves from their servile obligations. Then, too, although the last part of this period was a time of almost constant war, it was also a time of great extension of trade. This was due in a great measure to the fact that the king could no longer seize the property of the merchants to pay his expenses, but was obliged to get their consent to taxes through their representatives in the House of Commons.

It must not be supposed, however, that men's ideas on commerce were in those days like our own. At that time men saw, as some think they see to-day, that as gold and silver could be exchanged for anything, they formed a nation's whole wealth. Going one step *Financial* farther, they believed that a country would be *policy.* rich according to the amount of gold and silver actually within its borders. The more gold and silver England could draw from France and other countries, the richer she would be. The way to accomplish this was to sell as much wool, leather, and tin to foreigners, and buy as little from them, as possible; the balance being paid in gold and silver. But we now know that gold and silver are only commodities, like wool and leather, and that a nation cannot become richer by piling up within its borders more of any one thing than it can use.

Now, these wars of Edward the Third introduced England to the outside world, and gave Englishmen *Clothes.* an idea of the comforts and fashions of foreign lands. The effects were soon seen. Instead of the coarse, rough English cloth they formerly wore, men now began to wear colored clothes. The hose, which used to reach from the waist to the foot, were now divided at the knee, and the upper portion came to be called small-clothes. The most ridiculous things were the new-fashioned shoes, which sometimes were three feet long. Then, too, rugs and carpets began to take the place of rushes on the floors of the wealthier classes, and furniture, which up to that time had been very poor and scarce, began to be more plentiful and of much better quality.

All these new fashions gave rise to an extended commerce, which the king encouraged as well as he *Com-* could. But he saw with alarm the wool of *merce.* England exchanged for fine clothes and carpets rather than for gold, and many attempts were made to regulate this foreign trade. It was determined, in the first place, that certain towns should be designated as "staple towns," from the German word *stapel*, because in them a fair, or market, was kept open the whole year. Only in these places could wool, leather, lead, and tin be sold. At one time the laws were so strict that only a portion of the price of English goods could be exchanged for foreign goods, the remainder being paid for in gold and silver. At that time England was almost the only country where wool and tin were produced in large quantities. And as long as these laws could be carried out, gold and silver flowed into England. Gold was then very scarce, and silver was the principal medium of exchange. This silver was coined into money at the rate of two hundred and forty pennies to each pound of silver by weight. Thus we see the origin of the name "pound," which is still used in England as the standard of value, though a pound of silver would purchase much more wool and leather then than it will now.

It must not be supposed that any one could go to a town where a fair was kept, and buy and sell for himself; far from it. Rights to trade and to manufacture were then granted to certain per- *The guilds.* sons or sets of persons, either for money or as favors. Sometimes the merchants of one town would combine into one trade-society, or guild; but more often there were several guilds in each town, as of leather-dressers, tailors, silversmiths, etc. Each of these guilds governed itself, and took full charge of all goods made by its members, oftentimes putting its mark, or stamp, on the goods as a proof of their purity and goodness. The guilds of each town often had a share in its government, and the guildhall often answers very well to our town-hall. At this time, however, the beginning of the end of the guild system could be seen. This was due to the rise of a free laboring class, who worked by the day. They were hence called "journeymen," from the French word *jour*, or *journée*, a day. These and other laborers flocked to the towns in great numbers, largely because of the privileges enjoyed by those living in towns; and their presence in the end gave a severe blow to the exclusive system of the guilds.

This century also marks the rise of the English language as we now know it. This was the time of Geoffrey Chaucer, the first great English poet, and of Wycliffe, who may be regarded as the father of English prose. English was also used in the courts, and took the place of French as the language of the upper classes.

PORTRAIT OF GEOFFREY CHAUCER.

Rise of the English language.

CHAPTER XIII.

THE FIRST TWO LANCASTRIAN KINGS.

NEXT to Richard, the rightful heir to the throne was Edmund Mortimer, Earl of March, since he was descended from the second son of Edward III. Henry was really a usurper, and ruled merely as being the king elected by Parliament. He was thus obliged to keep on good terms with Parliament, and also with the Church. To please the Church he assented to an Act against heresy. Under this law a man once declared to be a heretic by the Church was handed over to the civil government for execution. This was commonly by fire; and the first Englishman burned as a heretic was William Sawtre. *Henry IV. (1399-1413).*

Henry was obliged to consent to the demands of Parliament. In this way the Commons obliged him to have the money voted by them accounted for. The Commons also obtained the right to originate all laws granting money, and the king was even forced to allow perfect freedom of debate in both Houses of Parliament. Henry made these concessions in order to secure the support of the people in maintaining himself on the throne. *Rise of the commoners.*

In 1399 there was a sudden rebellion of the great lords friendly to the Earl of March. But as the king, with a force of Londoners, was driving them to the

West, the people of Cirencester, led by their mayor, surrounded and captured them, and executed several before the king arrived. The same year witnessed Richard's death; though whether he was murdered or not, no one really knows. In time, however, events turned in Henry's favor, and by 1400 he was secure on his throne.

<small>Rebellion (1399).</small>

Henry's last years were not happy. A dreadful disease tormented him, and it seemed as though his eldest son, the Prince of Wales, wished to be king before his time. At least that is the story; and the old king was so jealous of his son that he had him removed from the council. In 1413 Henry IV. died.

One of the greatest evils of this time was what was called the "right of maintenance." The great lords were accustomed to have in their service large bodies of men, often old soldiers, who attended them when they went to Parliament, into court, and on other occasions. These men wore the liveries, or badges, of their masters, and were always armed and ready to fight. It thus happened that the great earls and dukes had small regular armies always at call, and it was this force of retainers that formed the foundation of the armies which fought in the Wars of the Roses.

<small>Maintenance.</small>

The new king came to the throne so quietly that it seemed hardly possible he was the son of a usurper. He had led a wild life in his youth, which is described in Shakspere's play of "Henry IV.;" but when he ascended the throne he became serious and patriotic. There was great discontent under the surface. The religious reformers called Lollards especially were so active that Henry may

<small>Henry V. (1413–1422).</small>

have thought this the beginning of another Wat Tyler's rebellion. At any rate, he took sides with the churchmen against the Lollards, and forty of the reformers were burned at the stake as heretics.

For the moment the effort after reform seemed to be suppressed. Still, it might break out again at any time, and Henry resolved to divert Englishmen's minds from their own wants and grievances by the conquest of France,— as if causing distress to any one nation would make another happier. Apart from this motive, which, after all, may not have been the true one, it was a good time to invade France. The French king was insane, and his eldest son, called the Dauphin, who ruled during his father's madness, quarrelled with the king's brother, the Duke of Burgundy. Now, this Duke of Burgundy was the most

EFFIGY OF A KNIGHT AT CLEHONGER, SHOWING DEVELOPMENT OF PLATE-ARMOR. DATE, ABOUT 1460.

powerful man in France, and he and Henry of England, working together, soon had France at their mercy.

Just as Henry was about to leave England, however, a plot to set the young Earl of March on the throne was discovered. Henry's uncle, the Duke of Cambridge, and some of the king's most trusted advisers were in the plot. They were executed, and the expedition set sail. The campaign was very much like that of Cressy. A great battle was fought at Agincourt, — a battle well described in Shakspere's "Henry V." The English were victorious, and, laden with booty and prisoners, they returned to England.

<small>Agincourt (1415).</small>

Two years later, in 1417, the invasion was renewed. This time the English advanced as far as Rouen unopposed. The Dauphin and the Duke of Burgundy now made peace, but the latter was soon after murdered by order of the faithless Dauphin. Then the new Duke of Burgundy forgot all love of country in a desire for revenge. At Troyes he and Henry made a treaty, by which the English king agreed to marry the French king's daughter Katharine, and to rule France during her father's life as regent. After his death, Henry was to be king of France, and his son after him. The Dauphin was thus disinherited. All patriotic Frenchmen gathered round him; but at the time they could do nothing but wait. Two years later Henry died, and was buried with the greatest magnificence in Westminster Abbey. Above his tomb may still be seen his helmet and saddle.

<small>Treaty of Troyes (1420).</small>

Henry V. should be remembered not only as a great soldier. He saw the real path to greatness for

England, and by extending commerce in every possible way he contributed to the material prosperity of the next century. He also increased and reformed the English navy, which has since risen to such great power.

THE CLAIMS OF YORK AND LANCASTER.

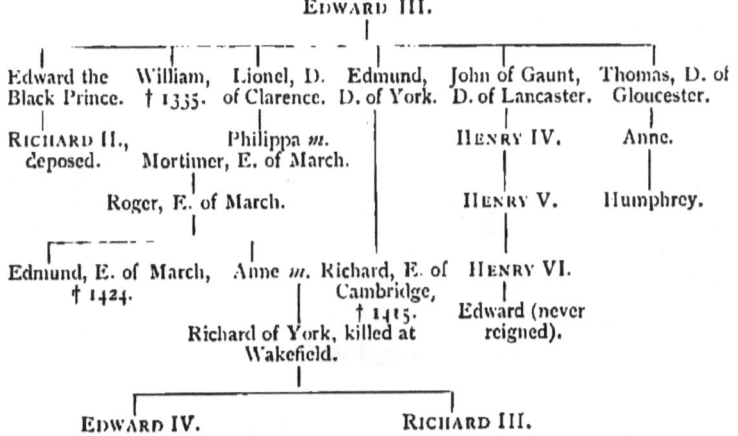

Thus, Richard of York inherited not only the claims of the House of York, but, through his mother, those of the older House of Clarence.

CHAPTER XIV.

HENRY VI.

1422-1461.

THE abilities of Henry V. were so great, and his conquests so splendid, that the bad policy of his French invasion did not appear until after his death. His son, an infant of eleven months, succeeded to the throne, and during his minority his uncles, the Dukes of Bedford and Gloucester, governed for him.

<small>Regency of Bedford and Gloucester.</small>

Bedford was an exceedingly able man, and for a time all went well. In 1428, however, he laid siege to Orléans. The English would probably have taken the town, had not a new foe appeared in the most unexpected way. This was Joan of Arc, a peasant girl of Lorraine. She believed that Michael the archangel and other holy personages had personally ordered her to go to the Dauphin's aid. Her appearance at court aroused the enthusiasm of the soldiers; and seeing this, the counsellors of the Dauphin gave her an army, and told her to save Orléans. Now, this spirit of enthusiasm was what the French soldiers most needed. Adversity and practice had made them good soldiers, and able leaders were not lacking; but hitherto they had fought without spirit. Joan of Arc put new life into them. She marched to Orléans, and attacked the English first on this side, then on that. The Englishmen were as

<small>Joan of Arc.</small>

superstitious as the French. They believed Joan of Arc to be a witch. The siege was abandoned, and soon after the Dauphin was crowned king of France. The next year, however, Joan of Arc fell into the hands of the English, and was burned alive. But the spirit she had aroused did not perish with her. In 1435 the Duke of Bedford died, and after his death one place after another was lost, till, in 1453, of all the English conquests Calais alone remained in their hands; and thus ended the Hundred Years' War.

During these later years of disgrace and failure William de la Pole, Earl of Suffolk, had ruled the kingdom through his influence with the young king's wife, Margaret of Anjou. Upon him the people laid the responsibility for the loss of France. The king, to save his life, banished him for five years; but on his way to France he was seized and executed. Earl of Suffolk.

This was in 1450, and in the same year a rebellion broke out in Kent. Led by Jack Cade, who called himself Mortimer, the rebels marched to London. They murdered many nobles and other persons obnoxious to them, and then began plundering London. The Londoners turned them out, and some time after Jack Cade was captured and executed. It has been thought that the king's cousin, Richard, Duke of York, was at the bottom of this plot. Jack Cade's rebellion.

This Richard of York was the son of that Duke of Cambridge who had plotted against Henry V. as he was setting out for France. Through his mother he inherited the claims of the Earl of March, who had been passed over when Henry IV. ascended the throne. His right to the English Richard of York claims the throne.

crown was better, therefore, than that of the reigning king. Now, it happened at this time, as it had so often happened before, that the Plantagenets not in power opposed those who were. And it is a little singular to see the same families fighting for the Duke of York as had fought for Henry IV. against Richard II. before Henry became king. In other words, a certain portion of the great families of England were always in opposition to the existing government. The Lancastrians took for their badge a red rose, while the Yorkists adopted a white rose; and it is for this reason that the troubles which followed are called the Wars of the Roses.

If Henry VI. had been a strong, able man, like his father and grandfather, these wars would probably never have occurred. He was not only always weak and feeble, but unfortunately was subject to fits of insanity. These attacks gave the Duke of York abundant opportunity to carry out his schemes. The two parties soon came to blows. In 1455 the Lancastrians were beaten, and the king fell into the hands of the Yorkists; but he was soon released. In 1459 he was again captured, and now the Duke of York came forward and claimed the crown in right of his mother. Finally, it was agreed that the king should continue to rule during his lifetime, but that at his death the crown should pass to the Duke of York and his heirs.

The Wars of the Roses begin.

In this way the young Prince of Wales was disinherited. It could hardly be expected that the queen would see her son thus treated. Gathering an army in the North, she marched towards London. At Wakefield she met the Yorkists and defeated them,

Edward IV. of York.

the Duke of York being killed during the battle, or put to death immediately after it. But his son Edward, a lad of nineteen, was still alive. Getting a small army together, he pushed on to London, reaching it before the queen, whose soldiers wasted time in plundering by the way. The people of London declared for Edward, and he was proclaimed king at Westminster as Edward IV. And thus ended the reign, though not the life, of Henry VI.

The most important constitutional event of this reign was the restricting the right to vote in counties for members of the House of Commons to those who owned land in the county to the value of forty shillings a year. In this way copyholders, as such, were deprived of the right to vote; and this remained the law until 1832.

ROYAL ARMS AS BORNE BY HENRY IV. AFTER ABOUT 1408, AND BY SUCCESSIVE SOVEREIGNS DOWN TO 1603.

CHAPTER XV.

THE YORKIST KINGS.

1461-1485.

THE crown was scarcely on Edward's head when he left London, and marched northward to meet the Lancastrians. He found them at Towton, and there overthrew them. He now felt reasonably secure on the throne, and so he might have been, but for his marriage with Elizabeth Woodville. She was a beautiful woman, but did not belong to any of the great families. The marriage angered the Yorkist nobles, who became more angry when Edward raised her father to the peerage, and in many other ways increased the importance of her family. This was especially displeasing to the head of the Neville family, the great Earl of Warwick. He had really placed Edward on the throne, and was known as the king-maker. Finally he secured the aid of the King's brother, the Duke of Clarence. Small insurrections broke out, and for a time Warwick even kept Edward a prisoner; but in 1470 Warwick was forced to flee to France. There he found Queen Margaret, and changing sides, he placed himself at the head of the Lancastrians, and returned to England. Edward in turn was forced to fly, and for a time Warwick ruled in the name of poor mad Henry VI. The next year, however, Edward came back, overthrew Warwick at Barnet, and

Edward IV. (1461-1483).

Queen Margaret at Tewkesbury, and once more ruled as king. Warwick the king-maker perished at Barnet, the young Prince of Wales at Tewkesbury, and only the old king remained. And he too soon died, murdered, it was said, in the Tower by Edward's brother, Richard of Gloucester.

His rivals and enemies being out of the way, Edward set out on an invasion of France. He got some money in a regular way from Parliament, and raised more by what were called "benevolences;" that is, he summoned the merchants before him, and asked them for money under this name. No one dared refuse, and he set out for France. Now, the king of France at that time was Louis XI., one of the most crafty men who ever sat on the French or any other throne. Seeing Edward's greed for money, he thought it would be much cheaper and better to buy him off than to fight him. Edward was not unwilling, and in this way his invasion of France came to an end. *Invades France.*

The only other striking event of his time is the murder of the Duke of Clarence. Edward had long suspected his brother of treason. He now formally accused him, and the Peers convicted him of treason. A few days later he was found dead in the Tower, drowned, the story is, in a butt of Malmsey wine. Not long after Edward himself died, a victim to intemperance. In some ways Edward was not a bad king. He preserved order throughout the kingdom, at least during the latter part of his reign. This was of great advantage to the producing classes. In many other ways the king showed himself the friend to commerce, even engaging in it himself. *Murder of the Duke of Clarence.*

Edward the Fourth left two sons,— Edward, Prince of

Wales, and a younger brother Richard, Duke of York. Edward was but thirteen years old, and he reigned less than three months. Indeed, he can scarcely be said to have reigned at all. From the very first, his uncle Richard, Duke of Gloucester, seems to have determined to make himself king. Getting possession of the two boys, he sent them to the Tower, which was then used as much for a palace as a prison. He then made himself Protector, ruling in his nephew's name. Next he got rid of the principal members of the queen's party, and then claimed the crown for himself. On July 6, 1483, he was crowned at Westminster as Richard III.; and not long after the young King Edward V. and his brother disappeared, smothered, it was said, by Richard's order. But this, like other stories of Richard, may be false. Until recent years almost all historians have given Richard a very black character. They have also added that he was a humpback, and was very ugly in person. We really know very little about him, and most that we do know is derived from writers of the Tudor period, whose interest it was to say all they could against Richard. At all events, his reign was so short and troubled that he had little chance to show whatever good there may have been in him. It is now supposed, however, that he was by no means bad looking, and that his back was straight. Very likely some of the other stories about him had as little foundation as his hump.

All the old rivals of the House of York had been killed on the field of battle or murdered; but a new rival now appeared in the person of Henry Tudor, Earl of Richmond. Through his mother

Edward V. (1483).

Richard III. (1483-1485).

The Tudors.

he was descended from John of Gaunt, though his
family had been excluded from the succession; but
the Beauforts, of course, had never acknowledged the
right of Parliament to do this. The claim at its best
was not good for much. But Henry Tudor determined
to win the throne for himself if he could. He soon
won many Yorkists over to his side by promising to
marry Edward IV.'s daughter Elizabeth; but his early
attempt ended in failure.

The people of England, however, were fast coming
over to Henry's side; for Richard had raised money
by means of a forced loan, and had shown favor to new
men who were dependent upon him for their position
and wealth. Especially he had placed great confidence in three men named Ratcliffe, Catesby, and
Lovel. So much favor had he shown them that people
went round shouting this doggerel:—

> "The Rat, the Cat, and Lovel our Dog
> Rule all England under the Hog."

In fact, he became so unpopular, and his own party
cared so little for him, that when Henry Tudor came to

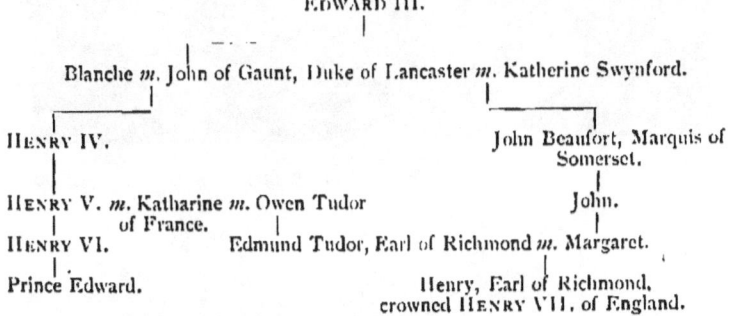

LANCASTERS AND TUDORS.

EDWARD III.
|
Blanche *m.* John of Gaunt, Duke of Lancaster *m.* Katherine Swynford.

HENRY IV.   John Beaufort, Marquis of Somerset.
| |
HENRY V. *m.* Katharine *m.* Owen Tudor   John.
| of France. | |
HENRY VI.   Edmund Tudor, Earl of Richmond *m.* Margaret.
|
Prince Edward.   Henry, Earl of Richmond,
                              crowned HENRY VII. of England.

England in 1485 he marched almost unmolested to the middle of the island. The two rivals met on Bosworth Field. Richard's two most powerful adherents proved faithless to him, Lord Stanley even joining his stepson Henry during the fight. In the battle Richard was killed, and at its close the Earl of Richmond was greeted as Henry VII.

Battle of Bosworth.

A FIFTEENTH-CENTURY SHIP.

CHAPTER XVI.

SOCIAL CHANGES DURING THE FIFTEENTH CENTURY.

AS we have already seen, the feudal system had begun to break down as early as the Second Richard's time. The introduction of gunpowder, by which a common man, armed with a fire-arm, became as dangerous as the knight in full armor, perhaps more so, hastened this decay. During the Wars of the Roses the great feudal families practically destroyed one another. And in this way, by the beginning of Henry VII.'s reign, the feudal structure of society in England may be said to have perished. A new era opened, not only for England, but for the civilized world. Columbus, sailing westward from the Canaries in search of a passage to India, first saw the New World in 1492. Five years later John Cabot, sailing under a license from Henry VII., discovered the northern continent. Upon this discovery of John Cabot rested the claims of the English sovereigns to the most habitable part of America.

<small>End of the Middle Ages.</small>

This discovery of a new world beyond the Atlantic might have produced little result, and even been forgotten, had not another discovery already come into common use. This was the art of printing, which was introduced into England in 1477 by Caxton, who had acquired the art in Flanders. Before this time the only way of multiplying books was by

<small>Printing.</small>

copying by hand. This was not only slow, but very expensive. When Caxton set up his printing-press he was by no means a young man. Yet so eager were people for books that before he died he had either written or translated and printed sixty works. Learning began to flourish, and in the next century England emerged from a state of semi-barbarism, and during Elizabeth's reign produced the greatest works in the English language.

Another thing which marked the beginning of a new era was the decay of villeinage, or serfdom. This was brought about in part by the Roman Catholic priests, who induced many rich men to free their serfs. Of course, in the long run, this was beneficial to the lower class and to the country; but for a while there was much suffering. In feudal times a man's importance depended upon the number of his followers. His only desire then was to make his land support as many persons as possible. Now, however, with the growth of trade and commerce, a man's importance depended more upon his wealth than upon any other single thing. Men only desired to get as much profit from their land as possible. In old days when the serf became sick or feeble he was taken care of, though not very tenderly, by his master. Now he was free, and was turned off, if he became useless, and another hired in his place. Then, too, it was often more profitable to raise sheep for their wool than to raise wheat. But it takes fewer men to tend sheep on a hundred acres than it takes to raise crops on those same acres; and in this way many men lost their occupation. Then again, under the old system of landholding, agriculture was very

Abolition of villeinage.

slack. Now, however, under the leasehold system it was for the interest of the tenant to make as much as he could out of his holding. He therefore hired as little help as possible, making those in his employ work a great deal harder than they had worked before. In one way or another, therefore, vast numbers of men were thrown out of employment in the country. They flocked to the towns, where the capitalists stood ready to hire them by the day or week. We have already seen the beginning of this. Now, however, laborers streamed to the towns in such numbers that what was called the "guild" system, by which each trade managed its own affairs, was weakened, and the system of open competition, such as we now have, began to prevail.

During this century Parliament, instead of gaining more power, had lost much that it had possessed. In the House of Lords the old nobility had almost disappeared. In its place was a new nobility, as yet dependent on the king and devoted to him. The House of Commons, too, had lost much of its strength. We have seen how the right to vote had been restricted in the counties. In the towns, or "boroughs," too, the same process had gone on. In the older time all freemen in the boroughs had voted. But gradually, in many boroughs, a small circle of men secured all powers of government; and in this way, while the town, or borough, grew, its ruling class remained stationary or decreased in number. As these men elected the members of the House of Commons for their borough, the commoners ceased to represent the people at large. Now, it is easy to see that the smaller the number of men voting for

[margin: Loss of power by Parliament.]

a member of Parliament, the easier it was for the Government to intimidate or bribe enough voters to give them a majority in the House of Commons. In this way Parliament, during the whole Tudor period, became little better than a tool of the king and his ministers.

One important gain had been made, though it did not bear fruit till later times. In the old days the two houses had drawn up petitions asking the king to grant certain laws. The king often consented to a petition, and then, after getting the money he wanted, and dissolving Parliament, so changed the law that, when it was finally passed, those who had asked for it could not recognize it. Now the two houses began to draw up the laws themselves, and present them to the king for his consent. At first, however, it was a change only in form. But the time was coming when the Commons would refuse to grant money for the king's use until he had assented to their bills, as these petitions now came to be called. The machinery, in other words, was all ready for the government of the country by the House of Commons; it only remained to bring a class into power which could and would use the machinery. And discerning men could already foresee the coming importance of the middle class, composed of merchants, shopkeepers, and small farmers, — a class destined in time to rule the House of Commons, and through it to govern England. That time was to be long deferred; but the beginnings were now made. And that is why with the reign of Henry VII. modern English history may be said to begin. Let us now study the doings of these Tudor sovereigns.

Money bills.

CHAPTER XVII.

HENRY VII.

1485-1509.

THOUGH Henry had been brought to the throne as the leader of the Lancastrian party, he really became king because there was no one to oppose him. To make his title more secure he had himself elected king by Parliament, and married Elizabeth of York, daughter of Edward IV. In many respects his position was like that of Henry IV., and throughout his reign he was always careful to keep within the law. He also enforced the law with great strictness, encouraged commerce in every way, and avoided war as much as possible. In short, his quiet, strong rule was precisely what England needed to enable her to make good the waste of the civil wars. It must not be supposed, however, that Henry was left to enjoy the throne in peace. *Henry's position.*

One of his first acts had been to imprison the young Earl of Warwick, son of that Duke of Clarence who was said to have been drowned in a butt of Malmsey. In 1487 a young man appeared in Ireland, and pretended to be this same Earl of Warwick. His real name was Lambert Simnel; and, invading England, he was captured, and made an assistant to Henry's own cook; but his followers were treated with great severity. *Attempt of Simnel.*

A more dangerous claimant soon appeared, styling himself Richard Plantagenet, Duke of York. He declared that when his brother, Edward V., was murdered in the Tower, his own life had been spared. His real name was probably Perkin Warbeck. But whoever he was, he had been so well schooled in his part that he deceived many people who should have been able to detect an impostor. After living in France and Burgundy, he went to Scotland and married Lady Katharine Gordon, a kinswoman of the Scottish king. He then tried to invade England, first from Scotland, and then by way of Cornwall, where there happened to be some discontent. Both attempts failed. In 1498 he was captured, taken to London, and he and the Earl of Warwick, trying to escape, were both executed. No one, even to this day, really knows whether Perkin Warbeck was an impostor or the son of Edward IV.

Attempt of Warbeck.

The remainder of his reign Henry devoted to strengthening his position by marrying his children to foreign princes and princesses. Some of these marriages were of great importance, especially that of his daughter Margaret to James IV. of Scotland, as their descendant was Mary, Queen of Scots, whose son, James VI. of Scotland, afterwards became king of England.

Henry's foreign policy.

Owing to the disturbance of the civil wars, crime had for a long time gone on unchecked. Indeed, it seemed impossible to carry out the laws, one reason being that juries would not convict. Henry therefore instituted a new court, called the Court of the Star Chamber, where offences were

The Court of Star Chamber.

tried without a jury. At first this court was used to suppress crime. But during later reigns it became an instrument of tyranny, and was then greatly detested. In 1509 Henry VII. died, and was succeeded by his son, Henry VIII.

TUDOR ROSE (WHITE AND RED): FROM THE GATES OF THE CHAPEL OF HENRY VII.

CHAPTER XVIII.

HENRY VIII.

1509-1547.

The Spanish marriage.

THE young king — for the eighth Henry was only eighteen years of age when his father died — had many things in his favor. He was handsome, well-educated, and soon rendered himself popular by persecuting the men his father had employed to extort money. These men had always kept within the law, but they were none the less hated. He then completed the marriage with his brother's widow, Katharine of Arragon, daughter of the king of Spain. This marriage, or rather the breaking of it, proved to be of such great consequence to England and to all Englishmen that we must stop a moment and see who Katharine was, and why Henry had delayed for years to carry out his part of the marriage agreement. In the first place Katharine was the daughter of Ferdinand and Isabella, under whose license Columbus had sailed on his famous voyage for India. It was in their time, too, that all of what we now call Spain was united under one rule. Katharine's nephew Charles, soon to become emperor as Charles V., was by far the most powerful man of his time. It was natural, therefore, that Henry should not wish to offend the great house of Spain, and besides, at that time Englishmen regarded Spain as

HENRY VIII.: FROM A PAINTING BY HOLBEIN ABOUT 1536, BELONGING TO EARL SPENCER.

their natural friend. How this last feeling came to be changed we shall see before long. There was one thing against this marriage, and that was that the law of the Roman Catholic Church — the canon law, as it is sometimes called — did not allow a man to marry his brother's widow. This prohibition was based on the Old Testament, and is still the rule in some countries, including England. The Pope, however, was very anxious to please Katharine's family, and granted to Henry and Katharine a release, or dispensation, from the operation of the law, and so they were speedily married.

It will be remembered that Henry VII. had wisely kept out of war whenever it was possible. His son, however, was less pacific, and was soon at war with France, fighting on the side of the Spaniards and Germans. The war amounted to little, though the English won a strange victory at Guinegaste in Flanders, where the French ran away so fast that it came to be known as the "Battle of the Spurs." As had happened so many times before, the French king thought the best way to meet the English attack would be to stir up the Scots, so in this same year the Scots invaded England; but all Englishmen were not in France, though the king was. Led by Lord Surrey, the English attacked the Scots at Flodden Edge. King James IV. of Scotland, Henry's brother-in-law, was killed on the field, the Scottish force was completely broken up, and soon after a general peace was made.

War with France.

Henry's chief adviser during these first years of his reign was Thomas Wolsey. This great statesman was of respectable birth and well educated, and by his great talents and industry raised himself from one position to another till he became chancellor, Archbishop of York, a cardinal, and even legate of the Pope in England. As legate he possessed all the power which the Pope would have exerted had he been personally in England. From his decision in matters of religion there was no appeal. In this way the English people became accustomed to having all power in church and state centred in their own government; and when, in a few years, the king was declared the head of the English Church, instead of the Pope or his legate, it did not seem so strange to the people as it would have at one time seemed. Wolsey was a very far-seeing man. He saw that the time was not far off when a reformation of the Catholic Church would be demanded in such a way that it could not be resisted. He wished to save the Church by reforming it from the inside rather than by having the reform forced upon it by those outside. For this reason he had become legate, and he actually began reforms in the Church in England. For the same reason, too, he desired to become Pope. It so happened that at this time there was an election for the crown of the Holy Roman Empire. Charles I. of Spain, who was also Archduke of Austria, had the best claim; but Francis I. of France also put in a claim, and so did Henry. Charles was elected, and war between him and Francis was sure to follow. Both tried to secure the aid of England, and Francis entertained Henry in a most regal way on a plain afterwards called the Field of the Cloth of Gold, because of the splendor there displayed; but Wolsey and Henry had other plans. Even before this meet-

Cardinal Wolsey.

ing, Charles had visited England secretly, and by promising his aid to Wolsey in the matter of the election of a new Pope, had led England again to take the side of Spain and Germany. Soon, however, there was a change. Charles beat Francis so completely as to no longer need the aid of England; and when the election for a new Pope came off, he worked against Wolsey. So Henry and Wolsey changed sides, and in 1528 made an alliance with France. In other ways, too, Henry abandoned the Spanish alliance.

He had never loved Katharine, and as years went by, and son after son died soon after birth, he began to have conscientious scruples about the rightfulness of the marriage. These scruples, even if they were genuine in the beginning, which many people doubt, were greatly increased when he fell violently in love with Anne Boleyn, a lady of his court, and a granddaughter of that Thomas Howard, Earl of Surrey and Duke of Norfolk, who had won the great victory at Flodden Edge. The king first applied

<small>The divorce from Katharine.</small>

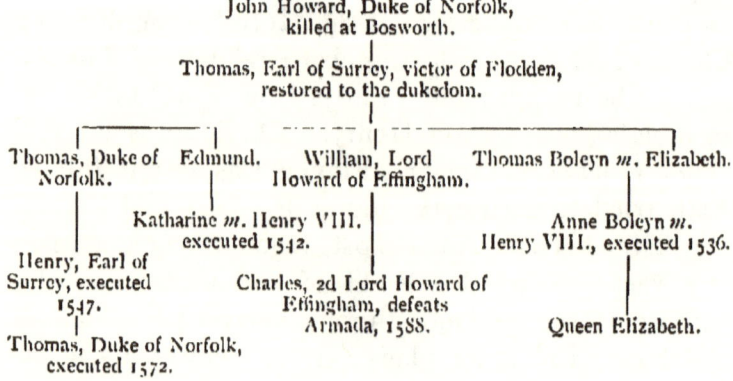

THE HOWARDS.

John Howard, Duke of Norfolk, killed at Bosworth.

Thomas, Earl of Surrey, victor of Flodden, restored to the dukedom.

Thomas, Duke of Norfolk. — Edmund. — William, Lord Howard of Effingham. — Thomas Boleyn *m*. Elizabeth.

Katharine *m*. Henry VIII., executed 1542.

Anne Boleyn *m*. Henry VIII., executed 1536.

Henry, Earl of Surrey, executed 1547.

Charles, 2d Lord Howard of Effingham, defeats Armada, 1588.

Queen Elizabeth.

Thomas, Duke of Norfolk, executed 1572.

to the Pope for a divorce from Katharine, asserting the original marriage to have been illegal. Ordinarily the Pope would have made no difficulty in complying with such a request; but just at this time it happened that he was actually shut up in the Castle of St. Angelo in Rome by Charles the Fifth's army. It could hardly be expected that he would still further offend Charles by declaring his aunt Katharine's marriage illegal; so he tried to put off any decision, and finally, in 1529, ordered the matter to be tried before him at Rome. Wolsey had assured the king that the divorce would be granted, and when it was not allowed, Henry lost all patience. Wolsey was dismissed from all his offices, and his property was confiscated to the Crown. It is true that by accepting the office of legate he had done an illegal act; but he had done it at Henry's special request. Henry the Eighth, however, never remembered such things when a man had offended him. Wolsey had extorted money in many illegal ways, and it was attempted to make his offences treason. The first attempt, owing to the exertions of his former servant, Thomas Cromwell, failed, and while coming to London to stand trial on a later charge he died.

When Wolsey was out of power and place, the king, for the first time in his reign, looked about him with his own eyes. From that moment, though he employed able men in his service, Henry the Eighth ruled England. And he ruled England as few kings have ruled before or since. His political instincts and abilities were indeed remarkable. In many ways Henry was a brute and a tyrant. His mind was despotic, and he did many things that no

Henry's personal rule.

one likes to recall. Let it be said, therefore, to his credit, that it was owing mainly to his sagacity and firmness that England was spared the religious wars and persecutions to which France, Germany, and Spain were subjected. Henry saw very clearly that the people would be on his side in a struggle with the Pope. Not that Englishmen were not Catholics so far as doctrine and belief went. But they wished for some reformation in the government of that Church in England. A few years before, Henry had become so angry with Luther, the German reformer, that he had actually written a book against him, for which the Pope had given him the title of "Defender of the Faith." The title is still borne by English monarchs; but it was not long before the Pope must have thought Henry very undeserving of it. In 1529 a Parliament met, and the House of Commons, under the guidance of Thomas Cromwell, entered heartily into the work of reforming the Church in England. Sir Thomas More, Wolsey's successor as chancellor, was unwilling to go as far as Henry desired, and before long Cromwell became the king's chief adviser.

In 1532 all appeals to the Pope were forbidden; and this being against the wish of the Archbishop of Canterbury, he resigned. In his stead was placed Thomas Cranmer, a scholar of Cambridge, who had already suggested many things to Henry. The question of the legality of the marriage with Katharine was immediately brought before him in his archbishop's court, and a decision given in Henry's favor. The king then acknowledged his marriage with Anne Boleyn. In a short time a daughter, the Princess Elizabeth, was born, and Parliament,

The Statute against appeals to Rome.

SIR THOMAS MORE, WEARING THE COLLAR OF SS: FROM AN
ORIGINAL PORTRAIT PAINTED BY HOLBEIN IN 1527,
BELONGING TO EDWARD HUTH, ESQ.

declaring the children of Henry and Anne to be the true heirs of the crown, disinherited Katharine's daughter, the Princess Mary.

The reformation of the English Church, however, did not stop with the divorce of Katharine. The Pope excommunicated Henry, and declared the divorce to be of no account. Almost in self-defence the king was obliged to break with the Pope. Parliament passed law after law. Payments of any kind by the clergy to Rome were forbidden. For the future all such payments must be made to the king. Bishops should no longer be appointed by the Pope, but should be chosen according to the king's command. Many changes, too, were made in the discipline of the Church in England. Even the clergy were glad to admit the right of Parliament to regulate the affairs of the Church, to pay a large sum of money to the king, and even to acknowledge him to be "Supreme Head on Earth of the Church of England." In fact, it was dangerous to deny this title; for the Act of Supremacy, passed in 1534, declared any one who should do this guilty of high treason. Among the first to refuse this recognition was Sir Thomas More, and by his prompt execution Henry showed how terribly in earnest he and his advisers were.

The Church of England.

In England, as in all other Catholic countries, there were then two classes of persons called, technically, "ecclesiastics,"—the secular and regular. The former were the parish priests or their superiors, as far as the archbishops. The latter were men or women who had taken vows to live according to certain rules and regulations. With few exceptions, these were gathered into convents and monasteries and other places where they lived together. Now the monks and friars had great influence with the people, and so far the reforms in the English Church had not touched them. On the contrary, they were working hard to arouse the people

Destruction of the monasteries.

against Henry and his reformation. Probably it was necessary for his own safety to put a stop to this; but Henry acted here, as always, with harshness, urged on, no doubt, by Cromwell, and inspired by the thought of the riches to be obtained. For years it had been known that in some of these monasteries the monks led far from holy lives. It was determined to send a commission to inquire into the condition of them all. This commission acted in a very despotic manner, and obtained evidence oftentimes in most discreditable ways. There probably was some truth in its report, but there must have been a great deal of falsehood. At all events, it was decided to suppress the monasteries and other like establishments. In 1536 the smaller ones were suppressed, and three years later the larger ones shared their fate. The wealth poured into the king's treasury was enormous. Some of it was used for religion, some for new fortifications; but most of it found its way into the pockets of Henry's ministers and friends. As it turned out, this was the very best thing that could have happened. Had the king and his successors kept this wealth in lands and goods, and managed it with any shrewdness, there would have been no more appeals to Parliament for money. The English king would have been as despotic as any monarch of Christendom. Whoever obtained in this way the lands of an abbey or monastery became a firm opponent of the Roman Church, and a supporter of the Reformation in England. Many of the most important families in England date their worldly prosperity from this time. This suppression of the monasteries produced another great result. The control of the House of Lords passed into the hands

The effect of this destruction.

of the lay peers. Up to this time three classes had sat in the upper house,— the lay peers, like the Earl of Surrey, the archbishops and bishops, and the mitred abbots. These last two, forming the spiritual peers, outnumbered the lay lords. But when the abbots disappeared, the House of Lords took on its modern shape of a body composed of the wealthy landowners and great soldiers and statesmen of England. And as the lay peers from this time on increased with much greater rapidity than the spiritual peers, the political importance of the latter has decreased, till now they have almost no political importance at all.

Before the suppression of the monasteries had proceeded very far the cause of the break with Rome herself disappeared. It is possible that Anne Boleyn may not have acted with all the dignity becoming a queen. It is more likely that Henry had become tired of her, and charged her with evil conduct as the easiest way of getting rid of her. At all events, in 1536 she was beheaded. The king then married Jane Seymour, who lived long enough to give birth to a boy, afterwards King Edward VI.

Execution of Anne Boleyn.

Meantime the Reformation had been making rapid progress. Everywhere there was great eagerness to read the Bible. Neighboring families joined in the purchase of one, and a copy was kept chained to the reading-desk in every parish church. In fact, the Reformation had gone farther than Henry or the great mass of Englishmen desired it to go. In all matters of doctrine and belief he was a good Catholic, and refused to allow any change in those respects. His opinions were expressed in a statute, called the Act of

The Six Articles.

the Six Articles, passed in 1539. But Henry would allow no persecution, and several times when the bishops had put this Act into execution, Henry interfered, and released those imprisoned. By this time the influence of Cromwell, who wished to go much farther, had become greatly weakened. It had been one of his pet schemes to marry Henry to one of the Protestant princesses of Germany, and thus bring him under the influence of German Protestantism. Unfortunately the princess selected, Anne of Cleves, proved to be very ugly. Henry was obliged to marry her; but he soon separated from her, giving her a pension. For Cromwell the affair was more serious. Like Wolsey, he had been very arbitrary, and had made many enemies. The king was furious with him on account of the marriage; so he withdrew his favor, and Cromwell was declared guilty of treason by an Act of Parliament, and executed without any trial. This was done by an "Act of Attainder," which was passed like any law. It is a little singular that the precise form this took at that time had been devised by Cromwell, and further that he was the first to be thus put out of the way. *Fall of Cromwell.*

The king had two more wives, — Katharine Howard (Anne Boleyn's cousin, who soon turned out to be undesirable), and Katharine Parr. The latter was already a widow, and was a woman of uncommon sagacity. She humored Henry in every way, and so pleased him by her care and attention that she not only contrived to outlive him, but even to secure a great influence over him. Henry was now getting old and feeble. He had grown so stout that it is said he could not walk. Every one but himself *Last years of Henry VIII.*

saw his end was soon coming, and a great strife began as to who should rule during the minority of his son. The Howards, with Norfolk at their head, thought they had the best right; but the king's jealousy was aroused, and Surrey was executed. Norfolk would have followed him, had not Henry died before the time set for the execution. The Howards were quite opposed to all reform in religion, and they were resisted by the Seymours, the uncles of the Prince of Wales, and liberals in religion. By Henry's will and an Act of Parliament the succession to the crown was given to Edward, then to Mary, then to Elizabeth; and if these had no children, to the heirs of Henry's younger sister Mary, thus passing over the descendants of his sister Margaret, who had married the King of Scots.

THE TUDORS.

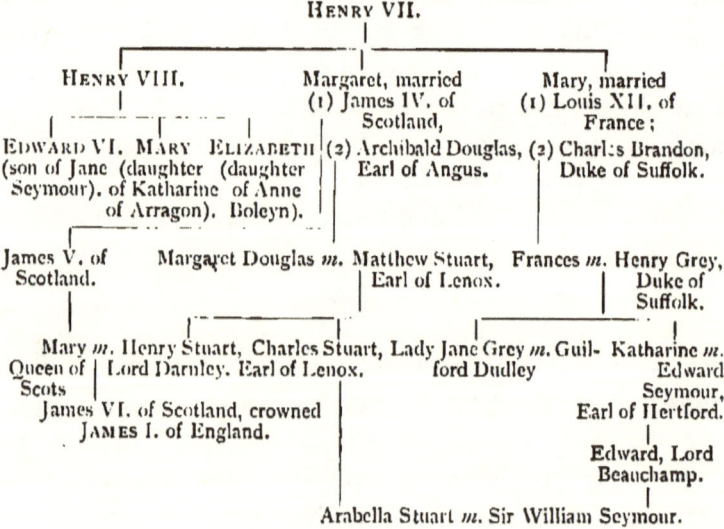

CHAPTER XIX.

EDWARD VI.

1547-1553.

WHEN Henry's will was opened it was found that he had appointed sixteen executors to govern the kingdom during his son's minority. He expected these executors to act in a very cautious way, so that there should be as few changes as possible when Edward took the government into his own hands. As a matter of fact the very opposite was done. The Seymours got all power into their hands, and the Earl of Hertford, the head of the family and uncle to the young king, was made protector. He soon made himself a duke, with the title of Somerset, and is known in history as the Protector Somerset. *[Protector Somerset.]*

Now Protector Somerset was an able man, and a very well-meaning man too. But he lacked the necessary patience and steadfastness of purpose to govern a great kingdom in such troubled times. His first failure was in connection with Scottish affairs. Henry had very much wished to marry Edward to his cousin, Mary Queen of Scots. In this way the two kingdoms would have been united; but the prejudices of the Scots had prevented the marriage. By waiting, these prejudices might have been overcome; but Somerset would not wait. He sent an army to Scotland, defeated the Scottish forces, and so *[The Scottish war.]*

"by the manner of the wooing" disgusted those hitherto favorable to the marriage that they sent the young queen to France, and married her to the Dauphin.

Somerset, too, tried to push on the reformation of religion faster than people wished. Images were pulled down, the painted walls of the churches covered with whitewash, a new service-book was prepared, and the Articles were repealed. There were other causes of discontent, and the result of everything was a series of rebellions which Somerset proved unable to suppress. Dudley, Earl of Warwick, now came to the front. Taking command of the army, he crushed the rebellions, and then overturned Somerset, making himself protector.

Progress of the Reformation.

Fall of Somerset.

A few years later, Somerset tried to regain his power, and was beheaded. Warwick and the other executors now set themselves to work to make their own fortunes, regardless of the welfare of the kingdom. They also found it necessary still to press on the Reformation. Among those who refused to change their religion was the Princess Mary. This made it all the easier for Warwick, now become Duke of Northumberland, to persuade Edward, who was an ardent reformer, to appoint Lady Jane Grey his heir. This Lady Jane was descended from Henry VIII.'s younger sister Mary. She was a Protestant and the wife of Northumberland's son, Lord Guilford Dudley. Soon after he had signed this will Edward died of consumption, though there were not wanting persons who thought he had been poisoned. The Lady Jane was crowned queen, but her reign, if reign it can be called, lasted only nine days, as will presently be seen.

Lady Jane Grey.

The Princess Mary had managed to keep out of Northumberland's grasp, and people flocked to her from all sides. No one then knew what a narrow and bigoted person she was. They did know what a hateful person Northumberland was, and they were resolved to deprive him of power. Then, too, Mary's right to the crown was the better, and England was resolved, whatever might happen, that the Wars of the Roses should not begin again.

Mary Tudor.

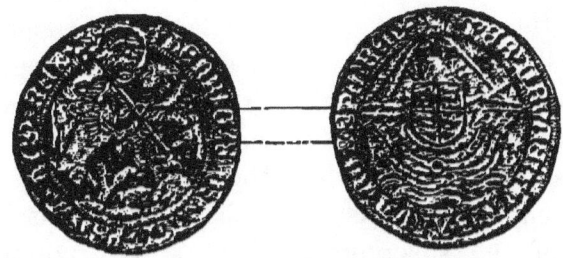

ANGEL OF HENRY VIII., 1543.

CHAPTER XX.

MARY THE CATHOLIC.

1553-1558.

THE central idea of Queen Mary's short reign, which lasted for only five years, was the restoration of the old religion in England. She wished, not merely to restore things as they were at the beginning Mary's of Edward's reign, but to connect England once policy. more with the Roman Catholic Church as it had been connected before the time of Henry VIII. Parliament, as was usual in those days, was in the hands of the sovereign's friends. Everything was done as Mary wished, till it came to restoring the property confiscated from the monasteries. But so many members of Parliament were interested in keeping those lands in their own hands that any such general restoration of the property of the Church was plainly impossible. Mary, however, gave back whatever the Crown still possessed of the spoils, which, indeed, was not very much. Before long, Northumberland was beheaded, though he tried at the last moment to save his miserable life by declaring that he had always been a good Roman Catholic.

Mary then married her cousin, Philip II. of Spain, like herself a strong Roman Catholic. But English-

QUEEN MARY TUDOR: FROM A PAINTING BY LUCAS DE HEERE, DATED 1554, BELONGING TO THE SOCIETY OF ANTIQUARIES.

men were so much opposed to this match that Philip was given no share in the government of the country, and it was agreed that England should never be called on to defend Philip's possessions.

She marries Philip of Spain.

It could hardly be expected that the friends of the Reformation would stand idly by and make no attempt to stop these proceedings. A rebellion broke out, and was put down with some difficulty. The rebels designed placing Anne Boleyn's daughter, the Princess Elizabeth, on the throne. But so prudent had been her conduct, guided as she was by William Cecil, that she could not be connected directly with the plot, from whose success she would have been the chief gainer. For the remainder of Mary's reign, however, she was kept a close prisoner at Woodstock. The unfortunate Lady Jane Grey and her husband did not fare so well. Although but seventeen years of age, Lady Jane Grey was executed, and within a few days at least eighty persons were hanged in London alone.

Risings in England.

Her rivals being thus killed or imprisoned, Queen Mary thought she could with safety coerce the people of England into becoming good Roman Catholics, or burn them if they resisted or refused. It was easy enough to get Parliament to pass laws by which this might be done legally, though Parliament probably never once dreamed of the length to which bigotry would be carried. The Pope, on his side, gave way a little, and received England back into the bosom of the Roman Church, though the Church lands were not restored. The most notable victim of this persecution was Archbishop Cranmer, who had presided at the trial at which Mary's mother was divorced from King Henry. Cranmer was now a feeble old man, and to the feebleness of age might perhaps be attributed his brief submission to the Pope. But it did not last long; and when the time came for him to make his con-

The martyrs.

fession in a public manner, he recanted everything, and declared that his unworthy hand, which had written the letter of submission, should be the first part of him to be burned, and so indeed it was. The other bishops then burned were Hooper, Ridley, and Latimer. The last two were burned at the same time; and it is related that as the fires were lighted, Latimer said to his companion: "Play the man, Master Ridley; we shall this day light such a candle in England as by the grace of God never shall be put out." He was right; for to these and other similar burnings was due, more than to any other one thing, the permanent severance of England from the Roman Church. In all, more than two hundred persons were burned. When compared with similar persecutions on the Continent, these numbers seem small, and it must always be remembered that it was a time of great bitterness of feeling; and that we know of these persecutions mainly through writers who were disposed to make the most of everything which was to the disadvantage of the Roman Catholics and Mary. It is certain, at any rate, that the people of England did not at all like such proceedings, and that nothing did more to make Englishmen into Protestants than these same burnings and other cruel punishments.

In fact, Mary is to be pitied as well as blamed. She was personally so unattractive that Philip soon left her to look after his own affairs on the mainland. No child was born to them, and it soon became evident that the time was not far off when Mary's diseased body and mind would pass away, and her hated Protestant sister Elizabeth, Anne Boleyn's daughter, become queen. To add to these misfor-

Mary's death.

tunes, in spite of the agreement made when Philip and Mary were married, England became involved in war with France; and in the course of that war Calais was captured by the French, and never after regained by the English. Whatever else she was, Mary was a true Englishwoman and a Tudor, and she once said that if any one could take out her heart and look at it, the name of Calais would be found written on it. This blow, added to her other griefs, was too much for her, and the worn-out, wretched, and almost insane woman died.

A MOUNTED SOLDIER: FROM A BROADSIDE PRINTED IN 1596.

CHAPTER XXI.

ELIZABETH.

1558-1603.

IT has been customary to speak of Queen Mary as "Bloody Mary," and of Queen Elizabeth as "Good Queen Bess." The truth is that they were very much alike. Both were cunning, deceitful women, Elizabeth being by far the abler. Mary was almost of necessity a believer in the Pope's supremacy, while all Elizabeth's interests pointed in the other direction. In religion, apart from this question of the supremacy of the Pope, Elizabeth seems to have thought herself a good Catholic. She had no sympathy with those who wished even a moderate reformation of the church service. During the first part of her reign, at all events, she had religious service in her chapel with all the ceremonies of the Roman Catholic Church. But she was determined that the Church of England should be separated from the Roman Catholic Church, as it had been separated in the time of Henry VIII. Elizabeth inherited from her father all his great powers of government and of state management. Like him, she knew how to surround herself with strong, able men, and, like him, she knew how to place on their shoulders the responsibility of questionable or unpopular actions. In her dealings with the Parliament and with the nation she was as

Character of the reign.

QUEEN ELIZABETH IN 1588: AFTER A DRAWING BY ISAAC OLIVER.

arbitrary as her father had been, but she also knew when to yield. Her reign, therefore, was one of the most successful, if not the most successful, in English history. A moderate reformation was effected in the Church, though her refusal to go a step farther prevented that Church from ever becoming national except in name, and gave rise to the Puritan opposition, of which we shall learn more hereafter. Then by her steady refusal to go to war, except in self-defence, Elizabeth gave to England a long period of comparative peace, at a time when great inventions and discoveries were coming into common use, and while England's commercial rivals were engaged in the most destructive of all wars, those for religion. This gave England a chance to grow so strong that when the struggle came, as it did come, even the power of Philip of Spain could not harm her. This period of growth also enabled England to take that lead in commerce and the arts of peace which she has ever since maintained. More important, perhaps, than the progress in these various directions were the reforms in the administration of the government. Elizabeth's reign, too, is renowned as the time of Shakspere and the other writers of the Golden Age of English Literature.

Elizabeth was undoubtedly a great ruler. But she had in her service men whose counsel more, perhaps, than her own powers, kept England free from foreign entanglements, and permitted the nation to work out its own salvation. Chief of these was William Cecil, afterwards Lord Burleigh. He had been Elizabeth's adviser even before she became queen. To his counsel it is probably due that she had held aloof from the plots of Mary's time, and could

William Cecil, Lord Burleigh.

never be connected directly with them. These plots had always revolved about her, their aim having been to set her upon her sister's throne: yet she could never

WILLIAM SHAKSPERE: FROM THE BUST ON HIS TOMB AT STRATFORD-ON-AVON.

be implicated. If much of this good fortune was due to Cecil, as much was probably due to Elizabeth's own cunning and power of deceit. Indeed, no English sovereign seems to have excelled her in this ability to deceive. It was partly born in her; but the circumstances of her early life were congenial to its growth. In fact, after her coronation, she and Cecil had need of all their ability and shrewdness to keep their country free. Never had the position of England and England's ruler been more precarious than during the first thirty years of this reign.

The hardest task Elizabeth and Cecil had to face was the reformation of religion. Elizabeth was declared to be the supreme governor of the Church in England. Thirty-nine articles of faith were drawn up, and a service-book was put forth. This last was based on that of Cranmer. The service was to be in English. By the Act of Uniformity this book was required to be used in all churches throughout the land, and no other service was allowed. Any one not attending the regular church was fined. It seems that Elizabeth and Cecil wished to build up a really national Church, and to have a form of service that all might attend. Thus the celebration of the mass was forbidden, and the service was to be read in English. This was to please the advanced reformers. Then, to please the Catholics, the dress of the clergy and many ceremonies disliked by the radicals were retained. Nor would Elizabeth consent to the marriage of the clergy. In fact, she wished to take a position between the two extremes which her father had occupied. But the times had changed. Mary's harshness had driven many to the Continent. There these exiles became intimate with the Calvinists and other advanced reformers. It is important to understand what Calvin's doctrines really were, for their influence

The Church of England.

The Calvinists.

upon England, and upon our own country also, has been immense.

First of all, Calvin was a religious reformer. As such he went far beyond Luther in his plans, and wished to throw away all the ceremonies and associations which had grown up around the Roman Catholic Church, except such as were commanded in the Scriptures. But it is as a social reformer that he is more interesting to us. He desired to remodel society, so that it might represent the society described in the Old Testament. He thus introduced a form of government which was then new in Europe. He thought that all society, whether in church or state, should be founded on the individual man. He believed that the best form of government would be obtained through men collected in congregations, and through congregations governed by elected councils. The heads of a Church founded on this model would be supreme in the land. They could explain the law of God to king or peasant. The power of these men proceeded from below, and the historian John Richard Green has therefore said: "It is in Calvinism that the modern world strikes its roots; for it was Calvinism that first revealed the dignity of man." This equality of baron and shoemaker before the law of God and man is the basis of all democratic society; but it is really incompatible with monarchy. Now these ideas of Calvin were being introduced into England by the reformers returning from abroad, and numbers of men were eagerly accepting them.

The Puritans. These men were called Puritans, because they wished to purify the Church. They regarded themselves as good members of the Church of England. They had no desire to separate from that Church, but only refused to conform to all its ceremonies. For example, the use of the surplice was to them very distasteful, as it reminded them of the Pope and their former connection with the Roman Church. They disliked many other ceremonies which were retained, but in all matters of doctrine they seem to have believed very much as did other members of the Church. As time went on, other sects arose. Especially there were some Puritans who went farther than the great mass of them were then willing to go. They refused longer to remain in the Church, and separated from it, and were hence called Separatists, and were also known as Brownists, from the name of an early leader. But the Puritans, whether merely Nonconformists or Separatists, saw that in Elizabeth's continued occupation of the throne lay their only chance for safety, or even for toleration of any kind. The next heir to the throne was Mary, Queen of Scots, and she was an ardent Catholic. So the Puritans supported Elizabeth loyally, although they had persecutions to endure even under her. In the reign of King James these persecutions continued and increased, and led, some years later, to the colonization of a New England across the Atlantic Ocean.

As has been already said, the Puritans felt the need of supporting Elizabeth, even if she did persecute them; and so Elizabeth and Cecil felt, on their side, the need of support from the Puritans, even if their doctrines tended to the overthrow of government by king and bishop. It seems probable that at her accession two-thirds of the English people were Roman Catholics. Her changes in the ritual were so few that the great mass of them attended without

The Roman Catholics.

difficulty the new service. It is said, indeed, that only two hundred out of nine thousand priests resigned their livings. In time, as the old priests died, and others took their places, a gradual change came over the Church, and men almost without knowing it became really Protestant. But a powerful minority remained true to the old faith. To them the divorce of Mary's mother had been illegal, and Elizabeth was an illegitimate child. As such she had no right to the throne. To them, therefore, Mary, Queen of Scots, was the real queen of England, Elizabeth being a usurper whom it was their duty to overthrow. At the beginning of the reign, however, it happened, fortunately for Elizabeth, that her good-will was necessary to Philip of Spain, and so she was given time to consolidate her power before any further struggle came.

We have seen how the Scots married their queen to the French Dauphin. In 1559 he became king of France, though he ruled only a year. If his queen should become queen of England too, France, Scotland, and England would be united under one ruler. That was something Philip of Spain could not allow, and he offered to marry Elizabeth. But she could not consent, without recognizing the right of the Pope to grant a dispensation. This of course she could not consistently do, and the project fell through. But for many years Philip and Elizabeth remained the best of friends. In 1560 Francis II. died, and Mary, Queen of Scots, returned to Scotland. Before long she married her cousin, Lord Darnley. Their child was afterwards James VI. of Scotland and I. of England. But before long, Darnley was murdered, and in 1568 Mary

Philip II.

Mary, Queen of Scots.

MARY, QUEEN OF SCOTS: FROM THE MEMORIAL PORTRAIT DONE IMMEDIATELY AFTER HER DEATH, AND NOW AT WINDSOR CASTLE.

fled to England and asked protection from her kinswoman Elizabeth. Now we really know very little about Mary, except that she was beautiful, fascinating, and inherited the Scottish throne by clear right. Some people say that she was an accomplice in Darnley's murder, and rewarded the murderer, Bothwell, by marrying him. Others tell a somewhat different story. She may not have been so bad as many think, but she probably was false and treacherous. At all events, she did not gain much by coming to England. Elizabeth alone would certainly have been a match for her. But with Elizabeth, Cecil, and Walsingham leagued together against her, Mary of Scotland was doomed from the first.

It is not easy to understand this part of Elizabeth's reign. But if a few points are kept in mind, the story will not seem so complicated as it at first sight looks. As yet the fate of English Protestantism hung on Elizabeth's life. Parliament urged her to marry, or at least to name a successor. Both these things she steadily refused to do. To us looking backward it is now clear that this was wise. As long as Mary was the next heir to the throne, she was almost compelled to keep quiet, that she might become queen on Elizabeth's death. Elizabeth declined, therefore, to name any one else as her successor, and either from jealousy or for some other cause, refused to name Mary. For the same reason Elizabeth was unwilling to marry. Should she marry a foreigner like Philip, there was sure to be trouble of one kind or another. Should she marry an Englishman, all other Englishmen of equal rank would be offended. So she would marry no one, though she held out great hopes to many. Then with regard to foreign relations, at first sight her whole policy seems in confusion, Elizabeth doing this thing to-day, that to-morrow. But she

Foreign policy.

had a difficult part to play, to keep on the good side of France and Spain, and at the same time to do all in her power to hurt and weaken them. It happened that the religious wars in foreign countries were a great help to her, for they kept the foreigners so busy at home that there was no time to attack England. In France the Protestants, or Huguenots, were struggling for existence, and Elizabeth sent aid to them in various ways, though really she aided them as little as possible. As long as the Huguenots seemed to be doing well, she acted rather defiantly with regard to Spain. But when the Catholics began to get the upper hand in France there was nothing too good to be said to Philip. At last the Protestants of the Netherlands revolted against Spain. This was a great help to Elizabeth, and she encouraged them with money, for whose repayment she took possession of certain towns. Beyond that she would not go. So in every way Elizabeth had to be very careful, and the Pope was not long in adding to her cares.

Mary had hardly arrived in England before the Roman Catholics formed plots to put her on the throne. The earlier plots were put down, and Mary was kept in strict confinement. But in 1570 the Catholics were roused to action by a bull, or proclamation, of the Pope of Rome excommunicating Queen Elizabeth, and releasing her subjects from their allegiance. Priests and emissaries of all kinds were sent to England to stir up the Catholics and to recall the lukewarm Protestants to their ancient faith. The nation was called upon to take sides in religion, and it took the Protestant side. This bull roused against the Roman Catholic Church the independent

Roman Catholic plots.

spirit of the English people, and England was lost to the Roman Church. From that moment there was little hope of recalling her to the old faith by peaceful means. Plots were discovered to assassinate the queen, and a panic swept through England. These schemes were made, of course, in the interest of Mary, and Parliament wished to put her out of the way by a Bill of Attainder, as though she were an English subject. But Elizabeth would not consent. While Mary lived, she felt that there would be peace. But an association was formed for the queen's protection, and to avenge her death in case she should be murdered. Severer laws were made against the Catholics, and the fines against non-attendance at the authorized service were enormously increased. There seems to have been little attempt made to carry out these laws against laymen. But woe to the priests who fell into the hands of the Government! For them a special court was set up. Elizabeth was the supreme governor of the English Church, and she delegated a portion of her authority to a commission consisting of the archbishop and other leading men, ordering them to inquire into and punish offences against the Acts of Supremacy and Uniformity. Before this court the accused person was brought, and compelled to answer under oath whatever questions might be asked him. Those who did not answer were tortured. All forms of law and all the safeguards of English liberty were forgotten. While this great engine of oppression was directed against the Catholics only, there was little outcry. When, however, it was later used against the Puritans it aroused fierce opposition. Neither the queen nor the archbishops

Court of High Commission.

seem to have cared very much about a man's thoughts, but they were determined he should keep them to himself, unless they were in harmony with the ideas of the Church. This the Puritans refused to do. They preached and taught on all sides as long as they were allowed to preach and teach. In truth, it was not long before the bishops silenced the outspoken ministers. The Puritans then resorted to the printing-press; and as nothing could be printed without the consent of the archbishop, they used a press which was kept moving about the country. It seemed as though nothing could stop these attacks on the bishops and the English Church. The most famous pamphlets were signed Martin Mar-Prelate. Even to this day the name of the writer is not known, but a man named Penry was executed as the author.

It had been impossible to connect Mary directly with any of the earlier plots to kill the queen. But in 1586 the Government was able, by its spies, to prove that Mary knew of a plan to assassinate her. Whether the plot really existed is not absolutely clear. Some writers have thought it was merely a scheme got up by the Government to entrap Mary. At all events she was convicted, and, Elizabeth's consent having been obtained, was executed. *Execution of Mary, Queen of Scots.* What Elizabeth had feared now came to pass. Mary, disliking her son, who was a Protestant, left her claims to the throne of England to Philip of Spain, and he, as a good Catholic, set about making them good. There were other and perhaps stronger causes that made him attack England. Elizabeth had sent aid to the Dutch; and the English sailors, led by men like Hawkins and Drake, were endangering the Spanish control of the West Indies and the Pacific coast of America. The English were also beginning to found colonies on the Atlantic coast of North America, though up to this time their settlements had not been successful. So Philip decided to send a great fleet to England, and with it the army which, under the Duke of Parma, had been fighting in the Netherlands. It had been intended to send this Armada against England in 1587, and provisions and ships were actually gathered at Cadiz. But the English under Drake sailed into the harbor one day, and destroyed so many of the vessels and so much of the provisions that the attempt was abandoned for that year. The next year, 1588, the Armada actually sailed from Lisbon for Dunkirk, where the army was to join it, and a joint descent was to be effected on the English coast. The Armada numbered about one hundred and fifty vessels, most of them large ships.

The Invincible Armada.

At that time England had nothing properly to be called a navy. When the queen wanted vessels she called upon the seaport towns to furnish them. This was not so difficult then as it would be now, for in those rough days all vessels were obliged to go armed to protect themselves from sea-robbers and pirates. So a fleet of about seventy-five sail was collected, and with it Lord Howard of Effingham, Elizabeth's kinsman, went forth to meet the great Armada. With him were Hawkins and Drake and others experienced in fighting on the water. At the same time two large armies were made ready on shore to repel the Spaniard if he should attempt a landing. The Armada was soon seen sailing up the Channel in the form of a crescent. Hanging on its rear, the English cut off and captured

SIR FRANCIS DRAKE, IN HIS FORTY-THIRD YEAR; FROM THE
ENGRAVING BY ELSTRACKE.

or sank every ship that lagged behind. The Spaniards then anchored off Calais. But the English sent fireships among them, and compelled them to weigh anchor and run northward. The English fleet had by this time increased to perhaps one hundred and forty vessels of all sorts and sizes. But if their ships were smaller, they sailed better. Besides, the English even then were great sailors and sea-fighters. Their guns were better aimed than were those of the Spaniards. Indeed, it seems probable that had Queen Elizabeth not been so stingy with her powder and provisions, the English would have completely destroyed the Armada. As it was, after driving the Spaniards to the north, the English turned homeward, and many sailors who had nobly fought for their country and religion died of starvation on the way back. As for the Spaniards, many of them never returned home. Trying to regain Spain with their shattered ships by the north of England and the Irish Channel, they were met by a furious storm. Ship after ship was wrecked on the coasts of Scotland and Ireland, and it is said that of that mighty Armada only fifty-four vessels ever returned to Spain. The destruction of the Armada broke the power of that nation. The supremacy of the seas passed into other hands. Even with that supremacy it had been difficult for her to hold her vast empire together. From this time one possession after another was torn from her grasp. With the control of the Channel in English hands, troops could not be sent to the Netherlands, and the independence of the United Provinces was assured. Another Protestant power thus arose in Europe, destined ere long to stand side by side with England in the struggle for liberty. From the day when Drake chased the Armada north from Calais, England's power has gone on ever increasing, till on her empire, exceeding in extent even that of the second Philip, the sun never sets. We must now turn from this glorious scene, and begin our study of the most objectionable chapter in England's history, — her misgovernment of Ireland.

As far back as the times of the Normans there had been some kind of an assertion of the right of the English king to be considered the ruler, or "overlord," of Ireland. But the relations between the two islands and the two peoples did not become close till the time of Henry VII. It was in 1494 that, a Parliament of some kind having met at Drogheda, an Act, called "Poynings' Law," named after the English king's deputy, was passed. By this law no bill could be brought into the Irish Parliament until it had received the approval of the Government in England. Thus Ireland was put, as far as legislation went, completely under subjection to England. During Henry VIII.'s reign little attention was paid to Ireland, except to give to some of the Irish chieftains the title of earl. But during the minority of Edward VI. an attempt was made to establish the Reformed Church in Ireland. The attempt was a failure from the beginning, — partly because the Irish could not understand the service in English any better than when it was read in Latin, but more especially because the Roman Catholic Church was well suited to their habits and needs. Of course the attempt was abandoned at the accession of Mary.

As we have already seen, Queen Elizabeth was determined that there should be one religion in England, and only one. She soon became equally determined that there should be but one religion in England and

"Poynings' Law."

Ireland, and that this should be the religion prescribed by the English Church, of which she was the head. So the Acts of Supremacy and Uniformity were extended to Ireland. Wherever English law could be enforced there, the Roman Catholic clergy were turned out, and Protestants put in their places. It was very difficult to get good men to go to Ireland, in fact difficult to get any one to go. It resulted that in many places the churches went to ruin, and no services were held at all. English law, however, could be enforced only in a very small part of Ireland. In the rest the Roman Catholic service was kept up. The Protestant Established Church was weak from the beginning, and was an object of contempt and hatred to the bulk of Irishmen. Thus was introduced an element of discord which has lasted to our own time.

The Elizabethan settlement of Ireland.

There were other causes of jealousy. At this time Ireland was under the control of three families, — the Geraldines, descended from the Norman Fitz-Gerald; the Butlers; and the De Burghs, or Burkes. Now, of these, the Butlers, led by Ormond, were Protestant, while the Geraldines, headed by Kildare and Desmond, were Catholics. The opposing forces were so arranged that it was impossible for the Butlers to be of much use to the English, cut off as they were by the Geraldines from the English part of the island. It was now proposed to send over English colonists to occupy a large portion of the lands of Desmond, he having relinquished his title to escape being tried for treason. It was hoped also that the courts would find defects in the titles to much more land held by the Irish. In this way it was thought to make a large portion of the island English. But the first attempts were failures. To take an Irishman's land was to touch him in the tenderest part. A fearful insurrection broke out in Munster in 1569, and ten years later in Connaught. Both were put down with the greatest severities and almost unheard-of cruelties. In the northern province alone was the colonization a success. There was already a colony of Scots there; and Essex, the leader of the English in the enterprise, was an exceedingly able man. By 1584 the English were supreme throughout the island, though at a tremendous cost in suffering to the Irish.

When the Armada had been driven away from England, Elizabeth was already an old woman. She had reigned thirty years, and the men whose advice and help had so far made her reign a success were rapidly passing away. Leicester, her favorite though incompetent commander, died while the rejoicings over the defeat of the Armada were still ringing in his ears. Sir Walter Mildmay, the founder of the Puritan College of Emmanuel at Cambridge, — the college from which our own Harvard is in a manner descended, — died in 1589. Walsingham, whose marvellous skill in ferreting out plots had saved Elizabeth's life more than once, followed in 1591. Finally, in 1598, after forty years of service such as few men have given to their sovereign and country, William Cecil, Lord Burleigh, passed away. Young men were now coming to the front. Prominent among them was Robert Cecil, Burleigh's son. His most formidable rival was Robert Devereux, Earl of Essex. Essex was not in any sense a statesman, but he had succeeded to Leicester's place in the queen's

Elizabeth's last years.

affections, and become her favorite. Essex rapidly rose to prominence. In 1596 he and Lord Howard of Effingham led a successful expedition against Cadiz. But Essex did not gain all the advantages from this

WILLIAM CECIL, LORD BURLEIGH, K. G., 1520-1591: FROM A PAINTING IN THE BODLEIAN LIBRARY, OXFORD.

success that he had expected, as most of the credit was given to Lord Howard. It is related that some time after this, in 1598, when the appointment of a deputy for Ireland was being discussed in the council, the queen said something displeasing to Essex. He turned his back on her, which so enraged Elizabeth that she gave him a sound box on the ear. This story may be true or not, but one thing is certain, that when Burleigh died, in the same year, it was Robert Cecil, and not Essex, who succeeded to his place and power.

The next year Essex went to Ireland as deputy. There he used his power in a very mysterious manner. Exactly what he intended is not clear. Perhaps he expected to create a government for himself in Ireland. Perhaps he intended to use the Irish army against his enemies in England. At all events, he found it necessary to hurry back to England and try to regain the queen's regard. But with all her love of flattery, Elizabeth never allowed her personal feelings to interfere with her duties as queen. Essex was placed under restraint. Gathering about him several desperate characters (Sir Ferdinando Gorges among them), he tried to incite the Londoners to rebellion. The attempt failed. Gorges, with the most contemptible meanness, betrayed his friend. Essex was tried, condemned, and executed for treason. Whether he was justly executed or not, Elizabeth seems never to have recovered from the shock of his ingratitude. In 1603 she died, holding to the last the loyal love of the English people.

CHAPTER XXII.

STATE OF SOCIETY.

AS we have already seen, Queen Elizabeth's reign was very remarkable for the great material advancement then made by England. Her foreign commerce was greatly extended. The cruelties of the Spaniards drove many (it is even said one half) of the merchants of Antwerp to London. The decline of the former city and the supremacy of the latter date from this time. In Queen Elizabeth's time, too, the port of Archangel was discovered, and a trade with Russia opened. The East India Company and others like it were formed to trade with foreign parts, and from all directions wealth and luxuries poured into England. There was at the same time a great expansion of home industry. Hitherto English wool had been mainly worked up outside of England; now the cloth was made at home. The same was true, though in a less degree, of the manufactures of steel, and from this time on, the names of Manchester and Sheffield began to be heard more and more.

<small>Commerce.</small>

The country had been so long free from civil wars that the mode of domestic architecture had undergone a complete change. The turreted castle gave way to the hall of the Elizabethan time. Chimneys took the place of the hole in the roof, and the master no longer ate with his dependants in the great hall, but withdrew to his parlor, — called for this reason

<small>Architecture.</small>

a withdrawing-room, and afterwards a drawing-room. Pewter dishes were beginning to take the place of the old wooden trays, though forks were not common until some time after Elizabeth's death. Nor were these

COACHES IN THE REIGN OF ELIZABETH. FROM "ARCHÆOLOGIA."

improvements in the art of living confined to the very rich, for the moderately rich class, which was now coming into existence, enjoyed advantages which had been denied to the wealthiest of only a generation or two before. The lot of the laboring class, however, did not improve.

The changes in agriculture which we have already described had gone on with increasing rapidity. Undoubtedly one cause of this was the fact that people were beginning to live very differently. But the suppression of the monasteries had much to do with it. The monks had been easy landlords. They had taken care of the sick and poor of their district, even going so far as to encourage begging by their indiscriminate giving. All this was now stopped. The new owner of the forfeited monastery lands wished to get as great a return from them as possible. Some he turned into sheep-walks, the rest he cultivated with care, employing, either by himself or through his tenants, as few laborers as possible. Masses of men were thrown out of work. The country became infested by vagabonds and beggars. Several remedies were tried. At last it was determined to make each locality, whether called parish or town, take care of its own poor. In this way the old principle of local responsibility was once more brought into use. There were other reforms in the same direction, but this making the parishes responsible for the poor within their own limits is the most important. The principal law was passed in 1601, and remained in force till 1834. The immediate effect of the new system was startling. In the time of Henry VIII. some two thousand robbers had been hanged each year. This number was now reduced to three or four hundred, although the population had greatly increased.

The poor law.

It has been already said that English literature was carried to a high point in the reign of Elizabeth, Shakspere being its chief ornament. There was a whole circle of authors, — such as Marlowe, Ben Jonson,

Massinger, Ford, Chapman, Beaumont, and Fletcher,— who have never since been equalled, as dramatic poets, by any similar group in any other age. The modern form of prose fiction had not yet been created; but people were fond of reading long narratives of imaginary adventure, either in verse, like Spenser's "Faerie Queene," or in prose, like Sir Philip Sidney's "Arcadia." Sir Walter Raleigh was not merely a great explorer, but also an author; and wrote, while a prisoner in the Tower of London, his "History of the World." William Tyndale produced in this reign the first important translation of the Bible into English.

Scott's novel of "Kenilworth" gives a tolerably vivid picture of the society and manners of the Elizabethan period; but these can best be studied in the actual literature of that period.

THE STUARTS.

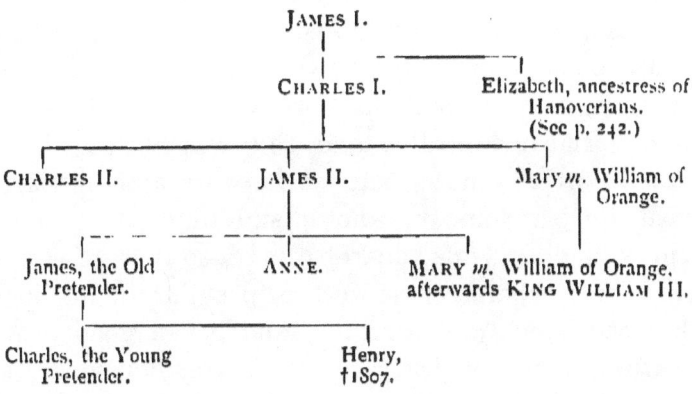

CHAPTER XXIII.

JAMES I.

1603-1625.

IT was well understood towards the end of Elizabeth's reign that James VI. of Scotland, son of Mary of Scotland, and descended from Henry VIII.'s sister Margaret, would be Elizabeth's successor. After Elizabeth's death he was proclaimed King James I. of England, and succeeded to the throne as quietly as had any heir-apparent before him. It is a curious fact that although he was the son of the most beautiful and attractive princess of that time, James was of very disagreeable and repulsive appearance. His face was plain and foolish, with a tongue so large that he could not help showing it all the time. His legs were very small and weak, so that he walked feebly and awkwardly; and this was noticed by the people all the more, because he wore a thick padded coat, for fear some one should stab him. He was very timid, and also false and obstinate, so that he was unpopular in character as well as peculiar in his looks. He had been well educated, and had a good deal of learning; but he had very little common-sense, and was called by the French minister Sully "the wisest fool in Christendom."

His character.

He was hardly seated on his new throne before plots began to be formed against him, especially by

SIR WALTER RALEIGH (1552-1618) AND HIS ELDEST SON WALTER, AT THE AGE OF EIGHT: FROM A PICTURE, DATED 1602, BELONGING TO SIR J. F. LENNARD, BART.

the enemies of Robert Cecil, his Secretary of State. Among those who joined in these plots was the celebrated Sir Walter Raleigh, so well known for the interest he took in colonizing the American continent. The plan of some of these conspirators was to dethrone James I. and give the crown to Lady Arabella Stuart, who, like James, was descended from Henry VII. The plot did not succeed; but it gave the king a great dislike to this lady, and when, some years later, she married Henry Seymour, a third descendant of Henry VII., James thought her so dangerous that he had her shut up in the Tower, where she died insane. Sir Walter Raleigh was also sent to the Tower, and lived there many years, writing books, some of which are famous. At last, in 1616, the king released him, that he might take command of an expedition to look for gold mines in South America. But James, with his usual deceitfulness, let the Spaniards, who had claimed the country where the mines were said to be, know just where Raleigh was going, so that the expedition was a failure. When Raleigh returned unsuccessful, he was first charged with misconduct in regard to the expedition, and then the old complaint was brought up against him that he had plotted against the king; and on this last charge he was beheaded at the Old Palace Yard in Westminster. The king's real object was to please the Spaniards, who found in Raleigh's enterprise a great danger to their colonies.

Execution of Raleigh.

The most famous of these plots is known in history as the "Gunpowder Plot." James's mother, it must be remembered, was a Roman Catholic; and before he became king of England he wrote to a prominent Englishman of that faith, the Earl of

The Gunpowder Plot (1605).

Northumberland, that when he came to the throne the Catholics should have freedom of worship. Perhaps he meant it sincerely, and for a time the Catholics were well treated. But the king soon found that there was in England a strong popular feeling against them, and that he himself was charged with being at heart of their faith. When he found out this fact, he began to deny that he had ever pledged himself that they should have freedom of worship, and he ordered his lawyers and judges to enforce the severe laws that existed against all who refused to attend the Protestant services. These persons were called under the law "Popish recusants," and they were subject to a fine of £50 — which would to-day be equivalent to $500 — for each month when they had failed to be present at the services of the Church of England. This severe persecution led to the formation of a plot, led by Robert Catesby, who belonged to one of the oldest families in England, to blow up the Parliament House at a time when the king, lords, and commons should all be there together. "In that place," wrote Catesby, "they have done us all the mischief, and perhaps God hath designed that place for their punishment." Catesby had followers, of whom the best known is Guy, or Guido, Fawkes, and they placed six barrels of gunpowder under the House of Lords without being detected. Then, while waiting for Parliament to assemble, they tried to hit upon a plan by which the Roman Catholic noblemen could be kept away from the House of Lords and their lives saved. But it was finally left to each person to caution those whom he thought fit; and thus it happened that Lord Mounteagle, a brother-in-law of one of the conspirators, just as he was sitting down to supper one evening, received a note, written without punctuation or capitals, advising him to retire into the country for a time. "God and man hath concurred," this strange note said, "to punish the wickedness of this time;" and it added, "though there be no appearance of any stir, yet to-day they shall receive a terrible blow, this Parliament, and yet they shall not see who hurts them." Lord Mounteagle sent this letter to the Secretary of State, and the very night before Parliament was to assemble, a search was made, and the gunpowder was found, with Guy Fawkes standing guard over it. Fawkes, on being seized, said to the man who arrested him that if he had only had the chance, he would have blown him up, his house, himself, and all. When taken before the king, he confessed the truth, saying that he meant to have blown up king, lords, bishops, and all the rest. He gave the names of the other conspirators, and they were all put to death. This made the greatest excitement, and led to still severer laws against the Catholics, most unwisely and unjustly, for it was the cruelty of the laws that first led to the plot; and although the conspirators were Catholics, Lord Mounteagle, who foiled them, was of the same religion. This happened Nov. 5, 1605; and to this day, in some parts of England, it is the custom to make bonfires on that anniversary, and to burn a stuffed image of Guy Fawkes, singing this rhyme:

> "Remember, remember the Fifth of November,
> Gunpowder Treason and plot;
> I see no reason why Gunpowder Treason
> Should ever be forgot."

It shows how long traditions last, that within a few

THE PURITANS.

years, on the banks of the Merrimack River in Massachusetts, these bonfires have still been made.

As the king was always in trouble with the Roman Catholics, so the same want of frankness kept him always in trouble with the Puritans. They presented to the king a petition signed, as was claimed, by a thousand persons, asking for changes in the Church usages. As James's early years had been passed in Presbyterian Scotland, they had reason to think that he, at least, would not be a very strict Episcopalian, and would treat them fairly. On receiving this petition he called a conference between the petitioners and the High Churchmen, as those were called who opposed the request. The conference was held at Hampton Court, and the king himself presided. From the beginning he took sides entirely with the Episcopalians, and with the bishops who represented them, and he said fiercely of the Puritans, "I will make them conform, or I will harry them out of the land." But although the Puritans got no fair treatment from this conference, the assembly had one good result, — an English translation of the Bible, better than any that had yet appeared. Forty-seven clergymen, it is said, began working on it soon after the conference was closed, and they finished their work in 1611. This translation is still in general use among Protestants who speak English. It is known as King James's version, and was one of the few good results of his reign.

James I. had three children. There was one daughter, Elizabeth, who married a German, Prince Frederick, called the Elector Palatine. This marriage was very important, as will be seen by and by. Then there was a son Henry, who soon died, and a son Charles,

KING JAMES I.: FROM A PAINTING BY P. VAN SOMER, DATED 1621, IN THE NATIONAL PORTRAIT GALLERY.

for whom it was necessary, in time, to find a suitable wife. James set his heart upon having a Spanish princess for a daughter-in-law. But the Spaniards thought he should show some favor to the English Catholics, which he could not well do. Prince Charles and a young companion, George Villiers, Duke of Buckingham, actually went to Spain to see the princess. But the match fell through. This greatly pleased the English people, and for a time Buckingham was the most popular man in the kingdom. *"The Spanish Marriage."*

One of James's follies was a belief in what used to be called "The Divine Right of Kings." He had come to the throne in defiance of an Act of Parliament, and merely because he was the nearest in blood to Queen Elizabeth. He did not regard himself in any way responsible to the people of England, but thought himself an absolute monarch. He would have had no such thing as a Parliament if he could have helped it. Fortunately for England, there was no safe way for a king to get money except from Parliament, and he was obliged to call it together much oftener than he wished. Now, during the reign of Queen Elizabeth, Parliament had been quite submissive on the whole, though once in a while some bold member would openly say what he thought. There was a feeling of loyalty towards Elizabeth, which was not the case with regard to James. Then, too, she was thoroughly a queen in her bearing, while in mind and body James was very far from being the Englishman's ideal of a king. So members of Parliament neither respected nor feared him. And they soon showed their independence by impeaching the Lord Chancellor, the highest judge in England. This was Francis Bacon, Lord Verulam, one of the most eminent men in the *The Divine Right of Kings.*

nation, and one of the few really great men whom James had about him. He was charged with taking bribes, and confessed to having received presents from those whose cases were being tried before him. He was declared guilty by the House of Lords, and sentenced to fine and imprisonment, from both of which he was almost entirely excused by the king; but he spent the rest of his life in retirement. It must be remembered in his behalf that the practice of taking bribes was then almost universal; and he was perhaps right when he claimed to have been the most honest lord chancellor for many years.

Impeachment of Bacon.

The House of Commons also turned its attention to foreign affairs, and informed the king that it was not safe for the nation to have a Catholic queen, as might be the case if his son should marry a Catholic princess. James became very angry, and called it an assembly of five hundred kings. He bade the Commons not to meddle with the "mysteries of state," and threatened even to imprison some of them in the Tower of London. The commoners had often listened to this sort of language from Queen Elizabeth. But they now drew up the "Great Protestation," claiming that the king's view of his own powers was quite wrong. They declared "their liberties and privileges to be the undoubted birthright of the subjects of England." They asserted also that they had a clear right to inquire into anything that concerned the public good. This enraged the king so much that he dissolved Parliament, and sending for their records, tore out this "Protestation" with his own hands. A few years later he died.

The Great Protestation (1621).

CHAPTER XXIV.

CHARLES I.

1625-1649.

AS soon as matters could be properly arranged, the new king married the Princess Henrietta Maria of France. She was a sister of the French king, and daughter of that Henry IV. portrayed by Macaulay in the ballad of the "Battle of Ivry." But Henry IV. had turned Catholic in order to become king, and Henrietta Maria had grown up to be a very strict Catholic. She was accompanied to England by several priests, who often advised her very ill. One day she went with them to Tyburn Hill, and prayed to some of the Roman Catholics who had formerly been put to death there, as if they were saints and martyrs. This Charles considered an insult to him and to his whole nation. Again, she refused, under the advice of her priests, to be crowned by the Archbishop of Canterbury, as the king had been. This enraged Charles above all, and he ordered Buckingham to send every one of the French priests out of the kingdom. He said, "If you can, by fair means; but stick not long in disputing. Otherwise force them away, driving them like so many wild beasts." This sending away the priests was against the marriage agreement, and so the French king made war against England.

The French marriage, and war with France.

It seemed to Charles and his favorite, Buckingham, that the best way to carry on the war was to help the French Protestants, or Huguenots, against their king. The stronghold of the Huguenots was at La Rochelle, a fortified city on the sea-coast; and the Duke of Buckingham led a great expedition to the relief of that place when it was besieged by Cardinal Richelieu.

Attempt to relieve La Rochelle.

This enterprise was at first popular; and though it cost a great deal of money, this would have been joyfully given, had the English people felt confidence in Buckingham. For want of this confidence, the House of Commons refused to provide the necessary funds unless he was dismissed. Charles was angry, dissolved Parliament, tried in vain to raise money on his own responsibility, and then called Parliament together once more in March, 1628. But the House of Commons, instead of voting money, drew up a paper called the "Petition of Right." This paper, which received the consent of the Peers, asserted the following principles: First, that no English subject could be compelled to pay any tax whatever without the consent of Parliament; secondly, that no one could be imprisoned without cause shown; thirdly, that no one could be compelled to receive soldiers or sailors into his house; and fourthly, that no one could be tried by martial law in time of peace. All these things had been done by the king; and for him to surrender the right to do them was to give up a great deal of what he and his father before him had regarded as kingly power. But his need of money was desperate, and the House of Commons held the purse; so at last, most unwillingly, he consented to the petition. Even then he tried to

Petition of Right (1628).

soften the fall by giving his consent in an unusual way. But the Commons were not to be put off in this manner, and at once set about adding an additional document, called a Remonstrance, or Statement, of

KING CHARLES I.: FROM A PAINTING BY VAN DYCK.

Grievances. Then the king sent them a message informing them that it was their business to vote money, and not to draw up remonstrances. Then followed some bold debates, in which Sir John Eliot was beginning to say something against the Duke of Buckingham, when the Speaker interrupted him, and said, "There is a command laid upon me to interrupt any that should go about to lay an aspersion on the ministers of state." Presently the Speaker asked permission to leave the House; and when he was gone, the members found their tongues. Sir Edward Coke stood up, and named the Duke of Buckingham as the source of all the people's troubles. Then the Speaker returned, and adjourned the House till next day. But the words that had been spoken, and the spirit shown, had such an influence on the Peers that they sent a deputation, with Buckingham at its head, to beg the king to give a prompt and clear answer to the Petition of Right. That very afternoon he answered by coming to the House of Peers, and giving his approval in the customary form to the petition. The clerk said in old Norman-French, which is even now used in many official proceedings in England, "Soit droit fait comme est désiré" (Let it be enacted as prayed for); and henceforth the Petition of Right became the law of the land. It was so great a step in the direction of popular government that it has been called "the second Magna Charta." After all, when the House had voted the money desired, it went on with the "Remonstrance;" but the House had now lost its hold on the king, as he had all he wanted, and so he dissolved it.

Another expedition for the relief of Rochelle was now fitted out with all speed, and the Duke of Buckingham went down to Portsmouth to take command. But he was there murdered by an officer in the army who felt himself ill-treated by Buckingham.

Parliament came together again in 1629, amid disaster abroad and discontent at home. The House of

Commons, instead of voting money, began by adopting a complaint against Laud and two other clergymen who favored more elaborate religious cere- monies in the Church of England. Then came up anew the question of the Petition of Right, which had been disregarded. The Speaker tried to prevent action by the House, even breaking up the sitting by leaving his chair. A few days later, after having twice adjourned the House in this same way, he again refused to keep his place. This could be endured no longer; and two members, Denzil Holles and Benjamin Valentine, seized him, and held him in his place by main force, Holles saying, "You shall sit until we please to rise." Then Sir John Eliot made a bold speech, defending the House against any charge of disrespect to the king, and presenting a series of resolutions, on which he demanded a vote. Several members rose to leave the House; but a member locked the door, and put the key in his pocket. Then Eliot again called upon the Speaker to do his duty, and put the resolutions to vote, reminding him that every one who had thus far defied Parliament had been broken down by it. The Speaker said he dared not do it. At last Denzil Holles, standing by the Speaker's chair, and while the royal messengers were pounding on the door, read the resolutions himself, put them to vote, and saw them passed by an overwhelming majority. They asserted that every one who tried to introduce new ceremonies into the Church, or who advised the levy of taxes without the express grant from Parliament, or who paid taxes so levied, was a betrayer of the liberties of England, and an enemy to the kingdom. The door was then flung open, and the members

Sir John Eliot's Resolutions.

went out, meeting the soldiers whom the king had sent to force their way in. The work of this Parliament was done. It was now the king's turn, and for eleven long years no House of Commons was called together in England. Sir John Eliot was placed in confinement, and refusing to make his submission to the king, died there a martyr to the cause of English liberty. Among the members who spoke for the first time in this Parliament was Oliver Cromwell.

Charles was now resolved to govern without parliaments, if it were possible. The money question was the only difficult one. But he had a treasurer named Weston, who had great skill and ingenuity in getting money out of the people of England without driving them into rebellion. To begin with, Weston and his friends looked up and enforced certain old laws which people had long since forgotten. For instance, there was an old law which required that when a new king was crowned, all men who owned land to a certain amount must be raised to the rank of knighthood, whether they desired it or not. Now, as years went by, and the value of money decreased, it became impossible for such landowners to support the dignity of knighthood. They had not asked to be knighted, and the existence of the law itself had been wellnigh forgotten. Weston now compelled all who had broken this law to pay large fines. Another way he had of raising money was by the sale of monopolies, or the exclusive right to sell or make a certain article. There was now no Parliament to object to the creation of monopolies, so Weston sold the right to make and sell innumerable things, even soap, to those who would pay a large sum to the king,

Personal government of the king.

and a smaller sum to himself. In these and other ways Weston kept the king supplied with money for several years.

The king had another and worse adviser in William Laud, Archbishop of Canterbury. After Weston's death, he became the real head of the treasury, and the most powerful subject in England. He was honest and sincere, but narrow, harsh, and arrogant. To him "Church and King" were everything, while the people seemed a body to be trained, amused, and kept down. He especially wished to restore the Church and clergy to the high power in the state they had once held, and to bring back many of the ceremonies that had been given up since the Reformation. He wished to replace in the churches the stained glass windows that had been destroyed or removed. He wished also to encourage dancing, the theatre, and Sunday afternoon sports. He even persuaded Charles to reissue a certain "Declaration of Sports," which King James had withdrawn, for fear of offending the Puritans and their friends. The clergy were now ordered to read this declaration from their pulpits. Some refused, and were punished. One man read the offensive document and the Ten Commandments in succession, and then said to his congregation: "Ye have heard the commandments of God and man; obey which ye please." When it came to play-acting, there was more to be said for the Puritan view. The stage was degraded, and reflected the moral tone of the people, which was low. All this displeased the Puritans, whose moral tone was good, though their views might sometimes be narrow. One of them, William Prynne, wrote a book

Archbishop Laud and the Puritans.

against stage-plays. Laud declared this an insult to the queen, who sometimes had taken part in private theatricals. So the Star Chamber sentenced Prynne to be placed in the pillory, where everybody might insult him, to lose his ears, to pay a fine, and to be imprisoned during the king's pleasure. And this sentence was executed without arousing much remark.

During all this time the need of money became more and more pressing. All the extreme measures resorted to by Weston and his successors were not enough; so a new device was invented. This was called ship-money. The English navy had become very much reduced, and it was decided to revive it. In Queen Elizabeth's day she used to call upon the seaport towns or counties to furnish ships for the navy, as they were needed. This was now done; but the ships demanded were so large that only London could furnish them, the other seaport places being let off with paying a sum of money instead, to be collected from the individual taxpayers. A large sum was thus raised without much opposition, and there is no reason to doubt that it was honestly spent on the navy. The trouble was that it created a very strong temptation to go a little farther, and raise money in this way for all the expenses of the court.

Ship-money.

Accordingly, during the next year (1635) there came another call for ship-money. This time it was ingeniously argued that the inland counties were as much interested in the defence of the kingdom as the rest, and why should they not pay their share? This they did, with some farther grumbling. But when there came, in the next year, a third call for ship-money, addressed to all the coun-

Hampden's Case.

ties, and payable by individual taxpayers, the people began to open their eyes. It became plain that the king had hit upon a method for raising just what money he pleased, even while refusing to call together a Parliament. The excitement spread fast, and many prominent men refused to pay their share of the ship-money, believing that the Parliament alone had the right to tax them. Among them were Lord Say and Sele, Lord Brook (for whom Saybrook in Connecticut is named), and John Hampden, one of England's greatest men. Hampden's case was brought to trial. Seven of the "twelve judges" decided against him, giving their opinions in favor of the king. We shall see what became of the "ship-money judges," and their decision in Hampden's case, when the Long Parliament met. For the present the ship-money was collected.

The king's triumph seemed complete; but his best advisers cautioned him that the popular feeling was *Public opinion against the king.* with Hampden, and that he would do well to call a Parliament. Soon Prynne was again brought before the Star Chamber, this time for speaking his mind very freely about Laud and his bishops. Others were brought up at the same time, — Burton, a clergyman, and also a physician named Bastwick. This last man had gone even farther than Prynne, and had prayed: "From plague, pestilence, and famine, from bishops, priests, and deacons, good Lord deliver us." All three were condemned to stand in the pillory, Burton and Bastwick to lose their ears, and Prynne what was left of his; and the last-named to be branded on each cheek "S. S.," for Sower of Sedition. When the prisoners went through the streets to meet their punishment, they found the pavements strewn with flowers and green wreaths in their honor. A groan went up from the whole assembly when the cruel punishment was inflicted; and when the prisoners were afterwards carried to distant parts of England, the same deep sympathy met them everywhere.

Between Prynne's two punishments a great change had taken place in public opinion. The great middle class now stood behind Hampden and Prynne, though Charles and his favorite archbishop had not discovered it. The great Puritan emigration to America was going on all this time (1630-1640); and we cannot understand the bitter feeling that the emigrants carried with them, not merely against bishops, but against kings, without remembering how Laud and Charles were associated in their minds. Before long these two men took a new step in what the people called tyranny. They resolved to strengthen the Episcopal Church in Scotland. They found the Scots less loyal and patient than the English. In Scotland, at the Reformation, the bishops had generally left their flocks, and, under the lead of John Knox, the Church of Scotland, or Kirk, as it was called, had come to be governed, according to the methods of Calvin, by representative assemblies, "presbyteries," and the like. King James had established bishops in Scotland, but they had obtained little influence. The king and Laud now resolved to make the Scottish Kirk uniform with the Church in England. So the Scottish clergy were ordered to wear surplices, which they hated, and a new prayer-book was sent to them from England, with orders for every minister to buy two copies, and use

The Scottish Church.

the book every Sunday. On July 23, 1637, the Dean of St. Giles's Church in Edinburgh began to read from the new prayer-book. A riot followed, and it did not take long to put all Scotland in open rebellion. An old agreement, called "The National Covenant," was revived. It was signed by all the leading men except a few royalists in the North. Its signers agreed to stand by their own religious faith and forms. The Covenanters soon raised an army, seized Edinburgh Castle, and went to war with the king.

The war, however, did not last long. Neither party really wished to fight, and a treaty was made at Berwick. Unfortunately the Scots had no confidence in Charles. They kept their army together, and applied to the French king for aid. Charles wished to renew the war, but he had no money; and at last, after eleven years of refusal, he made up his mind to call Parliament together once more. In doing this he acted under the advice of Thomas Wentworth, Earl of Strafford. Men called this statesman "the apostate," because at one time he had seemed to be on the people's side. But his opposition to the court at the time of the Petition of Right had been merely because of his dislike to Buckingham, after whose death he fell into his natural place as the chief defender of royalty against the rising spirit of liberty. He wished to preserve the king's power as it had existed under the later Tudors. While Weston and Laud had been at work for the king in England, Strafford had been doing the same in Ireland, where, under his favorite watchword, "Thorough," he had oppressed the Irish most cruelly. He had advised the king against the treaty of Berwick,

The first Bishops' War (1639).

Strafford.

and he now urged him to call a Parliament. That body met in April, 1640. It utterly refused to vote money until the popular grievances were redressed. But the king refused thus to give up all the principles at stake; and after a twenty-three days' session Parliament was dissolved. It is hence known as the Short Parliament. *The Short Parliament (1640).*

In one way or another Charles and Strafford got together some soldiers and armed them. At their head Strafford set out to meet the Scots. But the English soldiers hated Laud more than they did those against whom they were marching. They called the war "The Bishops' War." They tore down the altar railings which Laud had caused to be erected in the parish churches. They deserted by hundreds, and sometimes killed their own officers. The Scots poured over the border, took possession of the coal-mines of the North of England, and were only prevented from coming farther southward by the king's promising to pay them £25,000 per month until peace should be made. The king could not possibly pay such a large sum, and he was compelled to call a Parliament. It met at Westminster Nov. 3, 1640, and sat, with intermissions, for nearly twenty years, until March 16, 1660. It is for this reason known in history as the Long Parliament. *The second Bishops' War (1640).*

The new Parliament was differently situated from any other that had ever come together. In the first place, the great mass of the English people was behind it, for men were weary of paying taxes to which their consent had not been given, while many were tired of Laud and his innovations. Then again, and what was most important, *The Long Parliament (1640–1660).*

Parliament had an armed force behind it, — not the English army, to be sure, but the Scottish army. The king could not pay the Scots; and as long as Parliament paid them only enough to secure their staying in the North of England, and not enough to induce them to return to Scotland, so long Parliament held a sword hanging over the king's head. If Parliament were dissolved, and the Scots came south, no one could tell what might happen. Or again, if Parliament refused to pay any money, and they came south, it was uncertain how many Puritans would join them; so the king was obliged to do and hear many things he did not like.

Recognizing in Strafford the one man capable of opposing them, the patriot leaders determined to overthrow him. On November 11, therefore, John Pym — "King Pym" his enemies called him — appeared before the House of Peers, and in the name of the Commons accused Strafford of high treason. Even while Pym was speaking, Strafford entered the House, intending to bring the same charge against Pym on account of certain dealings with the Scots. He was forbidden to speak, and was sent to the Tower to await trial. Laud, too, was arrested, though his trial was long delayed. When Strafford's trial began, it soon became evident that it would be hard to convict him on the charge of treason. So the trial before the Peers was abandoned. A bill declaring Strafford a public enemy, and providing for his execution, was brought into the Commons and passed. This was called a Bill of Attainder, and, like any other bill, required the consent of the Commons, Peers, and king, to become a law. The excitement during its passage

Execution of Strafford (1641).

was intense, and once when a board in the floor of Parliament creaked under the weight of a very heavy member, the other members drew their swords, as if the Gunpowder Plot were begun again. Charles was very slow to give his consent to the Bill of Attainder, and when he did so, he tried to put off the execution. As soon, however, as it became known that Strafford had tried to bribe his jailer with £20,000, — a sum that would be worth, in these times, several hundred thousand dollars, — the House of Commons demanded that his execution should be hurried, and refused to wait. So on May 12, 1641, the great earl was beheaded.

During the year 1641 Parliament made many other changes, aiming to overthrow the whole system of arbitrary government built up by Strafford and Laud. The courts which had been misused were abolished, — the Star Chamber, the High Commission, and the Council of the North. Prynne and his fellow-sufferers were released from prison. Ship-money was declared illegal, the judgment in Hampden's case was annulled, and the ship-money judges who did not get away were impeached. Then a law was passed arranging for more frequent parliaments in the future, even if the king did not summon them. When the king's consent was obtained to a bill providing that the present Parliament should not be dissolved except by its own consent, the two Houses went to work to pay off both armies and to disband them.

Constitutional reforms.

Charles now went to Scotland, found he had very little authority there, and then came back to England, where he was better received than before. This was due partly to the concessions he had made, but still more to the fact that the reformers themselves had now begun to disagree as to what to do with the Church of England. Some of them, like Falkland and Hyde (afterwards Earl of Clarendon), wished simply to have the Church service as it was before Laud had meddled with it. Others, like Pym, Hampden, and Cromwell, desired that it should be completely reformed; a few, like Lord Brook, stood for a middle course. Moreover, a fierce rebellion had broken out in Ireland. After Strafford's iron rule had been removed, the Irish peasants, who had been driven from their homes by the English, drove out the English in return; and these last were either killed or made their way to Dublin half-starved and naked. It was plain it would never do to give Charles an army to put down this rebellion, for he would surely use it against the patriots in England, who were now having a hard time to maintain themselves. To revive the resentment of the people against the king, the reformers carried through the Commons the "Grand Remonstrance," reciting all Charles's illegal acts since the beginning of his reign. Their majority in the Commons, where at first they had met with almost no opposition, was now only eleven, and they came near drawing swords among themselves. Two days later the king returned from Scotland, and found himself so well received that he believed his power to have revived, and refused to make any concessions whatever.

The patriots disagree about religion.

The Irish Rebellion (1641).

The Grand Remonstrance.

On Jan. 3, 1642, the king's attorney-general came into the House of Peers and impeached of high treason one peer, Lord Kimbolton, and five commoners,—

ATTEMPT TO ARREST THE FIVE MEMBERS.

Pym, Hampden, Haselrig, Holles, and Strode,— the complaint being that they had intrigued with the Scots during the late troubles. When the king demanded the persons of the five accused commoners, the House of Commons voted to take the matter into consideration. Not satisfied with this, Charles decided to go the next day to the House and seize the five members. When the moment came, his heart failed him, and had not the

The attempt to arrest the five members.

A COACH OF THE MIDDLE OF THE SEVENTEENTH CENTURY:
FROM AN ENGRAVING BY JOHN DUNSTALL.

queen called him a coward, he might not have gone. At last, however, he entered the House, and standing before the Speaker's chair, told the members that he had come to take the traitors. Not seeing them, he asked the Speaker if they were there. William Lenthall, the Speaker, kneeling before the king, answered bravely, "May it please your Majesty, I have neither eyes to see nor tongue to speak in this place, but as the House is pleased to direct me." "Well, well," said Charles, "'t is no matter. I think my eyes are as good as another's." Then, finding, as he expressed it, that the birds were flown, he departed amid cries of "Privilege! privilege!" This was to remind him that it was the legal privilege of members not to be arrested for what they said in Parliament. He soon found that the five members had taken refuge in the City of London, by order of the House, and he accordingly went and demanded them of the Common Council. The same cry of "Privileges of Parliament" met his ear, and this was all he could get from the City, which had lately received him so cordially. These attempts, too, made all the reforming party in Parliament feel that their own freedom was in danger; so that the peers, the city merchants, and the moderates, like Falkland, were once more united with the Puritans. The Commons left Westminster, and sat as a committee in the Guildhall of the City of London. They appointed a general to command the London train-bands, or militia, who were loyal to the people's cause; and even the Thames watermen pledged themselves to protect the Commons. After this they thought they could safely return to Westminster, and did so, Jan. 11, 1642.

Charles I. had not waited to see the triumph of "King Pym" and the Puritans, but had fled with the queen and their children; and when next he entered his palace of Whitehall, it was as a prisoner. Meanwhile, the Parliament made one more demand upon him, — to place the control of all the militia in the hands of officers chosen by

Civil War begins.

Parliament. Refusing this, Charles raised his royal standard at Nottingham, and called on all loyal subjects to aid him against his rebellious Parliament. It was thought a bad omen for his success when the great flag, blown by the furious wind, fell to the earth. But it was again set up, and the great Civil War began.

TENTS AND MILITARY EQUIPMENT IN THE REIGN OF CHARLES I.

CHAPTER XXV.

THE CIVIL WARS.

1642–1649.

PARLIAMENT found no sort of difficulty in raising an army. The City of London held to the Parliament's side, and so did the people of the Southern and Eastern counties, then the richest and most thickly settled parts of the kingdom. As for arms and ammunition, the Parliamentary party had seized whatever the king had collected. Yet their soldiers were inexperienced, and the king was therefore generally successful at first. The first battle at Edgehill was indecisive, and the royal army advanced as far as Brentford, a few miles from London; but there the city train-bands stopped him, and he turned back to Oxford, where he spent the winter, and where, indeed, he had his headquarters during most of the war.

The Civil War begins (1642).

The next year neither side gained much. The greatest loss to the Parliament was in the death of John Hampden, who was killed in a skirmish at Chalgrove Field, near Oxford. Not very much is known of Hampden's private history; but the respect he won both from friend and foe shows his character to have been high. At last the aid of the Scots was secured by the Parliamentary leaders. This was the last achievement of "King Pym," and he

Death of John Hampden (1643).

also died at the end of 1643. A year or two later came the execution on the scaffold of Archbishop Laud, who had done more than any one, except, perhaps, Charles himself, to bring civil war upon the country. Hampden and Pym upon the one side, and Strafford and Laud upon the other were thus removed. But a new personage, more powerful in his way than either of them, had meantime appeared upon the scene. Death of Pym.

Years after, it was related that when the members were leaving the House of Commons after the passage of the "Grand Remonstrance," a man of good stature, very plainly dressed, with a sharp, untunable voice, and a red and swollen face, was heard to declare that had the Remonstrance been rejected, he, for one, would have sold his all the next morning, and never have seen England more. He added: "I know there are many other honest men of the same resolution." That was Oliver Cromwell, known to his neighbors as "The Lord of the Fens," for the manful way in which he had asserted the rights of his friends against both king and noble. Cromwell was not a great Parliamentary leader, like Eliot or Pym, but he had a wonderful way of seeing the needs of the moment, and of seeking a remedy with immense energy and strength. Oliver Cromwell.

He saw that the Parliament's troops, who were, as he said, mostly "old, decayed serving-men and tapsters, and such kind of fellows," were no match for the adherents of the king. "You must get," he said to Hampden, "men of a spirit that is likely to go on as far as gentlemen will go, or else you will be beaten still." Soon after Cromwell's Ironsides.

this, Cromwell was made a colonel of cavalry, and he took good care that none but "godly men," by which he meant honest, well-behaved men, should enlist in his regiment. He never asked them what

OLIVER CROMWELL: FROM A PAINTING BY SIR PETER LELY.

Church they preferred, but only made sure that they were honest, sober Christians, who had an interest in the welfare of the country. These men he drilled until they obeyed orders as men have seldom obeyed before or since. "Truly they were never beaten at all," he said at a later day. They went into battle singing psalms, and were known as the "Ironsides."

At the head of these men he helped the Earl of Manchester to drive the king's forces from the eastern counties. He then marched into Lincolnshire, and beat the Royalists at Winceby Fight. Soon after, he joined Fairfax and the Scots, and the united armies laid siege to the city of York, whither the Marquis of Newcastle, the king's commander in the North, had retreated. Before long, Prince Rupert came to the marquis's aid. The two armies met on Marston Moor. Cromwell, with his Ironsides, dashed through Rupert's hitherto unconquered troopers as through a field of growing corn. "God made them as stubble to our swords," he wrote to the Speaker of the Commons. Recalling his men from the pursuit, he rode to the aid of the Scots, who were hard pressed on the other flank. In a few moments the day was won. Soon after, York surrendered, and Cromwell was a power in the land.

Marston Moor (1644).

Meantime, in the south of England, the king had been very successful, and had captured the greater part of the main army commanded by the Earl of Essex. And even Cromwell was not always so fortunate as at Marston Moor. At Newbury, when he and Manchester had driven the king off the field, Cromwell had begged to be allowed to make one charge with his Ironsides on the retreating army. "No," said Manchester, "if we should beat the king ninety-nine times, he would still be king, and his posterity after him, and we should be subjects still; but if he should beat us only once, we should be hanged, and our posterity undone." To Cromwell this lukewarmness seemed little better than treason to the cause of freedom. What though he should be hanged, if the cause was gained? As for the king, Cromwell declared that if he met him in battle, "he would fire his pistol at the king, as at another." He rose in his place in the House of Commons and declared: "It is now a time to speak, or forever hold the tongue;" adding, "I do conceive if the army be not put into another method, and the war more vigorously prosecuted, the people can bear the war no longer, and will enforce you to a dishonorable peace." It was determined to put the army into a new method, and to get rid of Manchester, Essex, and others who were afraid to beat the king too thoroughly. This was done by the passage of the "Self-denying Ordinance," depriving all members of Parliament of their military commands. The army was also reorganized, or "new modelled," as the phrase was, on the plan of the Ironsides. Fairfax was placed at its head. He soon enlisted twenty thousand "godly, honest men," never asking what were their religious preferences. Cromwell's presence was felt to be so necessary that the officers petitioned Parliament to relax the "Self-denying Ordinance" in his favor. The request was granted, and on June 13 he rejoined his Ironsides, who gave "a great shout for joy of his coming to them." In truth, he came in good time, for the very next day the "New Model" army met the king at Naseby. As at Marston Moor, so at Naseby, Cromwell's Ironsides won the day. The king's cause was utterly ruined; he never found himself at the head of an armed force again. But more fatal to him than the loss of his army was that of his writing-desk,

The Self-denying Ordinance (1645).

"The New Model."

Naseby (1645).

which proved to be filled with papers showing his terrible faithlessness to his promises and his people. The war was virtually ended at Naseby; but it was not until two years had passed away that Harlech Castle, the last royalist stronghold, surrendered. Then, at length, in the words of one of Charles's faithful followers, "the conquerors might go to play, unless they fell out among themselves." Unfortunately, this last was just what they did.

The Puritan leaders may have expected that the king, after so many defeats, would yield to their demands. But no such idea seems to have crossed the mind of Charles. On the contrary, seeking refuge with the Scottish soldiers, he tried by promises to induce them to take his side, and to make war on their English allies. If Charles had not deceived them already so many times, they might have done as he wished; for they were discontented at the growing strength of Cromwell and his Ironsides, who were no Presbyterians. As it was, however, they put no faith in the word of a king, and, on condition that their expenses should be paid, handed him over to the commissioners of Parliament. The king now saw that his best course was to come to terms with the Presbyterian leaders in Parliament; so he agreed to do what they wished with regard to religion. But this did not at all suit the army. *[Charles flees to the Scots.]*

It will be remembered that Fairfax and Cromwell, when they enlisted the soldiers of the "New Model," asked no man what his religion was. It turned out, however, that a majority of the soldiers were, like their great leader, Independents. That is, they thought that every Christian had a *[The Independents.]*

right to worship as he saw fit, always excepting the Roman Catholics. They had no wish to have a Presbyterian Church thrust upon the nation. So one evening, before any treaty between the king and the Parliament was concluded, an army officer appeared at Holmby House, where the king was imprisoned by Parliament. He called upon the king to accompany him. The next morning this demand was repeated, as the king had at first refused to comply. "Where is your commission?" asked the king. "There, behind me," answered Joyce (for that was the officer's name), pointing to his soldiers. "Your instructions are written in a very legible character," said the king, and he went with the officer.

The army seizes the king.

The army next turned the Presbyterian leaders out of Parliament; and when the London mob interposed in their favor, the army marched through the City, and put an end to all opposition. Meantime Cromwell and the other officers had been trying to get Charles to consent to certain propositions, securing to all Englishmen, except the Roman Catholics, freedom of worship and a more equal representation in Parliament and on the juries. But Charles, believing that London would prove too strong for the army, refused his consent. When he saw his hopes dashed to the ground, he escaped from his jailers, and rode rapidly to the south of England, where he was arrested by Colonel Hammond, and locked up in Carisbrooke Castle, on the Isle of Wight.

There now came another attempt to induce the king to agree to a treaty; but before anything was concluded it became known that Charles was negotiating with the Scots. Indeed, he had promised that if they would set him on his throne again, he would establish Presbyterianism for three years as the state church. This was perhaps the worst thing that he could have done; for however much they differed among themselves on religious affairs, the great body of the patriots was united against having these questions decided for them by the Scots. They forgot their differences, and bent all their energies against the Scots and the Royalists. But first the soldiers held a prayer-meeting, and resolved that if they were victorious, they would bring "Charles Stuart, that man of blood, to account for that blood he had shed, and mischief he had done to his utmost against the Lord's cause, and people of these poor nations." *The Scots invade England (1648).*

While Fairfax was beating the Royalists in the eastern and southern counties, Cromwell captured Pembroke, and then went in search of the Scots. He came upon them near Preston, in Lancashire, as they were marching southward, unsuspicious of danger. They were scattered along many miles of road, and the Ironsides dashed down first on one body, and then on another, until, after three days of hard fighting, the Scottish army was no more. *Battle of Preston (1648).*

Now, while the army was thus employed, Parliament had been negotiating with the king. But he, hoping even to the last, had delayed too long before yielding. The army returned to London, and told Parliament to stop their negotiations, and to bring the king to justice. Parliament refused. Then one morning the members found Colonel Pride's regiment surrounding the Parliament House. Colonel Pride himself was at the door, and as fast as the Presbyterian members appeared, they were arrested *"Pride's Purge" (1648).*

and taken to a neighboring tavern. This was repeated the next day, until at length the House of Commons was "purged," as they called it, of all members opposed to the army. The Commons then voted that there should be no more debate with the king, but that he should be brought to London and tried for his life before a court established for that purpose. The Lords — for there were twelve peers who still sat in the upper house — refused their consent. The Commons then voted that the consent of neither king nor Lords was essential to legislation. The army, to make sure of its control, had again taken possession of the king. He was brought to London. He refused to recognize the authority of the court, and, being found guilty of treason, was beheaded before his palace of Whitehall on the 30th of January, 1649. Whatever may be thought of the previous faults of Charles I., he met his death like a king. In the words of the poet, Andrew Marvell, —

The king executed.

> "He nothing common did or mean
> Upon that memorable scene,
>   But with his keener eye
>   The axe's edge did try;
> Nor called the gods, with vulgar spite,
> To vindicate his helpless right;
>   But bowed his comely head
>   Down, as upon a bed."

The army was now supreme in England and Scotland, so that Cromwell was at liberty to turn his attention to Ireland. The Puritans had never forgotten the massacres of 1641; and the Irish had added to the hatred with which they were regarded, by entering into an engagement to fight in the king's army. They plainly could expect no mercy from the Ironsides, and they got none.

Cromwell landed at Dublin in August, 1649. A month later he took Drogheda by storm. In the heat of the action he ordered his soldiers to spare no one found with arms in his hands; and so none were spared, not even the priests, whom the Puritans hated with the most bitter hatred. Cromwell felt that some explanation was required for such a barbarous act, even in an age when the horrors of the Thirty Years' War in Germany were still fresh in men's minds. So he wrote to the Speaker of the "Rump," as Parliament was called after Pride's Purge, that this slaughter was a righteous judgment upon the Irish for the massacres of 1641. He added that the remaining garrisons, seeing what their fate would be if they resisted to the end, would surrender before the storm, and that thus bloodshed would be avoided. There may have been some truth in this, for the future conquest was easy, and in a few months Cromwell was able to leave it to other hands, and to return to England, where his presence was much needed. In the end, the Irish were mainly driven out of three of the four provinces into which Ireland is divided, and were left to starve, as they had left the English settlers to starve years before. The only difference was that, as there were more Irish than English, there was now more suffering. Some years later, the Irish again tried to uphold the Stuart cause, and were again defeated; but the complete subjection of the island really dates from this "Cromwellian settlement."

Massacre of Drogheda (1649).

CHAPTER XXVI.

THE COMMONWEALTH.

1649-1653.

THE Scots had never given up the hope of living under a Presbyterian ruler; so they invited Charles I.'s eldest son, Prince Charles, or Charles II., as they called him, to be their king. He came; but before he was allowed to land, he was compelled to swear to the Covenant and to promise to be a good Presbyterian. The young Charles cared very little for religion, and was very desirous of being a king. So he promised everything they asked of him, and was allowed to land and to be declared king. For a time the English leaders hardly knew what to do. Here was a young Charles ready to march through England, and there was every reason to suppose that many who had fought against the old king would not fight against his son, as he had never yet done anything despotic, and indeed had never had the opportunity. And besides, the Presbyterian leaders in the first rebellion were so dissatisfied at being governed by the Independents in the army that it was probable they would welcome the prince with open arms as a deliverer. It was therefore decided by the English leaders that he must be captured or driven back to France, and that Scotland must be brought under English rule. Fairfax refused to lead the Eng-

Charles II. in Scotland.

lish army, as he could not see why the Scots should not manage their own affairs as they chose. But Cromwell was of a different way of thinking, and he led the army to Edinburgh.

But the Scots, who had learned the strength of the Ironsides at Preston, retired to the city, carrying with them all the food from the surrounding country. Cromwell dared not attack them in their strong position, and retreated to Dunbar, where he could get provisions from his fleet. The Scots followed, and posted themselves on top of a hill, where Cromwell could not get at them, and whence they could attack him whenever a good chance offered, and especially if he should try to march back to England. At last it seemed that their opportunity had come. So, late one afternoon, when they thought Cromwell could not see them, they descended the hill, and prepared to surprise him the next morning. But he had seen them; and, as they were setting out on their march to surprise him, the Ironsides burst upon them, and in one short hour swept the Scottish army to utter ruin. *Battle of Dunbar (1650)*

The next winter and spring Cromwell passed in Scotland, capturing some strong places, and trying to force into action another army which the young king had raised. The Scots were too wary for him, and suddenly turning southward, they marched into England. Charles probably hoped that his father's friends would rally to his aid. But they had been so roughly treated after Preston that they dared not show their faces. Cromwell overtook the Scots at Worcester, and after a severe fight routed them. *Battle of Worcester (1651).*
Almost alone, and after many hair-breadth escapes, the

young prince found his way to the sea-coast, and thence to France. It is related that during his flight he sought refuge amidst the leaves of a wide-spreading oak; and, until within the recollection of men now living, he who wished to show respect to the Stuart cause would hang an oak-branch over his doors. But the victory at Worcester put an end for a time to the hopes of the exiled prince. It was indeed, as Cromwell said, "a crowning mercy;" for it was the last battle of the civil wars. So long as the best-disciplined army of the day remained of one mind, and under the guidance of the greatest commander of his time, no one dared, after this, to oppose it in battle.

Upon the death of Charles I., Parliament had declared that there should be no more kings in England. In the future the country should be governed by a Parliament of one house. They called this new form of government "The Commonwealth." In reality, however, it was no republic, but a government by an oligarchy, or small number of persons. For what with "Pride's Purge," and the abolition of the House of Lords, the Long Parliament had dwindled down to an assembly of only about fifty members, the Rump Parliament, as it was called. Now, among these there were many dishonest men, who voted to exempt from confiscation the property of any Royalists who paid them a sufficiently large bribe. This, of course, made all honest men very angry.

The Rump Parliament.

After the great victory at Worcester, Cromwell put himself at the head of this opposition. He and the army demanded that there should be a new election. The "Rump" seemed to agree to this. But one day

JOHN MILTON, THE PURITAN POET.

Cromwell found that, in spite of promises which the leaders had made to him, they were about passing a bill to make themselves members of the new Parliament, whether they should be re-elected or not. Cromwell thereupon went into the House, and standing in his place, accused them of dishonesty. He declared that they had forfeited the respect of the country, and had no right to sit longer. Then, calling in his soldiers, he turned them out, and locked the door. No one was sorry for them, and, as Cromwell said, "We did not hear a dog bark at their going." The army officers then formed a council of state, and upon their advice Cromwell, as head of the army, summoned about one hundred and fifty of the leading Puritans to London to help him govern the country.

<small>The "Rump" expelled (1653).</small>

Years after, when it had become the fashion to laugh at the Puritans, people called this assembly "Barebone's Parliament," after Praise-God Barebone, a wealthy leather-dresser who had a seat in it. But all its members were not mechanics, nor did they all bear such grotesque names. Yet they had little practical ability, and by trying, in a few short weeks, to reform the abuses of a hundred years, they accomplished nothing, and were glad to resign their power into the hands of Cromwell.

<small>Barebone's Parliament.</small>

The army officers next drew up an "Instrument of Government," or constitution, as we should now call it. Some time before, Cromwell had declared that "a settlement with somewhat of monarchical power would be very effectual." And this constitution made the chief ruler a monarch in reality, though only called Lord Protector. He had all executive power, although he was obliged to consult his council of state upon important matters. The power to raise money and to make laws was given to a

<small>The Instrument of Government (1653).</small>

Parliament of one house, which was to meet once every year. But the Lord Protector and the Council, when the Parliament was not sitting, could make temporary laws, to which the consent of Parliament must be obtained at its next session.

It was impossible that, during these civil wars, literature and art should flourish, as had been the case during the great reign of Elizabeth; but John Milton, the Puritan poet, has always ranked second among the great poets of England.

WAGON OF THE SECOND HALF OF THE SEVENTEENTH CENTURY: FROM LOGGAN'S *Oxonia Illustrata*.

CHAPTER XXVII.

THE PROTECTORATE.

1653-1659.

Oliver, Lord Protector.
OF course, there was but one man who could have secured the support of the army, and that man was Oliver Cromwell. So he was invested with the office of Lord Protector with as much pomp and ceremony as ever had been witnessed at the coronation of a king. In fact, since the days of the "Grand Remonstrance," Oliver had procured a new tailor; and one writer, who describes him as being at first harsh and rough, says that he now possessed "a great and majestic deportment, and a comely presence."

Oliver's first Parliament came together in September, 1654, and immediately denied the legality of the new constitution. The Protector, after a little while, went to them and told them that if the "Instrument of Government" was illegal, they had no business there. He then excluded all who did not agree to recognize his government, and, as soon as the constitution allowed, dissolved the Parliament itself.

Scarcely had these over-zealous republicans left the House when two Royalists, Wagstaff and Penruddock, rode into Salisbury at the head of about two hundred men. They turned out the judges, who were then holding a court in that town, but they gained nothing, for a troop of Ironsides, which chanced to be in the neighborhood, soon killed or captured most of them. This little rising convinced Cromwell that the Royalists needed to be watched with greater care; so he divided England into military districts, to each of which he assigned a major-general and a sufficient number of soldiers. The Royalists were made to pay the cost of this supervision; but the major-generals acted so harshly, "like so many Eastern Bashaws," that all good people were offended. In addition, Cromwell held it necessary to forbid the celebration of divine service according to the Episcopalian rites, as he thought that such meetings were the rallying points of those hostile to his rule. But this order was never strictly carried out, and meetings in private houses were seldom suppressed. The opening chapters of Scott's novel, "Peveril of the Peak," give a graphic description of the condition of affairs in England at this time.

The major-generals (1655).

When Cromwell became Protector he found England at war with Holland. It might seem at first sight that as both countries were inhabited by Protestants, and had similar governments, they would have been good friends. But this was not so, for they were commercial rivals. It chanced, too, that at this time the English were trying to get the carrying trade away from the Dutch, and, under the lead of Sir Harry Vane, once governor of Massachusetts, Parliament had passed a Navigation Act, compelling English merchants to import goods in English vessels, or else in those of the country where the goods were produced. This was aimed directly at the Hollanders, and the two nations were soon at war. The Dutch

War with Holland.

fleet was very strong, and soon drove the English ships into harbor. Then the Dutch admiral, Van Tromp, sailed up and down the English Channel with a broom lashed to his masthead, to show that he was able to sweep the English from the seas. But this did not last long; for, after a series of desperate sea-fights, Admiral Blake compelled the Hollanders to cease their opposition to the Navigation Act, and to salute the English flag in the "narrow seas" surrounding the British Isles.

Van Tromp and Blake.

Cromwell and Blake then turned their attention to the Spaniards, who had been harboring Prince Rupert and his privateers. Blake soon stopped that proceeding; and Admiral Penn, father of Penn, founder of Pennsylvania, failing to capture San Domingo, seized the island of Jamaica; while still another fleet took possession of some Spanish treasure-ships which had so much silver on board that it took thirty-eight wagons to convey it through the streets of London.

It required a great deal of money to fit out these fleets and to pay the sailors. Cromwell could have wrung this from the Royalists by the aid of his major-generals, but he preferred to get it in a more constitutional way from a Parliament. No one was allowed to sit in this Parliament who was hostile to him, and therefore he had little difficulty in getting the money he wanted. In return, he recalled the major-generals. The Parliament then adopted a "Petition and Advice" to the Lord Protector, which was really nothing but an amendment to the constitution. In some ways this restricted the Protector's powers; in others enlarged them. It provided also for a new body to take the place of the old House

The Petition and Advice (1657).

of Lords, gave Cromwell the right to name his successor, and asked him to take the title of king. This last he refused, as the soldiers did not wish him to accept it. The new House of Lords did not turn out well. In the first place, not many of the old peers were willing to sit in it, and some of those created by Cromwell hardly deserved the distinction. Then again the new House of Commons, which was elected to work with it, called it in contempt "The Other House," and refused to have anything to do with it. In an angry speech, exclaiming, "The Lord judge between you and me," Cromwell dissolved the Parliament. For the remainder of his life he ruled England by the strength of the army and by the silent consent of a majority of the people.

If Cromwell was strong enough at home to rule without a Parliament, that "greatness was but a shadow of his glory abroad." He became the head of Protestant Europe, and his alliance was sought by the greatest monarchs of the time. He decided to support France in her war with Spain. The Ironsides, under the generalship of the great French commander, Turenne, proved irresistible. Dashing over fortifications that had before been thought impregnable, they scattered the best infantry of Spain, just as they had routed Prince Rupert and his Cavaliers years before. Dunkirk was turned over to Cromwell as the price of his assistance.

This was Oliver's last triumph on earth. It was in the same summer (of 1658) that George Fox, the Quaker, interceded with him on behalf of his fellow Quakers. "Before I came to him," wrote Fox, "as he rode at the head of his Life Guards, I saw and felt a waft of death go against him; and when I came to him he looked like a dead man." In truth, anxiety and private sorrow had worn him out; and on the 3d of September, as the anniversary of Dunbar and Worcester was drawing to a close, he died.

<small>Death of Cromwell (1658).</small>

We might almost wish that Cromwell had died at Worcester fight. Then he would have come down to us as the leader of the victorious army in the cause of freedom. As Protector, he was the slave of a party, the army; and he ruled, not as he desired, but as the army wished. The minds of Strafford, Cromwell, and Laud were cast in the same mould. The first and last tried to force upon England forms of government and religion which it had outgrown. Cromwell, many years in advance of his time, tried to force upon his countrymen the government and religion of the future. Both attempts were failures, for successful revolutions are not made in that way.

At first it seemed as if the revolution was to last longer than Cromwell, and his eldest son, Richard, succeeded him as quietly as ever a king's son had succeeded his father. But this quiet did not last long. A new Parliament, attempting to assert its power over the army, was turned out of the Parliament House. Richard then tried to rule the army, and it put an end to the protectorate. The officers meantime had brought back the "Rump." But the members of that body had learned nothing by experience. They, too, tried to govern the army, and they, ere long, were turned out by it.

The officers then governed the country without any attempt at concealing their usurpation. Men of all parties began to sigh for a settled form of government.

Even then the army might have maintained itself, if it had remained united. Fortunately for English liberty, however, the troops in Scotland, under General Monk, could not see what right their fellow-soldiers in England had to rule over them. So they marched to London, where they found the "Rump" once more in place.

Now, however, there came another complication. The Londoners refused to pay taxes levied by the "Rump," on the ground that, as their members had been excluded at the time of "Pride's Purge," they were not represented in the Parliament, and therefore were not bound to pay any taxes levied on its authority. The army easily put down this little rebellion. But Monk saw clearly enough that the mass of the nation was impatient of the rule of the army; so he declared for a free Parliament. It is possible that he did this because he thought that the return of the Stuart family would aid his own advancement. At all events, many people were delighted at the prospect of getting rid of the army and the "Rump," and fell to roasting rumps of beef on the street corners in London with such vigor that Pepys, who wrote a diary of the events of this period, relates that he counted thirty-six fires at one time. The Presbyterians once again took their places in the House of Commons, and after making provision for a new election, the Long Parliament dissolved itself on March 16, 1660.

At this, the most favorable time he could have chosen, Charles II. issued a Declaration from the little town of Breda, in Holland, where he was then living. In this declaration he offered a general

Monk's policy.

pardon to all who should not be excepted by Parliament from forgiveness, assured holders of the confiscated Royalist estates that they should not be disturbed in their possessions, and promised to persecute no one on account of his religion. The new Parliament came together in April, and at once invited the young Charles to return to England, and sent a fleet to convey him to his native land. He embarked on the flag-ship, whose name he changed from "Naseby" to "Charles," and after a pleasant voyage entered London on the anniversary of his birth, May 29, 1660.

<small>The Restoration (1660).</small>

> "Oh, the twenty-ninth of May,
> It was a glorious day,
> When the king did enjoy his own again!"

Scott's novel of "Woodstock" gives an animated description of this scene.

The army that had so fiercely beaten Charles at Dunbar and Worcester, now disunited and powerless, received him, and then dispersed. But even then the Ironsides showed how unlike ordinary soldiers they were; for instead of becoming paupers and a burden on the community, they resumed their old occupations; and if one saw a particularly industrious farmer or mechanic, it might very well happen that he would turn out to be one of Cromwell's old soldiers.

Many persons suppose that the Puritans made severer laws than any persons who had ruled England before them, and that the time of the Commonwealth and Protectorate was a period of great intolerance in religious matters. But this is quite untrue. On the contrary, the Puritan state was in most respects more tolerant and humane than any previous English

<small>Puritan ideas.</small>

government had been, and many great legal reforms date from that time. After 1558 no person was ever burned in England for his religious opinions, — a thing which had before been common, — and no one was put to death in any way for such opinions, except when returning to England after being previously banished. Of course this fell very far short of complete toleration, but it was a great advance on what had been the earlier custom. Cromwell, moreover, allowed Jews to live in England for the first time since the reign of Edward I. Torture was abolished as a means of obtaining confession, though it lasted nearly a century longer in most European countries, and was legal in one German state down to 1831. The principles of the Habeas Corpus Act were established under the Commonwealth, although the Act itself did not follow until later, as will hereafter be shown. It also became the practice to examine all witnesses in open court, instead of condemning men, as had sometimes before been done, upon evidence taken in secret. All these were great steps in human progress. And though the Puritans forbade some innocent amusements, yet that was but a trifle compared with what they did to reform the terrible cruelty of the early English courts.

CHAPTER XXVIII.

THE RESTORED STUARTS.

1660-1688.

The Restoration: Charles II. (1660-1685).

CHARLES II., the "restored" king, and his principal adviser, Edward Hyde, Earl of Clarendon, now acted as though nothing had happened since 1641. They even called the first law that was passed after the "Restoration," the Act of the 12th year of Charles's reign, just as if he had been reigning since 1649. Now it was easy enough to print such a figure in a book, and to make believe that all the laws of the Protectorate and the Long Parliament were no laws at all. But the Cavaliers soon found that it would be as easy to make everybody around them really twenty years younger as to undo all the work of those twenty years; so they found it necessary to confirm many of the laws of that period, among the rest the Navigation Act. They found, too, that it was impossible to revive many old customs which had gone out of use while there was no king in England. Thus, in old times, the king had the right to make the heiresses of the great landowners marry any one who pleased him, whether the bride liked the man or not. This and other similar rights had bound the landowners to the king, and had made it advisable for them to be attentive to him, and to vote as he wished in Parliament. These rights were now swept away in a legal manner, and it was soon found that the ties which had hitherto bound the coun-

CHARLES II.: FROM THE PORTRAIT BY SIR PETER LELY IN CHRIST'S HOSPITAL, LONDON.

try gentry to the king were greatly loosened. Before long, indeed, a country party began to be formed to oppose the king and his courtiers by their votes in the Commons.

During the civil wars the lands of the Church, of the king, and of the Royalists had been mostly confiscated. The king and the Church now had their estates restored to them, but the poorer Royalists were left to recover theirs as best they might through the courts of law. If a sale of any kind could be proved, they could not get their estates again. Even when they did recover their homes they could not collect any rent for the use of their farms and houses during all these years. Moreover, all who had taken part in the Great Rebellion, except the king's judges and a few others, were pardoned. These things were done by what is called "An Act of Oblivion and Indemnity to those who had taken part in the late disorders." But the disappointed Cavaliers declared that it was an Act of indemnity, or reward, for the Puritans, and of oblivion, or forgetfulness, for the services of the king's friends.

<small>Act of Indemnity and Oblivion (1660).</small>

Many of those who had borne a prominent part in the execution of Charles I. were imprisoned for life, thirteen were hanged, while others escaped, some to Switzerland, some to New England. These last could never be found, though the king sent the strictest orders for their arrest, and although we now know a good deal about their movements in this country. The most unjust execution was that of Sir Harry Vane. He had not got on well with Cromwell, and had taken little part in the events of the past few years; but he was such an outspoken republican that the king was afraid of him, and he was beheaded. Yet when one considers how many

<small>The Regicides.</small>

were guilty of treason and murder in the eyes of Charles and the Royalists, fourteen executions seem a very small number, compared with the practice of earlier kings. Indeed, some years later, when the governor of Virginia crushed a little rebellion in that colony, Charles, in alluding to it, declared that "the old fool has taken away more lives in that naked country than I for the murder of my father."

In the day of their triumph the Presbyterians had often treated the Episcopalians with harshness; and if they expected that the Episcopalians, whom they had restored to power, would treat them as friends, they soon found that all such expectations were vain. It was in the spring of 1661 that the new Parliament came together. The House of Commons, elected in the midst of the reaction against the Puritans, was so completely in the hands of the Royalists that it went by the name of the Cavalier Parliament. Later on its members became so corrupt that they took bribes from all sides, and it then was called the Pensioned Parliament.

The Cavalier Parliament (1661–1679).

The first law against the Presbyterians and Independents was called the Corporation Act, because by it all but Episcopalians were turned out of the offices in the cities. The next year came the Act of Uniformity, requiring all ministers and teachers who did not accept everything in the Episcopal service-book to leave their places. Two years later all religious meetings, other than those of the Episcopalians, were declared illegal by the Conventicle Act. By these laws all the Puritans had been driven from the schools and churches. It so happened that the very next year (1665) a dreadful disease, called the Plague,

Corporation Act (1661).

raged with fearful violence in London. Every one who was able to leave the city ran away as fast as he could. Among the first to seek safety in flight were the ministers of the Episcopal Church. The Nonconformists thought it a pity that the poor in London should die without the consolation which a minister alone can give, and they took the pulpits left vacant by their persecutors. Their reward for this heroism was the Five-Mile Act, which forbade any minister who had not subscribed to the Act of Uniformity from coming within five miles of any place in which he had once been a minister. To make sure that these various laws were carried out, a single justice of the peace, without any jury, was given authority to try and convict these people, and to sentence them to transportation for seven years to any place outside of England, except to New England, for there they would find friends and sympathizers.

<small>The Plague (1665).</small>

It is difficult to describe the sufferings of these pious men. But Richard Baxter, one of their number, has left the following: "Many hundred of them, with their wives and children, had neither houses nor bread. Some lived on little more than brown bread and water, many had but eight or ten pounds to maintain a family, so that a piece of flesh has not come to one of their tables in six weeks' time. Many, being afraid to lay down their ministry after they had been ordained to it, preached to such as would hear them in fields and private houses till they were seized and cast into jails, where many of them perished." The result of this cruelty no one foresaw at the time; for in the end, instead of converting the Puritans to the Established Church, it gave them a hatred for that Church, and they ceased to regard themselves as a part of it. They formed little churches of their own, and from Nonconformists became Dissenters, or people outside of the regular Church. The Episcopalians, finding that the Dissenters no longer wished to change the forms of the Episcopalian service, relaxed law after law, until now religion is as free in England as in our own land, except that the Episcopal Church is established by law as the State religion, and the various forms of dissent are only tolerated.

The Dissenters.

The Great Plague was in 1665. In September of the next year many of those who had escaped the plague saw their homes and places of business burned down by the Great Fire of London, without being able to save anything. The fire began in the shop of a French baker, near the end of London Bridge. In those days the houses were built of wood, and thatched with straw. A furious east wind fanned the flames, and before the fire could be stopped by destroying houses in its path, London, from the Tower to the Temple, and from the river in some places a mile inland, was in ashes.

The Great Fire (1666).

Baxter has left us a vivid picture of this event: —

"It was a sight that might have given any man a lively sense of the vanity of this world, and all the wealth and glory of it, and of the future conflagration of all the world. To see the flames mount up to heaven and proceed without restraint; to see the streets filled with the people astonished, that had scarce sense left them to lament their own calamity; to see the fields filled with heaps of goods, and sumptuous buildings, curious rooms, costly furniture, and household stuff, yea, warehouses and furnished shops and libraries, all in a flame, and none durst come near to receive anything; to see the king and nobles ride about the streets, beholding all these desolations, and none could afford the least relief."

So wide was the sympathy excited by this great calamity that collections were taken up in the New England churches for the relief of the sufferers; and those of Charlestown, Mass., alone sent £105 sterling.

Meantime the English and Dutch had again come to blows about their commercial interests. This time the Dutch were successful. They entered the Thames, and sailing into the Medway, burned Sheerness and the shipping at Chatham. They then blockaded the mouth of the Thames for some weeks, although at the peace which followed, they confirmed England in her possession of the New Netherlands, which were now called the Province of New York, in honor of James, Duke of York, the king's brother. Now the English people did not at all like such defeats. They soon discovered that much of the money which Parliament had voted for the carrying on of the war had gone into the pockets of the worthless men and women by whom Charles was surrounded. They were too loyal to accuse the king of stealing, but they fell heavily on Clarendon, who had managed to offend all parties. Knowing that many of his acts would not bear investigation, Clarendon fled to the Continent, and passed the remainder of his life in writing his attractive, though untrustworthy, history of the Great Rebellion. The Commons then declared that no more money should be voted unless an officer in whom they had confidence should have the spending of it. This was a very serious limitation of the king's authority, and Charles resisted as long as he dared. But the Commons were in earnest, and as he above

War with the Dutch (1666-1667).

all did not wish, as he expressed it, to "set out on his travels again," he yielded to their demands, and a great step towards parliamentary government was taken.

There were many, too, who remembered the victories of the great Puritan Admiral Blake. They contrasted the gayety and license of the present time with the morality of the past, and "did not stick to say that things were better ordered in Cromwell's time, for then seamen had all their pay, and were not permitted to swear, but were clapped into the bilboes, and if the officers did they were turned out, and then God gave a blessing to them." In those old days Cromwell had been the arbiter of all Europe. Charles II. was now the paid servant of the King of France.

Louis XIV., who was then on the French throne, wished to make France the foremost country in Europe. As a step in this attempt he determined to seize the little strip of land on the north of France which we now call Belgium, but which was then known as the Spanish Netherlands. Spain was too weak to offer much opposition, but Holland was strong, and did not at all relish the thought of having France for such a near neighbor. Now Louis saw that, although as rivals in business, the English and Hollanders might quarrel, yet as fellow-Protestants it was hardly probable that England would stand still and see Holland defeated by France. He therefore offered Charles a considerable sum of money if he would help him against the Dutch, and declare himself a Catholic. Charles agreed, by a secret treaty, signed at Dover in 1670, to do both these things, for he wanted money, and was at heart a Catholic. Louis

The Secret Treaty of Dover (1670).

then invaded Holland. But the sturdy Hollanders were not easily beaten. The young Prince of Orange was given the command. He cut the dikes, and let the waters of the ocean flow over the country, except where the walls of the towns kept them out. And the French, to avoid being drowned, ran away as fast as they could. The English people now forced Charles to make peace with the Dutch. Some years after this, the Prince of Orange, William by name, came over to England, and married the eldest daughter of the Duke of York. We shall meet with him again, for he afterwards became King of England.

Nor did Charles succeed much better in an attempt to make things easier for the English Catholics. In 1672 he issued what was called a Declaration of Indulgence, because by it the king gave notice to the Catholic and Protestant Dissenters that the laws aimed against them would not be carried out. These last might have accepted this indulgence for themselves; but when it was offered to the Catholics also, the Dissenters refused to take any advantage of it. Moreover, they joined with the Episcopalians in Parliament, and compelled the king to recall it. They even went further, and passed the Test Act, requiring all the great officers of state to take part in the service of the English Church or resign. This was especially aimed at the Duke of York, who was supposed to be a Catholic, and he acknowledged the truth of the suspicion by resigning.

Declaration of Indulgences (1672).

The Test Act (1673).

It may be that even then the existence of the Secret Treaty of Dover was known, by which Charles had sold himself to the French king. But the full extent of his infamy was not known until the spring of 1678, when Ralph Montague, then English minister to France, suddenly appeared in his place in the Commons, and read a letter ordering him to tell Louis that, if he would pay Charles £24,000 a year for three years, England would remain neutral in the war which France was then waging against Holland. A postscript to this letter was in the king's own handwriting, and the date of the letter was only five days after the Commons had actually voted money to enable Charles to aid the Dutch. Naturally the whole nation was furious. The Commons could not touch the king, but they impeached Danby, the Secretary of State.

It was while the people were thus wrought up that Titus Oates appeared before Sir Edmondsbury Godfrey, and on his oath declared that the Roman Catholics were plotting to murder the king, in order to put the Catholic James, Duke of York, on the throne. In ordinary times no one would have placed any confidence in what Oates said, for he was a miserable wretch, and James was so unpopular that Charles said to him, "No one will murder me to set you on the throne." But these were no ordinary times, and a few days later the excitement grew into a perfect frenzy when Sir Edmondsbury Godfrey was found on a lonely hillside with a sword sticking in his lifeless body. To this day no one really knows whether he killed himself or was murdered. At the time, however, most Englishmen believed that the Catholics had killed him, and were very ready to believe anything that Titus Oates might say. There may, indeed, have been some truth in the story. At any rate, many Catholics were executed, and because

"Popish Plot" (1678).

Oates had declared that the London fire had been the work of Catholics, a lying inscription to that effect was placed on the monument which marks the spot where it was first discovered. This inscription was taken down at James's accession. It was replaced after the Revolution of 1688, and was not finally removed until 1831. Even more unjust was a law excluding Catholics from Parliament; and this was not repealed till 1829.

The Cavalier Parliament, which had been so loyal at its first assembling, had now become very hostile to the king. He dissolved it, and a new Parliament met in March, 1679. This lasted for less than three months; but in that short time it passed one of the most important laws in the whole history of the English race. This was the Habeas Corpus Act. Of course, ever since the days of Magna Charta, every free Englishman had possessed in theory the right to a speedy trial. But in practice so many obstacles could be interposed that the right was often denied. By this Act any judge was obliged to grant at any time a writ, or paper, addressed to the jailer, ordering him to produce his prisoner in court at such a time, and to show cause why the prisoner should not be released. The judge's order, or writ, began with the Latin words *Habeas corpus*, meaning, "You must have the body of such a person before me at such a time," etc. It is therefore called a writ of *habeas corpus*. The judge and jailer were subject to heavy fine if they disobeyed the Act; and therefore since that time no one has been imprisoned in England for any length of time without a good reason. In times of great public excitement, Parliament has sometimes

Habeas Corpus Act (1679).

suspended the operation of the Act, thereby giving the Government power to keep suspected persons in jail, even when a clear case could not be made out against them.

This Act was really passed because people were afraid of the Roman Catholic James; and they even went further, and tried to exclude him from the succession to the throne. Unfortunately, instead of naming the next heir, the Princess Mary of Orange, they named a worthless illegitimate son of Charles, the Duke of Monmouth. The scheme fell through; but the struggle gave rise to two party names that have ever since been famous. It seems that the Presbyterians in the west of Scotland were called "Whigs." The name spread to England, and was applied by the courtiers in derision to their opponents. These in turn called the king's men "Tories,"— a name under which some wild Irish Catholics had plundered their Protestant neighbors. And as Whigs and Tories the two parties have been known until recent times; and the same names were formerly used for political parties in America. *Exclusion Bills (1680-81).*

The bill to exclude James failed, and then there was a reaction in favor of the king. Indeed, for a while it seemed as though the times of Charles I. and his policy of "Thorough" had returned. Some of the Whigs, driven to desperation, planned to kill the king at a lonely spot near the Rye House. The plot was discovered, and Lord Russell and Algernon Sydney — to whom we owe the motto on the shield of one American State — were unjustly executed, while the Earl of Essex killed himself in prison. The defeat of this plot greatly *Rye House Plot (1683).*

strengthened the hands of the king, and he was fast becoming as absolute as his father, when he died. On his death-bed he professed himself a Roman Catholic. As he had no lawful descendants, his brother James, Duke of York, became king.

The first thing James the Second did was to revenge himself on Titus Oates and his fellow informers for the lies they had told about the Catholics. They were whipped so severely that one of them died. But Oates had strength to survive and be forgotten.

James II. (1685-1688).

The king then undertook to suppress the rebellion which had broken out in the North and West. In the North the revolt was easily subdued, and Argyle, the leader, executed. But the rising in the southwest of England, where Monmouth had put himself at the head of a considerable army, was not so easily quelled. Indeed, it seemed for a short time as if the young king — for such Monmouth declared himself to be — would succeed. His soldiers, however, were poorly armed and led. They were beaten in the battle of Sedgemoor, which should be remembered as the last battle fought on English soil. Monmouth himself was found partially concealed in a ditch, and was taken to London and executed, although he begged on his knees that his father's brother would grant his life. The king then ordered the persecution and death of all who had in any way helped the unfortunate duke. It is impossible to say how many were killed, but in one county two hundred and thirty-three persons were hanged. Probably at least four hundred lost their lives, and as many more were sold into slavery. All this was done by a judge named

Battle of Sedgemoor (1685).

Jeffreys, at a session of court which has ever since been called "The Bloody Assize." The name of Jeffreys has always been infamous in consequence of these trials; but it is now admitted that he was not more harsh and brutal than was the custom of English judges at his day. There was then a great deal of cruelty and brutality in the habits of the English race, and the courts shared this bad character.

YEOMEN OF THE GUARD: FROM SANDFORD'S *Coronation Procession of James II.*

CHAPTER XXIX.

THE "GLORIOUS REVOLUTION" OF 1688-1689.

AS soon as Monmouth was fairly out of the way, James threw off the mask, and devoted all his energies to making England a Roman Catholic country. Though the Test Act declared that no one but an Episcopalian could hold office, James appointed Sir Edward Hales, a Roman Catholic, colonel of a regiment. The judges, who had been appointed for this very purpose, declaring that the king could waive the penalties of a statute in a particular case, Sir Edward Hales retained his place until he became governor of the important fortress and prison, London Tower. Roman Catholics were by degrees given places in the Privy Council, the universities, and even in the English Church itself.

The case of Sir Edward Hales.

In 1598 Henry IV. of France had issued the Edict of Nantes, giving the French Protestants equal political rights with the French Catholics, and securing to them a certain measure of religious freedom. Louis XIV. revoked this edict in 1685. It is said that fifty thousand Huguenot families fled from France. Many of them took refuge in England, and set up the silk manufacture in the Spitalfields, now a part of London. They were very poor, and a collection was authorized in their behalf in the churches. But King James was so

Revocation of the Edict of Nantes.

afraid that the ministers would tell the truth about the way these poor people had been treated that he ordered the clergy not to preach against the Roman Catholics. The Bishop of London, refusing to punish one of his subordinates who had disobeyed this order, was himself summoned before a new and illegal High Commission Court, and suspended from office.

Now James determined to go one step farther, and grant general liberty of conscience to all Englishmen, whether Protestants or Roman Catholics. This was entirely different from dispensing with a single statute in a particular case. It is probable that James hoped to gain the Dissenters to his side by this Act. A few, indeed, took advantage of it. But it shows the bitterness of religious hostility at that time that the great mass preferred to suffer all the rigors of the law rather than to see the Roman Catholics well treated. The clergy had been ordered to read the declaration to their congregations, as that was the easiest way of making it generally known. The Archbishop of Canterbury and six bishops petitioned the king not to insist on their reading it. He did insist, however, and the declaration was read by a few ministers who were too timid to refuse. As for the archbishop and his companions, the Seven Bishops, as they were called, James had them arrested, on the ground that their petition was a seditious libel. They were taken to the Tower, where the Catholic Sir Edward Hales was sure to keep them safe. But the people were on their side. Even the soldiers on guard at the gateway of the Tower knelt before them, asking their blessing. Later they drank to their good health and acquittal. The excite-

Declaration of Indulgences (1688).

The Seven Bishops.

ment spread to the remotest corners of England; and the Cornish miners declared their intention of marching to London and rescuing their beloved bishop, Trelawney, one of the seven. They sang a song beginning, —

> "And shall Trelawney die?
> And shall Trelawney die?
> Then thirty thousand Cornish men
> Will know the reason why."

This sympathy was not confined to the Episcopalians. The Nonconformists visited the Tower, as did also an enormous number of persons of all grades and ranks, from the peers down to the humblest. It was in the midst of this excitement that the king's Catholic wife gave birth to a son who is known in history as the Old Pretender.

No one but Catholics had been present at the birth, and the English people generally declared that the boy was no son of the king's, but some spurious child palmed off on them by the Jesuits.

The Old Pretender.

It was plain that the child, if he was the real son of James, was the heir to the English throne, to the exclusion of the Protestant Mary of Orange, wife of the heroic William. So the people, especially the Whigs, refused to believe that he was a genuine son, and determined to rebel at the first good opportunity.

Every one was now waiting to hear the result of the trial of the Seven Bishops. For a long time the jury wavered. Eleven of the twelve were for acquittal. The twelfth was the king's brewer. He said that he should be ruined if he voted against the king. But he was at length brought over, and the verdict of "Not guilty" was received with an

The Seven Bishops acquitted (1688).

enthusiasm witnessed but once in a century. Even the royal army, which James had brought to London to put down a rising, should there be one, showed by their cheers that their sympathies were with the people. The Patriot leaders saw that now at last the time had come to act. Admiral Herbert, disguised as a common sailor, set out for Holland. He was the bearer of a letter signed by the most influential among the Whigs and Tories, asking William to come to England to protect the rights of his wife against the spurious son of James, and to save England from a Catholic tyranny.

The Invitation to William

William joyfully accepted the invitation. He loved his wife, and did not wish her to be deprived of her rights. But above all, he desired to be king of England, that he might use England's strength, both of men and money, in the grand struggle he was making against the power and ambition of Louis XIV. of France.

Everything favored William. His proclamation was received with rejoicings, while the concessions made by James were looked on with suspicion, as people saw that they had been extorted by fear. Louis, too, offered to help James, by attacking William, and thus keeping him at home in Holland. But James scornfully refused, and the French king, in a rage, sent his army into Germany. Even the winds helped William; for, though at first adverse, the breeze soon became favorable, and then increasing, the strong east wind — "the Protestant east wind," as they used to call it, — drove William's ships safely through the English Channel, while at the same time it kept the English fleet cooped up in the Thames.

William lands.

William landed at Torbay, in Devonshire, on the 5th of November, 1688, the anniversary of the Gunpowder Plot.

For several days no prominent men joined him, and it is said that he was on the point of returning to Holland, when they began to come. Among the first to arrive was Lord Churchill, afterwards the celebrated Duke of Marlborough. His wife was the most intimate friend of the Princess Anne. And so it fell out that when Lord Churchill deserted his master, the Princess Anne ran away from her father. "God help me!" cried the abandoned James, "even my children have forsaken me." So he sent his wife and son to France, and then escaped himself.

James runs away.

Unluckily, however, some fishermen caught sight of him as he was leaving the shore. Mistaking him for the Jesuit Father Petre, they seized him. Soon he was in London again,— much to the dismay of William, who would have had the field all to himself if he could have said that James had deserted his people. James was easily scared away again, however, and care was taken this time that he should not be stopped. Louis received him, and gave him a palace to live in. But the means used to get rid of him seemed to many good people so very much like force that they took his side, and were called, from James's Latin name of Jacobus, Jacobites.

He is brought back.

The Jacobites.

William now summoned the Peers, and all who had sat in the House of Commons during the reign of Charles the Second, to meet him at Westminster and advise him as to what he should do. Upon their advice he summoned a Parliament, though it was called a Convention for the time being. It met on the 14th of March, 1689, and after some discussion offered the crown to Mary. But she was too loyal to her husband to accept it, and he on his part declared that he would not be his wife's servant. So, after more discussion, the crown was offered to William and Mary as king and queen; William to have control of affairs. At the same time the Lords and Commons presented a Declaration of the Rights of the people of England. The main points of this great declaration, which was afterwards made into a regular law, were that the king had no power, without consent of Parliament, (1) to dispense with the laws, (2) to raise money, or (3) to keep a standing army. It was further declared (4) that the subjects had a right to bear arms, (5) to petition the king, and (6) to have freedom of debate in Parliament. (7) The High Commission Court was declared illegal, and (8) frequent Parliaments were declared necessary. On these terms the throne was offered to William and Mary, and accepted by them. Henceforth no English king could claim to rule by divine right, but only by the will of the nation.

The Convention.

Declaration of Rights.

CHAPTER XXX.

THE FIRST CONSTITUTIONAL MONARCHS.

THE Declaration of Rights did not seem to be all that was necessary to protect the people. So, to make sure that no king could again turn tyrant, Parliament granted William the revenues from customs for a few years, instead of for life, as had hereto-fore been done. Then, too, the Commons said that for the future money must be spent on the objects specified in the vote. This was to guard against the king's obtaining money for some particular purpose, like the navy, and then spending it to keep up a large army to hold the people down. Still further to guard against the same evil, Parliament voted the bill giving the army officers control over the soldiers — the Mutiny Bill, as it is called — for one year. If Parliament for any cause should wish to disband the army, it had only to refuse to pass a new Mutiny Bill; for when the old one expired, the army would drop to pieces, as the soldiers could not be punished for disobeying the officers. And this practice of passing money and mutiny bills has lasted to our own times. This is a very important fact, for in this way the House of Commons has obtained control of the government, as it is in that House that money bills are first passed. The king was, and is, obliged to have for his ministers

William and Mary (1689-1702).

The Mutiny Bill.

men who have the confidence of a majority in that House; in other words, men who can get these very bills through Parliament. In this way the great British Empire has come to be ruled by a committee of the party which for the moment has a majority in the House of Commons. This is called "responsible government," as these men are responsible to the House of Commons, and through it to the people of England.

The next thing Parliament did was to pass a law declaring that all officers in church and state must swear to support William and Mary as king and queen. Many good people still believed that James was the real king, and refused to swear. They were called non-jurors (non-swearers). They were sincere, and did what they thought was right; but their actions made William's position much more difficult. It was found impossible to repeal the harsh Acts which the Cavaliers had passed against the Dissenters. But one great step was made in the passage of the Toleration Act, allowing Dissenters to stay away from the Episcopal service without being fined.

The Non-jurors.

Now that William was firm on the throne, James was glad to accept the helping hand held out by Louis of France. The Irish were devout Roman Catholics, and were thus disposed to be friendly to James. It is probable, too, that the Irish leaders hoped that by aiding James they might free Ireland from the English yoke. At any rate, no sooner had James fled to France than they made war on the English and Protestant settlers in Ireland, and compelled them to seek refuge in two towns in the northern part of Ireland, Enniskillen and Londonderry. Soon James came over with some French soldiers, and siege was laid to the two towns. The garrison of Enniskillen, sallying forth, drove their assailants away. Those at Londonderry

WILLIAM III.: AFTER A PORTRAIT BY J. H BRANDON.

ate everything that was eatable in the town, including all the rats and salt hides. Then at length two London ships broke through the obstructions which the Irish had placed in the mouth of

Siege of Londonderry.

of the harbor, and the town was saved, after one of the most persistent defences in history.

The next year William himself went to Ireland with

MARY II.: AFTER A PORTRAIT BY J. H. BRANDON.

a famous French general,—Schomberg,—whom Louis had driven from France because he was a Huguenot. They fought with James and his French and Irish troops at the Battle of the Boyne, and

Battle of the Boyne (1690).

beat him so thoroughly that he fled to France as fast as horse and ship would carry him. Nevertheless, it took several years to reconquer Ireland thoroughly.

The news of this great victory reached England in good time, for Admiral Herbert — now Lord Torrington — had been badly beaten the very day before by the French off Beachy Head. The French admiral then landed his soldiers and set fire to the huts of some poor fishermen who lived in a little town in the southern part of England. This outrage so angered the English people that thousands who had hitherto been lukewarm now came to the assistance of William and Mary, and did all they could to save the land from James and his allies.

<small>Beachy Head.</small>

In fact, all danger from the Jacobites was for the moment at an end. William crossed over to Holland and took his place at the head of the European powers who were opposed to Louis. Now the French king thought that the best way to compel William's return to England would be to send James over there. So he gathered a great army at Boulogne. James was so sure of being successful that he drew up a proclamation, telling people what would happen when he was on the throne again. Among other things he said that the ignorant fishermen who had stopped him on his first attempt to escape would be treated as traitors, and have their heads cut off. Indeed, the proclamation was so ridiculous that the English Government reprinted it, and sent copies all over the country at its own expense. But James never got to England again, for an English fleet under Admiral Russell swept from the seas the French fleet that was to have conveyed him to England. The English sailors remembered the humiliation of Beachy Head, and now at La Hogue sank, captured, or drove ashore every French ship. They even rowed in small boats right up to some ships that had taken refuge under the guns of a fort, and set them on fire. All this was done under the eyes of James himself. There was no longer any need for William to feel anxious for England. At the Peace of Ryswick (1697) Louis was compelled to give back all the places he had seized. This was mainly owing to the pluck and skill of William; for though he seldom won battles, he knew how to prevent the French from making any use of their victories,—and that is sometimes as important as winning battles.

La Hogue (1692).

The fight which William was so manfully making was not merely a fight for the Protestant religion, but a struggle for English liberty. His success would benefit succeeding generations for hundreds of years. So the Government borrowed a portion of the funds needed to support the armies, the first loan being made in 1693. It was the beginning of the English national debt.

His financial advisers.

At this time there were no banks in England. All large sums of money were collected and paid through the goldsmiths and silversmiths of London, who in this way acted as bankers. Of course this was not a very secure way of doing business, as everything depended upon the honesty of some particular man. So a Scotchman named Paterson agreed to establish a national bank. As an inducement for the authorities to give him the necessary power, he proposed to lend to the Government one-half the capital of the bank. Thus the Government would be able

Bank of England.

to borrow money, and at the same time the shareholders and those who had deposited money in the bank would be interested in the stability of the Government of William, because if it should be overthrown they would never get their money back. In this way the Bank of England was established.

Another great reform was the recoinage of the currency. To-day an English gold sovereign is good the world over; but two hundred years ago this was not the case. The money then in circulation had been coined with smooth edges. Any one could clip off a little without its being noticed. In the end, however, so much might be clipped off that the coin would not be worth anything like its face value. The merchants refused to take these coins in payment, except by weight, so many ounces of gold or silver for so many pounds of bread and butter. Of course this was very inconvenient, and the Government employed Sir Isaac Newton, the great philosopher, to make some new coins. The new pieces had milled edges, and could not be clipped.

In this year, too, the "Licensing Act" of 1660, which had placed the control of printing in the Government, expired by limitation, and Parliament refused to renew it. Since that time every one has been at liberty to publish anything he chooses. But he is responsible for what he publishes, as he is for everything else he does.

Liberty of the Press (1695).

The one great blot upon William's name is the massacre of Glencoe. Ian MacIan, chief of the Macdonalds, who lived in Glencoe, in a fit of stubborn pride had waited until all the other chiefs had taken the oath of submission to William

Massacre of Glencoe.

and Mary. Then he went to the nearest fort, and offered to take the oath; but there was no one there who could administer it. Now thoroughly alarmed, because those who did not take the oath before a certain day were to be declared outlawed, he trudged over the snow to Inverary, only to find when he arrived there that it was too late. The sheriff, however, made out a paper to the effect that the chief had tried to take the oath at the proper time; indeed, he took it then only six days late. It chanced that the king's representative in Scotland at that time was a bitter enemy to the Macdonalds. He contrived to suppress the fact that MacIan had offered to take the oath at a proper time, and obtained from William an order to "extirpate the Macdonalds of Glencoe." This sentence was in the middle of a long document, and it is probable that William never saw it. At all events, one morning in February, 1692, a company of Scottish soldiers, led by Campbell of Glenlyon, after enjoying the hospitalities of the Macdonalds for two weeks, suddenly fell on them and killed thirty-eight on the spot. The remainder fled to the mountains. How many died from cold and hunger will never be known. The act was one of private revenge on the part of the Campbells. But it was done under orders, and William felt obliged to shelter the authors, and no one was ever punished.

Queen Mary died in 1694. This was a great loss to William, for she was very popular with the people, while he was very unpopular. Indeed, it might have gone hard with him, had not Louis of France, in defiance of treaties and promises, put his grandson on the throne of Spain. This aroused the jealousy of the English people, and William found himself at the head of another Grand Alliance of Europe against the Bourbons. Just at this moment the exiled James II. died in his borrowed palace of St. Germain's. In direct opposition to the Treaty of Ryswick, Louis acknowledged James's son James (the "Old Pretender") as king of England. All England was now anxious for war. But William was not again to lead the armies of Europe. In the winter of 1702 he was thrown from his horse, and a few weeks later he died. Suspended about his neck, where no one could see it, was a locket containing a gold ring and a lock of Mary's hair.

As William and Mary had no children, Mary's younger sister, the Princess Anne, became queen. She was more of a Stuart than Mary, and allowed herself to be ruled by favorites, as her ancestors had allowed themselves to be ruled. During the first part of her reign her favorite was the wife of the Earl, afterwards the Duke, of Marlborough. This Marlborough was a selfish man. But he saw that by carrying out the plans of William he might make a great name for himself. And, indeed, for the next few years he was the real ruler of England, and even took William's place at the head of the Alliance against Louis.

Queen Anne (1702–1714).

The first year he accomplished little. But in 1704 he broke away from the Dutch allies, who always prevented his doing anything at all hazardous. Marching up the Rhine and the Neckar, he crossed over the mountains to Donauwörth, on the Danube. There he was joined by an Austrian army under Prince Eugene. They encountered the French and their allies, the Bavarians, at the little town of Höchstädt. The two opposing forces had no sooner

Battle of Blenheim (1704).

come into contact than Marlborough saw that the enemy had stationed a large part of his army in the village of Blenheim, at the end of the line. He there-

QUEEN ANNE: FROM A PORTRAIT BY SIR GODFREY KNELLER.

fore made the middle of his own line as strong as possible. Then, while a false attack was made on Blenheim on the one flank, and while Prince Eugene kept the Bavarians engaged on the other flank, Marlborough threw his whole weight on the centre. He broke through, and turning half round, wrapped his army around the village of Blenheim. Not a Frenchman in the village escaped; they were all killed or captured. On the morning of that day the French and Bavarian generals had commanded an army of some sixty thousand men. At night but twenty thousand remained. The road from Ulm to Ratisbon runs through a part of this battlefield, and the pathway is said to be founded on the bones of men and horses who perished there. In fact, to this very day the skulls of men are sometimes turned up by the plough.

> "'T is some poor fellow's skull,' quoth he,
> 'Who fell in the great victory.'"

The victory of Blenheim placed England at the head of Teutonic Europe. To Marlborough it brought the thanks of Parliament and a magnificent estate.

Marlborough gained many other victories, but none so important as this. Nor was he the only English commander to gain victories, for Admiral Rooke, having with him a small land force under the command of a German prince, captured Gibraltar, the key to the Mediterranean Sea. The English held it through the war, retained it at the peace, and it is still in English hands, and is claimed to be the strongest fortress in the world. The Treaty of Utrecht ended this long war. The French prince kept his Spanish throne, but France had been greatly weakened by the struggle. The twenty-five years of peace which followed brought her little strength, though giving England time to grow, and to become the leading

Seizure of Gibraltar.

power in Europe. In America this war was usually called Queen Anne's War, and during its continuance Acadia was taken from the French. At the Peace of Utrecht it was retained by England, and this was the first step in the breaking up of the French empire in America.

One of the principal reasons for the prominence which England now gained was the union with Scotland. Ever since James VI. of Scotland became James I. of England, the two countries had been ruled by one sovereign. But, except for a short time during the ascendency of the Puritans, a Scottish Parliament, sitting at Edinburgh, had made laws for Scotland; a Scot had been regarded in England as a foreigner; and Scottish goods could be brought into England only on terms which made their profitable sale impossible. Of course the evils of such a state of things were apparent to every one. But so jealous were all parties of their rights that it was not until 1707 that the union of the two kingdoms was brought about. After that date, laws for the United Kingdom of Great Britain were made by a Parliament sitting at Westminster. The Scots sent one-twelfth of the new House of Commons, and in the House of Lords there were sixteen Scottish peers, chosen by all the Scottish peers. Besides these, however, many Scots sat in the House of Lords, because they possessed English titles of nobility, so that the disproportion was not so great as it at first sight appears. For purposes of trade and taxation the two kingdoms were placed on an equality. Many people thought that the less numerous Scots would be lost to sight among their more numerous neighbors. Such has not

Union with Scotland (1707).

been the case. By patience and energy the Scots have made Glasgow on the Clyde the rival of Liverpool on the Mersey. In colonial enterprises the two races have stood side by side, while in the government service, in the army, the navy, and even in the Church, the Scots have taken a leading part. And this, though the Presbyterian Church was recognized as the Established Church of Scotland. The old English flag had been the red cross of St. George on a white ground. The white "saltire" of St. Andrew, or cross, in the shape of an X, on a blue ground, was now combined with this, and the "union" flag became the symbol of the union between the two countries.

ROYAL ARMS BORNE BY JAMES I. AND SUCCEEDING STUART SOVEREIGNS.

CHAPTER XXXI.

GEORGE I.

1714–1727.

QUEEN ANNE was the last of the Stuart monarchs. She died in 1714, leaving no children. As long ago as 1701 an Act had been passed regulating the succession to the crown in such a way that none but a Protestant should ever become king or queen of England. The Protestant having the best right to the crown after Anne was the Electress Sophia of Hanover, that small country being governed by an elector; and on her and her descendants, provided they were Protestants, the crown was settled. A few things which had been omitted from the Bill of Rights were inserted in this new agreement between Parliament and the future kings and queens of England, especially one clause requiring the judges to be appointed to hold office during good behavior, and not merely during the king's pleasure. Electress Sophia died a few weeks before Queen Anne. So upon the latter's death, Sophia's son, Elector George of Hanover, became King George the First of England.[1]

Act of Succession, or Settlement (1701).

There were many persons in England, and even in the government itself, who would have preferred a Stuart king. But just before Queen Anne's death,

---

[1] For genealogy, see p. 242.

some noblemen favorable to the Hanoverian cause, suspecting the ministers of conspiring with the Stuarts, seized the government. That their suspicions were correct is shown by the fact that Lord Bolingbroke, who had been the leading minister, soon after ran away to France, and openly joined the Pretender, James Stuart. Then the elections to the new Parliament were scenes of such great disorder that the Riot Act had to be passed. When, a year later, it came to be time to elect a new Parliament, there was still so much opposition to the Hanoverian Succession that an Act was passed extending the duration of Parliament to seven years, unless sooner dissolved by the king. This was called the Septennial Act, and is still in force. No Parliament can sit for more than seven years, in any case, without a new election; and new elections may be held much oftener than this, as, for instance, when the ministry is defeated in any important vote, or when a Prime Minister thinks it a favorable time for his party. When a ministry is finally defeated, the sovereign sends for some leading member or members of the successful party, and they agree upon a new list of ministers.

Jacobite plot (1715).

Riot Act (1715).

Septennial Act (1716).

The next few years were marked by a desire among the people to grow rapidly rich. A great scheme for trade to South America and the islands of the Pacific was set on foot. The company which undertook to carry on this trade was called the South Sea Company, from the old name of the Pacific Ocean. It soon made some very corrupt bargains with the English Government, and thus attracted much attention. Its shares rose from one hundred pounds apiece

South Sea Bubble (1720).

1720.] SOUTH SEA BUBBLE. 231

GEORGE I.: FROM AN ENGRAVING BY VERTUE.

to one thousand pounds apiece; and there were not so many shares as people wished to buy at any price. New companies were quickly started: one to "trade

in human hair," for instance, another "to insure against
losses from dishonest servants," and still another for
the "making of iron with pit coal." Pit coal, or coal
as we call it, was then regarded as unfit for smelting
iron, which was done with charcoal. A few years
later a method of smelting iron with coal was introduced, and this industry is to-day the basis of England's prosperity. Alarmed at the sudden rise of
these companies, the South Sea Company procured
their downfall. When the distrust of the people had
been aroused in this way it was directed against the
South Sea Company as well as against its rivals. The
Government interfered, and the South Sea Company
was saved. During this fit of speculation thousands
had lost all their property, and there was much
discontent and misery throughout England. The
Jacobites thought the time had come to overthrow the
Hanoverian monarchy. But again their scheme fell
through. The leaders were executed, while others,
like Atterbury, Bishop of Rochester, were exiled.

The bursting of the South Sea Bubble brought Sir
Robert Walpole, a skilful financier, to the head of
affairs. He became First Lord of the Treasury,
and from that day to this it has been usual for
that official to be prime minister, or premier.
All the members of the Government, too, began
now to act together under the leadership of
the premier, the principal ministers forming a select
council, or cabinet.

<small>Sir Robert Walpole Prime Minister (1721–1742).</small>

Sir Robert Walpole saw that what England now
needed was a period of repose, during which the Hanoverian kings might become firmly seated on the throne,
and be associated in people's minds with prosperity

and quiet. He resolved to let well enough alone, and never to do anything which might arouse opposition. In this he was successful. He also bought, by gifts of money or easy places under the Government, the votes of a majority of the members of the House of Commons, and in this way secured his own power, and kept the two Houses of Parliament from

<ul><li style="list-style:none">Walpole's policy.</li></ul>

GROUP SHOWING COSTUMES AND SEDAN CHAIR, ABOUT 1720: FROM AN ENGRAVING BY KIP.

quarrelling. In 1727 George I. died, and his son, George II., succeeded to the throne as quietly as any son ever succeeded his father. The first George had been a dull and heavy man, who spoke English very imperfectly, because of his German birth, and had won very little affection or admiration from his people.

CHAPTER XXXII.

GEORGE II.

1727-1760.

IT seemed at first as if Walpole would be turned out of office; but he soon discovered that the new king was governed by his wife, Queen Caroline. So he promised her that if he should remain Prime Minister, she should have a larger allowance than any queen had before received. This pleased Queen Caroline, who also saw that Walpole was the ablest and safest man then in public life. She threw her influence on his side, and while she lived he was secure in his place.

Queen Caroline.

It was during this reign that the brothers Wesley began a great revival in the English Church. As they laid much stress on their peculiar methods, they were in derision called Methodists. But the Methodists grew and prospered, and now are a strong and influential body, not merely in England, but in our own country as well.

The Methodists.

In 1737 Queen Caroline died, and the mainstay of Walpole's power was removed. His peace policy, too, was becoming distasteful to Englishmen, who thought he yielded too much to foreigners. At last an English seaman named Jenkins appeared in London with one of his ears carefully preserved in a box. This, he declared, had been cut off

War with Spain (1739).

SIR ROBERT WALPOLE: FROM THE PICTURE BY VAN LOO
IN THE NATIONAL PORTRAIT GALLERY.

by a brutal Spanish sailor. When asked what his feelings were at the time of the ear-cutting, he replied: "I commended my soul to God, my cause to my country." This story aroused great ill-will among the people, and the king, too, was eager for war. He was still Elector of Hanover, and, being a German by birth and breeding, he cared much more for the interests of Hanover than for those of England. So in 1739 Walpole was compelled, quite contrary to his own judgment, to declare war against Spain. In the next year King Frederick II. — called Frederick the Great — of Prussia seized some valuable territory belonging to Austria, and the war became general, England and Austria fighting on one side, against Spain, France, and Prussia on the other.

<small>And with Prussia and France.</small>

In 1742 Sir Robert Walpole was forced from office, and before long Henry Pelham became prime minister, with his brother, the Duke of Newcastle, as his right-hand man. The war was now carried on with more vigor. The English took part in two noted battles, Dettingen and Fontenoy. The former is especially memorable as the last battle in which an English king took a personal share, and the latter as one in which Irish troops fought against England.

<small>Pelham Ministry (1742-1754).</small>

The war is important in English history, however, as giving occasion for the last attempt of the Stuarts to regain their lost throne by force. The French Government gave all the assistance it could, and many Scots rallied around Prince Charles Edward, the son of the Old Pretender, or James III., as the Jacobites called him. "Prince Charlie" beat the English at Preston Pans, near Edinburgh, and then, advancing south, marched almost unopposed to Derby, in the heart of England. In London all was confusion. The king made preparations to escape by sea, and Newcastle even thought of going over to the

<small>Stuart rising (1745).</small>

GEORGE II.: FROM THE PORTRAIT BY THOMAS HUDSON
IN THE NATIONAL PORTRAIT GALLERY.

side of the prince. But almost no one in England actually joined the prince, and without a fight he turned back, and retreated to Scotland. The Duke of Cumberland, brother to the king, now took command of the English forces, and pursuing the Scots to the northern end of Scotland, defeated them in the battle of Culloden. The slaughter did not cease with the battle, and earned for Cumberland the nickname of the "Butcher." After many romantic adventures, Prince Charles escaped. This was largely due to the bravery of Flora Macdonald, who later emigrated to the Carolinas. The Highland clan system was now broken up, and the warlike power of the chiefs destroyed. The war also led to a lasting change in the social condition of Scotland. Before this, the humblest Highland clansman had claimed a right in the soil; but he was now treated, under the English laws, as a mere tenant-at-will, and the Dukes of Athol, Sutherland, and Argyle entered, one after another, upon a series of "clearances," as they were called, expelling thousands of families to make room for grouse, sheep, and deer. The Scots never rebelled again, and in the next war they were found serving in the English army against the French. Before dismissing the Stuarts from our minds, let us recall for a moment how much they suffered and lost, mainly because of their religion. If we cannot sympathize with their despotic theories of government, we may perhaps honor them for their fidelity to their religious convictions.

This insurrection, "the Forty-five," as it was afterwards called, is vividly described in Scott's novel of "Waverley." During this war, the militia of Massachusetts and some of the other English North American colonies, with the assistance of an English fleet, had surprised and captured the French stronghold of Louisburg, on Cape Breton Island. This, with all other conquests, was given back by England at the Peace of Aix-la-Chapelle in 1748.

The year 1752 is memorable as being the first year in which English folk used the modern mode of reckoning time. The old calendar had been adopted in the days of Julius Cæsar, when people thought the year was shorter than it really is. In 1582 Pope Gregory had instituted a new calendar; but the English at that time hated the Pope so thoroughly that they would have nothing to do with it. It was adopted, however, by the Catholic countries of western Europe. In 1751 the difference in time between England and her neighbors was eleven days. The English year, too, began on the 25th of March, instead of on the 1st of January, and altogether it was very inconvenient. So in 1751 Parliament passed an Act providing that the year 1752 should begin on January 1st, and the day after September 2d should be called, not September 3d, but September 14th. In this way England caught up with her neighbors. But many people thought the Government had stolen the eleven days, and cried in public places, "Give us back our eleven days!" *New Style.*

During these years two young men — William Pitt and Henry Fox — pushed themselves to the front, and were taken into the Government, Fox as Secretary of War, and Pitt as Paymaster of the Forces. Former paymasters had used the money in their hands as their own, till it was actually needed. Pitt now refused to do this. He turned into *Pitt and Fox.*

the treasury the interest earned by the money, and thus won the confidence of the people. In 1754 Pelham died, and his brother, the Duke of Newcastle, became prime minister.

The Treaty of 1748 had really settled nothing. In America especially, the boundaries between English and French soil were vague and uncertain. France conceived the project of connecting her possessions in Canada and Louisiana by a line of posts extending down the Ohio River. If this were successfully done, Causes of the French and Indian War in America. the English colonies would be confined to the narrow strip of land between the Alleghanies and the Atlantic Ocean. Governor Dinwiddie of Virginia sent George Washington with a letter to the commander of one of the French posts, protesting against the whole scheme. No attention being paid to this, Washington led an expedition to seize Fort Du Quesne, which was erected at the junction of the two principal branches of the Ohio, near where Pittsburgh now stands. This expedition ended in disaster. The English Government then sent over regular troops under General Braddock to seize the place. But Braddock was killed before he came within sight of the fort, and his expedition, too, was totally wrecked.

By this time (1756) war had broken out all over western Europe. France took the part of Austria, and thus England was forced into an alliance The Seven Years' War in Europe. with Frederick the Great of Prussia. The war soon spread over the Christian world, and at first everything went against England. Newcastle tried to govern without Pitt, and failed. Then Pitt tried to carry on the government without

THE RT. HON. WILLIAM PITT, PAYMASTER OF THE FORCES, AFTERWARDS EARL OF CHATHAM: FROM A PAINTING BY HOARE.

Newcastle, and he in turn failed. The two then agreed to share the government between them, Newcastle to manage home affairs, and to secure by bribery, in which he was expert, a majority in the House of Commons, while Pitt should manage the war, and gain as many victories as he could.

William Pitt was probably the ablest war minister England ever had. He took the whole control of the army and navy into his own hands. For instance, the orders for the sailing of fleets were sent by Pitt *William* to the Admiralty (or navy department), and the *Pitt.* Lords of the Admiralty were compelled to sign them, without even knowing what they were. Once, it is said, Pitt told the Lords of the Admiralty to have a fleet ready to set sail the following Friday. The Lords said it was impossible. Pitt declared that if the fleet did not sail at the designated time, there would be a new set of Lords of the Admiralty. The fleet sailed at the appointed time, and a few days later won a glorious victory. Pitt especially sought for

---

THE HOUSE OF HANOVER.

James I., King of England.
    |
    Elizabeth *m.* Frederick, Elector Palatine.
        |
        Sophia *m.* Elector of Hanover.
            |
            George I., King of England.
                |
                George II.
                    |
        ┌───────────────────┴───────────────┐
    Frederick, Prince of Wales.   Duke of Cumberland.
        |
    George III.
        |
    ┌───────────┬───────────────┬───────────────┐
George IV.   *William IV.*   Duke of Kent.
                                                |
                                            Victoria.
                                                |
                            ┌───────────────────┴───────────┐
                    Albert Edward, Prince   Duke of Edinburgh
                        of Wales.
                            |
                ┌───────────┴───────────────────┐
            Albert Victor Edward.   George Frederick.
                †1892.

(For other descendants of James I., see p. 143.)

energetic, skilful young men, and promoted them over the heads of old and less efficient men, whose only recommendation was the influence their families possessed in Parliament. The result of this energetic administration was the expulsion of the French from the valleys of the St. Lawrence and Ohio rivers in America, and from one of the finest portions of India. Quebec and Plassey, associated with the names of Wolfe and Clive, were the two great victories won by the English in this war. They are still reckoned among the decisive conflicts in the world's history.

On the Continent, too, Frederick the Great, with the aid of English money, won campaign after campaign, and, though often sorely pressed, kept the French busy at home. Hence it is often said: "England conquered America in Germany." But before peace was made, George II. was dead, and Pitt and Newcastle were no longer in the Government.

COACH IN USE ABOUT 1700.

CHAPTER XXXIII.

GEORGE III.

1760-1820.

PART I. 1760-1783.

Character of the new reign. THE new king was quite unlike his Hanoverian predecessors. They were Germans, while he was born an Englishman. They were content to have England governed by constitutional ministers, as long as everything went well, and their pleasures were not restricted. But George the Third had been brought up by his mother with very high notions of the rights of an English king. She was always saying to him, "George, be king!" and he set to work to "be king" in earnest. This was now easier than it would have been in the earlier part of the century, for long years of power had split the Whig party into cliques, and it was no longer able to resist royal encroachment. In 1761 Pitt wished to declare war against Spain, which was plainly preparing to attack England. He was overruled by the influence of the king, and resigned. Soon after other changes were made, and Newcastle, in disgust, retired. These things were done by the advice of Lord Bute, the Scottish favorite of the king, who became Prime Minister.

The war with Spain followed, as Pitt had foretold. But the enthusiasm he had aroused remained, and Havana was captured from the Spaniards. In 1763

GEORGE III. IN 1767: FROM A PAINTING BY ALLAN RAMSAY
IN THE NATIONAL PORTRAIT GALLERY.

peace was made, England retaining nearly all her conquests, and exchanging Havana for the Floridas. In this way all of North America east of the Mississippi River, with the exception of New

Peace of Paris (1763).

Orleans, came into England's hands. In India was laid the foundation of her present splendid empire.

Nevertheless, many Englishmen thought Lord Bute had obtained less than England's due at the end of a long and successful war. The treaty was fiercely attacked in the House of Commons. Bute employed Henry Fox to buy enough votes to carry the treaty through. For his success in this dishonorable effort, he was raised to the peerage as Lord Holland, but he never recovered the esteem of men. Lord Bute now suddenly resigned, and Pitt's brother-in-law, George Grenville, became the real head of the Government. Bute's turning Pitt out of office, and then bringing the war to such a tame conclusion, made him very unpopular. He was attacked from all sides, and pamphlet after pamphlet was written against him.

Perhaps the boldest attack was made by John Wilkes, in a paper called, in direct allusion to Bute's Scottish birth, "The North Briton." This John Wilkes was a most extraordinary man. His character was as bad as it could be, and his personal appearance was so singular that one would have supposed he would have had no influence at all. But his conversation was so brilliant that in five minutes one forgot his evil looks, and his talents were so great that Benjamin Franklin once said: "Had Wilkes had a good character, and George the Third a bad one, the former would have turned the latter out of his kingdom." As it was, Wilkes gave the king and his ministers a good deal of trouble. The Government decided to punish him for writing the articles in "The North Briton." To make an arrest sure, a general warrant was issued to arrest the authors of the paper, not specifying any

one of the authors by name. Wilkes was arrested, but
Charles Pratt, Chief Justice of the Court of Common

A SITTING IN THE HOUSE OF COMMONS IN 1741-42: FROM AN ENGRAVING BY PINE.

Pleas, who later became Lord Chancellor Camden,
ordered his release; on the ground that as a member of

the House of Commons he was free from arrest except for certain things, of which writing newspaper attacks was not one. A little later, general warrants were also declared to be illegal. The majority of the House of Commons, however, was on the side of the Government, and by vote expelled Wilkes from his seat. Soon after he was wounded in a duel, and compelled to flee to France, and then was declared to be an outlaw. But "Wilkes and Liberty" became a popular cry, and before long the Government had more trouble with Wilkes himself.

The ministry now became involved in another quarrel, one result of which was the independence of the United States. The English colonies had been planted in the seventeenth century, either as commercial ventures or as places of refuge for particular religious beliefs. During their early years of weakness and poverty they had received little help or encouragement from the mother land. But as they grew in riches, and their trade became profitable, Parliament passed law after law to turn their trade and commerce to the advantage of England. Many of these laws were so severe they could not be enforced. This was especially true of the tax on sugar and molasses imported from the Spanish and French West Indies, which tax was so high as to prevent the profitable importation of such articles from those islands; that is, if the tax were paid. The only result was to encourage smuggling, which became a regular business in some colonies. George Grenville was an able lawyer, a hard-headed, narrow-minded man. To him smuggling was smuggling, whether on the coast of Old England or of New England. He lowered the

The North American colonies.

duty on sugar, and then ordered the English naval officers to carry out the law to the letter. This was done, but the harshness of the naval officers aroused much irritation.

Grenville also decided that a force of regular English troops must be maintained in the colonies to keep the Indians in order. He thought it only right the colonists should pay a part of the expense of maintaining them. This he told the colonial agents in London, and gave them a year in which to propose some method of raising the required sum. As they proposed none, he carried a bill through Parliament, laying a stamp duty on legal documents and newspapers in America. The Act was most ill-timed. The colonists refused to obey it. Newspapers were printed without a stamp, and, after a time, the courts went on without stamped documents, as if no law had ever been passed. *[The Stamp Act (1765).]*

As if these quarrels with Wilkes and the American colonists were not enough, Grenville now quarrelled with the king. George the Third's mind had never been very strong, and in 1765 he became for a time incapable of ruling. It seemed necessary to provide some one to take his place in case of future attacks. So Grenville drew up a bill to provide for the appointment of a Council of Regency. The king's mother was very unpopular, and it was thought best to omit her name altogether from the list of persons to be appointed, for if it were put in, the Commons would surely strike it out. The king consented to omit it. But when the bill came to the Commons they insisted upon its insertion. The king was furious. He dismissed Grenville on the first *[The Regency Question.]*

opportunity, and another Whig faction came into office under the lead of the Marquis of Rockingham, whose private secretary was an Irishman named Edmund Burke.

The Rockingham ministry was really disliked by the king, and had but a narrow majority in the Commons, so it accomplished very little. The Stamp Act was indeed repealed, but the repeal was accompanied by a Declaratory Act, declaring the right of Parliament to legislate for the colonies "in all cases whatsoever." The colonists, however, were so overjoyed at the repeal of the Stamp Act that they paid no attention to this other Act. The king then turned out the Whigs, and prevailed on William Pitt, now raised to the peerage as Earl of Chatham, to be the head of a new ministry. As he was getting feeble, the Duke of Grafton became nominal Prime Minister. Charles Pratt was in the new government as Lord Chancellor Camden, and Lord Shelburne, a friend of the colonists, was Colonial Secretary. Charles Townshend was Chancellor of the Exchequer, and Lord North held a subordinate office. In fact so many different elements were represented in this ministry that Edmund Burke laughingly called it a "Mosaic Ministry." Before the Government was fairly started, Lord Chatham became seriously ill, and retired to the country. In his absence, and in accordance with the Declaratory Act, Townshend passed a bill through Parliament laying duties on glass, paper, tea, and painters' colors imported into the colonies. Townshend did this merely to fulfil an idle boast, and almost immediately died. His place was taken by Lord North. Unable to prevent such measures, Shelburne resigned, and

Stamp Act repealed (1766).

Chatham, as soon as he recovered sufficiently to realize what was going on, also resigned. In 1770 Camden and Grafton followed, and Lord North became Prime Minister.

The king had now accomplished his object. By sinecure offices, bribes, and other corrupt means he had gathered about him a party, known as "The King's Friends," devoted to his interests. This party now supported Lord North, and from 1770 to 1782 King George III. governed very despotically, as no king had governed since the days of James II., and as none has governed since. Once in a while Lord North objected to the royal policy, and threatened to resign. But the king appealed to his personal loyalty, and Lord North, to his discredit, remained in office. Though including such men as Chatham and Camden in the Lords, and Burke and Charles James Fox in the Commons, the Opposition was able to accomplish nothing against Lord North and the King's Friends. One man there was who seemed singly a match for king and Parliament combined, and this man was John Wilkes.

In 1768 Wilkes had returned from France, and been elected to Parliament as one of the members for the County of Middlesex. The House of Commons declared him incapable of sitting in that House, and ordered a new election. Wilkes was again returned; and this was again repeated till the House ordered the man having the next largest number of votes to be considered the elected member. Up to this time the debates which took place in Parliament were not reported and published, because the two Houses would not permit it. Sometimes the speeches

"The King's Friends."

Wilkes again.

of members were printed as speeches delivered in "the Senate of Great Lilliput," or some such place, and the names of the speakers were never given in full. In 1770, however, some of the debates were published without any such attempt at concealment. The Commons decided to punish the printers, and sent their officers into the city of London to arrest the culprits. But the officers were themselves arrested and taken before the Lord Mayor, Brass Crosby by name, and Aldermen Wilkes and Oliver. These magistrates decided that the officers of the Commons could arrest no one within the limits of the city without the consent of a city magistrate. Then the Commons ordered Crosby and Oliver to appear in their places, for they were members of the House, and to justify their conduct. They also ordered Wilkes to appear at the bar of the House and defend himself. Crosby and Oliver did as they were ordered, and were sent to prison. But Wilkes refused to appear except in his place as member for Middlesex, and the House of Commons was afraid of another struggle with him, for the London mob took his side. It ordered him to present himself on a certain day, and then adjourned over that day, so that he could not appear. This was the end of the contest, and ever since, the debates in the Houses of Parliament have been published. The Opposition had sided with Wilkes. As time went on they took the part of the American colonists, and in this way the maintenance of the king's policy in England and America came to be regarded as a single question. This, of course, made reconciliation with America even more difficult than before.

The Townshend duties gave rise to so much irritation in the colonies that in 1770 they were repealed, with the exception of the tax on tea, which was retained at the command of the king. It chanced at this time that the English East India Company was in great need of funds. The Government loaned it money, and, in return, secured a voice in its affairs. To still further help it out of its difficulties, the Government gave it the privilege of exporting tea from its London warehouses to the colonies free of duty, except the tax which was to be collected in America, in accordance with the Townshend duties.

Tea sent to the colonies.

As there was a heavy tax on all tea sold in England, this arrangement would have enabled the Company to sell it to the colonists cheaper than to the people of England. In fact, this was one reason why the Government entered into the arrangement, as it was hoped that the Company would sell its tea so cheap that the Americans would stop buying smuggled tea from the Dutch traders. The colonists, on the other hand, regarded its very cheapness with suspicion, and felt that the Government was in effect bribing them to submit to taxation. They everywhere refused to buy the tea. In some colonies the ships were turned back, in others the tea was stored in damp cellars, where it soon spoiled. In Massachusetts, when Governor Hutchinson refused to allow the ships to sail before their cargoes were landed, the people threw the tea into the harbor, and then refused to pay the Company for what they had destroyed.

The Boston Tea Party (1773).

The English Government decided to make an example of the people of Boston and Massachusetts. Laws were passed through Parliament closing the port of Boston to commerce, and suspending the charter of the Province of Massachusetts Bay. Another Act, passed in the same year, extended the boundaries of the Province of Quebec to the Ohio River, and granted many privileges to the French Catholics living in Canada. By selecting Massachusetts for punishment the Government no doubt expected to separate her from the other colonies, and in this way to deal with one colony at a time. The colonists, however, acted in an entirely unexpected manner, for they made the cause of Massachusetts their own. This view was entirely just, for if Parliament could deal thus arbitrarily with one colony, it could with all. A Continental Congress, or meeting of delegates from all of the original English colonies on the continent, met at Philadelphia. It drew up a declaration of the rights of the colonists, and set on foot an association to prevent the importation and consumption of English goods.

The Boston Port Act and other oppressive measures (1774).

In 1774 a general election was held in England, and the voters showed their sympathy for the Government by returning a large majority to help the Government oppress the colonies. In fact, for the next six years, from 1774 to 1780, there was hardly an Opposition in Parliament. During the winter of 1774–1775, however, the colonists were active in preparing for defence. In the spring of 1775 occurred the skirmishes at Lexington and Concord, and the battle at Bunker's Hill (or Breed's Hill). All resulted practically in favor of the colonists, though they were obliged to retire from their works on Breed's Hill. Then followed the siege of Boston by the colonists, who were commanded by General Washington. In March, 1776, the British were forced to evacuate

Lexington and Concord (1775).

Boston, and the scene of warlike operations was transferred to New York.

Meantime, Ethan Allen and Benedict Arnold and their companies seized Ticonderoga and Crown Point, with their storehouses full of arms and ammunition; but later Montgomery and Arnold failed to capture Quebec, and the English General Clinton, with Admiral Hyde Parker, were in their turn frustrated in an attempt on Charleston, S. C.

In July, 1776, Congress issued a Declaration of Independence, and Articles of Confederation between the colonies were drawn up. Owing to various causes, however, they did not go into effect until five years later, in 1781. In July, 1776, came proposals for reconciliation from the English Government, but the terms offered could not then be entertained, and nothing came of the attempt. Washington and Howe once more confronted each other, this time in New York; but the British were now much the stronger party, and the Americans were driven from New York city and White Plains, across the Hudson, through the Jerseys, to the southern side of the Delaware River. With ill-timed caution General Howe, instead of following Washington across the Delaware and fighting him wherever found, stopped short and went into winter quarters, his line extending across New Jersey from Elizabeth to Trenton.

In December, 1776, affairs looked desperate for the Americans; but on Christmas night Washington recrossed the Delaware, and surprised and captured the British outpost at Trenton. Before long the British were obliged to concentrate within a short distance of New York. *The surprise at Trenton (1776).*

For the year 1777 a most elaborate plan was drawn up. The main army, under Howe, was to seize Philadelphia, while Clinton should protect New York city and capture all of the American forts he could on Hudson River. A third army, under Burgoyne, would march south from Canada and join Clinton. If this plan was successfully carried out, New England would be cut off from the other colonies, to be subdued at leisure. Burgoyne's march was disastrous to him. A detachment under St. Leger was turned back by the garrison of Fort Stanwix and by the militia of the Mohawk Valley under General Herkimer. Another detachment was defeated by the New Englanders, led by Stark, at Bennington, while Burgoyne was himself surrounded and captured, with his army, at Saratoga. The American commander was General Horatio Gates; but to Philip Schuyler and Benedict Arnold historians give most credit for this achievement. Clinton, on his end of the line, accomplished little.

<small>Burgoyne's surrender (1777).</small>

General Howe had better fortune. Placing his troops on transports, he carried them by water to the head of Chesapeake Bay, and approached Philadelphia from the south. Washington met him at Brandywine Creek, and was compelled to retire. Howe then occupied Philadelphia, and maintained himself there, although a portion of his army was surprised by Washington at Germantown. The Americans then retired to Valley Forge, a strong position on the Schuylkill. There they suffered terrible privations. But there they were drilled by Steuben and his under-officers till in efficiency the "continental line" became superior to its opponents.

The principal result, however, of the campaign of 1777 was the alliance between France and the Americans. The present time seemed to the French a good opportunity to deal a great blow at England's fast-growing colonial empire, and in this way to avenge the humiliations of the Peace of 1763. At first it seemed so doubtful whether the colonists could keep up their resistance that France was afraid openly to take their side. But the surprise at Trenton and the capture of Burgoyne put a wholly new face on the war. *The French alliance (1778).*

The French alliance caused great excitement in England. Chatham proposed to withdraw the troops from the colonies, win back the affections of the colonists, and oppose a united front to the power of France. Chatham was the only man who could have carried out this scheme. But the king refused to appoint him prime minister, though quite willing to consent to his taking office under Lord North, which of course Chatham could not do. Lord North, on his part, brought forward a plan for reconciliation, by which all the demands of the colonists, except independence, were to be granted. But this, like the former plans, came just too late. Chatham did not live to see the defeat of the English by the French and their American allies. While making a speech to arouse the spirits of the peers, he overtaxed his strength, and a few days later died. He was given a national funeral and a monument in Westminster Abbey.

The principal event in the campaign of 1778 was the evacuation of Philadelphia by the British. While marching across the Jerseys to New York, their rear was attacked by the Americans *Monmouth (1778).*

at Monmouth. Owing, however, to the treasonable conduct of General Charles Lee, the attempt was a failure.

In 1779 neither side attempted much in America. In England, however, the struggle was hot and fierce. General Burgoyne and General Howe were members of the House of Commons, and they endeavored to lay all the blame for their non-success on the shoulders of the ministry. In this attack they were assisted by Admiral Keppel, who, with a large fleet, had done absolutely nothing. Spain now joined France against England, and the Irish also bestirred themselves and demanded better treatment. In the face of all these difficulties Lord North wished to resign; but the king prevailed on him to remain in office for a while longer. The Opposition now adopted a new party cry. For years the Whig ministers — Sir Robert Walpole and the Pelhams — had maintained their power by bribery and corruption, and the Whigs had then seen nothing wrong in the system. Now, however, the king was using the same means to keep an obedient ministry in office, and to keep his opponents out. All the evils of government by corruption became at once apparent to the Whigs. They put themselves forward as the advocates of a more economical administration. They also advocated keeping government contractors out of the House of Commons.

In 1778 some of the laws against the English Roman Catholics had been modified or repealed. This was disagreeable to many Englishmen, and in 1780, at the head of a mob of sixty thousand persons, Lord George Gordon carried to Parliament a petition against the Catholics. For the next few

Lord George Gordon Riots (1780).

days London was at the mercy of the rioters. Houses were destroyed, shops broken open and plundered. At length the king took the matter into his own hands, and the mob was dispersed. Dickens's novel, "Barnaby Rudge," gives a vivid picture of all this excitement.

In 1779 Savannah and Georgia were taken by the British, and, in 1780, Sir Henry Clinton again came south, and in May captured Charleston. He, however, returned soon after to New York, to watch the movements of a French fleet which reached Newport in the summer of 1780. Cornwallis, Clinton's successor in the South, defeated General Gates in a battle near Camden, and to all appearance put an end to resistance in the Southern colonies. But not long after, a force of hardy pioneers from beyond the mountains captured an important detachment at King's Mountain, and in December, 1780, General Nathanael Greene took the principal charge of the campaign. The British, in January, 1781, under Cornwallis's lieutenant, Colonel Tarleton, were defeated at the Cowpens, and in a few weeks, after much manœuvring, the two main armies came together at Guilford Court-House. At the end of the contest Cornwallis retained the field of battle, but his losses had been so great in men and stores that he was compelled to retire to Wilmington. Thus Greene had won the campaign. The interior of North Carolina was clear of the enemy, and he marched to South Carolina. By the autumn of 1781 the British forces there were also withdrawn to the seaboard. Cornwallis marched north from Wilmington into Virginia, and Washington sent Lafayette with the light troops of the Continental line to watch him. Both sides ere long went into camp for the winter, Cornwallis at Yorktown, and Lafayette at Malvern Hill, and later at Williamsburg. In the summer of 1780 Marquis Rochambeau had arrived at Newport with a strong force of French veteran soldiers; but before the ships, which brought this army from France, could get away, the English fleet appeared, and blockaded them in the harbor of Newport. The French army was compelled to wait at Newport to protect the fleet, and for a year was practically useless. In September, Washington and Rochambeau held a conference. While Washington was away from his army, Benedict Arnold, who had taken offence at his treatment at Saratoga, formed a plan to surrender the strong forts at West Point, with its garrison and stores, to the British. Major André, a young officer of Clinton's army, came to West Point to conclude arrangements with Arnold.

COSTUMES OF PERSONS OF QUALITY, ABOUT 1783.

Arnold's treason (1780).

In disguise, and with compromising papers in his boots, he was captured by a party of Americans. Arnold escaped, but Washington was compelled to treat André as a spy, and as a spy he was hanged.

During the summer of 1781 it became known to Washington and Rochambeau that a powerful French fleet under Comte de Grasse would arrive at the mouth of Chesapeake Bay early in September. It was decided to march the allied army from Newport and New York to Virginia, to join Lafayette and any French troops De Grasse might bring, and, while the French fleet should prevent Clinton from reinforcing Cornwallis, to capture him and his army. This programme was carried out to the letter. The French ships at Newport slipped out of the harbor, and reached the Chesapeake safely. De Grasse and the allied armies arrived in good time to come together. De Grasse fought a battle with the English fleet; but while neither side was victorious, all the advantages of victory were gained by the allies, as the English fleet was obliged to return to New York for the purpose of refitting before it again put to sea. Cornwallis surrendered Yorktown, with its defenders, Oct. 19, 1781. This was the last important conflict between the English and the Americans. But the war was still vigorously prosecuted against the allies of the colonies.

Capture of Yorktown (1781).

The royal disaster at Yorktown not only settled the question whether America should be free, but it also decided the fate of the North ministry. Lord George Germaine, the Colonial Secretary, was the first to resign. He had had the principal direction of the war in America, and to his mis-

End of the North Ministry (1781).

management the failure of the British armies was largely due. He was now raised to the peerage as Lord Sackville. As he had been dismissed from the army during the Seven Years' War for disobedience to orders, many peers objected to his sitting in the House of Lords; but they could do nothing to prevent it. The Opposition in the Commons now rapidly acquired strength. The 20th of March, 1782, was selected for a great attack on the Government. But when that day came, Lord North seized a chance to speak, and announced the resignation of the ministry; and the House, as was its custom, adjourned, to give the Opposition leaders time to talk over their future plans. It was a harsh, wet night, and the members, expecting a long debate, had sent their carriages away. Lord North had retained his, and stepping into it, he remarked, with a smile, "You see, gentlemen, the advantage of being in the secret." In fact, this unbroken good nature was Lord North's most noteworthy characteristic. He even used to fall into a gentle slumber while Fox and Burke were attacking him and his Government.

The Marquis of Rockingham and the Whigs now took office. Charles James Fox and Lord Shelburne were the two Secretaries of State and the real leaders of the Government, in which Lord Camden, Admiral Keppel, and Edmund Burke had places. Lord Chancellor Thurlow alone represented the king. The ministry had three important questions to settle, — the conclusion of peace, the reform of the home administration, and the pacification of Ireland. The Irish question will be best considered later in connection with the union. To the Opposition

The Rockingham Ministry (1782).

in power the project of a reform of the administration in the direction of purity and economy seemed less desirable than it had seemed while others were enjoying the spoils. It was desirable, however, at least to seem to carry out their former promises. A bill was

EDMUND BURKE: FROM A PAINTING BY REYNOLDS IN THE NATIONAL PORTRAIT GALLERY

passed abolishing many abuses, though not till the Whigs had secured a good deal of spoil for themselves. Edmund Burke alone consistently refused to share in the general distribution.

The Rockingham ministry had come into power mainly on account of the disasters in America. Peace with America was their policy. They believed that the Americans might be detached from the French as the price of independence, provided ample concessions in the way of boundaries were made in return. Now it so happened that John Jay, himself of French descent, and John Adams, two of the American commissioners to negotiate a treaty of peace, distrusted the French Government. They believed that France was using the United States as a tool for her own ends, and was really opposed to the extension of the new state as far as the Mississippi River. It is probable that Jay was right in his belief; but for a long time the third commissioner, Benjamin Franklin, refused to believe him. The treaty of alliance provided that neither party should make peace without the other, and the instructions to the American commissioners ordered them to act in conjunction with the French Government. Finally, however, Jay prevailed. The commissioners broke their instructions, and, without the knowledge of the French Government, concluded an agreement, or set of articles, which should be made into a treaty whenever France and England should make peace. In this way the United States became an independent nation, with boundaries extending as far as the Mississippi on the west, and as far south as the thirty-first parallel of latitude. Before the treaty was actually concluded, Rockingham died, and Fox, who had quarrelled with Shelburne, withdrew from the Government with his friends. Shelburne became Prime Minister, and had for his Chancellor of the Exchequer a young man of twenty-three, — William Pitt, — the younger son of the Earl of Chatham.

Independence acknowledged (1782).

CONCLUSION OF THE WAR.

After the disaster at Yorktown, England was everywhere successful. Gibraltar, which the Spaniards and French had been besieging since 1779, was reinforced, and supplied with provisions in 1782. In the same year Admiral Rodney defeated, with great loss, the Comte de Grasse off Martinique. These two disasters made France and Spain willing to make peace on reasonable terms, and in September, 1783, the treaties were signed at Versailles and Paris. In the course of the war Spain had overrun the Floridas, and at the peace she retained all of North America south of the United States, as well as Louisiana, west of the Mississippi River.

Conclusion of the War (1783).

ROYAL ARMS, AS BORNE FROM 1801 TO 1816: THE HANOVERIAN SCUTCHEON, SURMOUNTED BY AN ELECTORAL BONNET.

CHAPTER XXXIV.

GEORGE III.

1760-1820.

PART II. 1783-1820.

FOR years Charles James Fox and Lord North had sat on opposite sides of the House of Commons, and had abused each other in the most outrageous fashion. They now joined hands, or coalesced, to turn Shelburne out of office, and put themselves in. Between them they possessed a large majority in the House of Commons. In 1783 Shelburne resigned, and North and Fox came in. The king was furiously indignant. He hated Fox, and did not wish to have anything to do with him. But he was enraged above all at the ingratitude of Lord North, for whom he had done so much. At first the king declared he would go to Hanover. But sober second thought convinced him it would be better to endure Fox and North for a while till something should turn up which would bring about their downfall. He did not have long to wait.

The "Coalition" (1783).

The English East India Company had made itself master of a large part of India. The Company was first of all a business venture, and must pay dividends to its stockholders. The hostility of the French, and the desire to extend the Company's boundaries, gave rise to incessant wars,

Fox's India Bill (1783)

which cost enormous sums of money. The Governor-general was now Warren Hastings. To meet the demands for funds in India and in England he had resorted to many tyrannical measures, and great hardship and oppression to the natives had resulted. It was perfectly plain that this state of things could not be allowed to exist indefinitely. Fox and Burke drew up a bill for the better government of India, by which the political control of the country was placed under the Home Government. This was all very well, except that Fox so arranged matters that the appointment to the offices in India would be in his hands, or in those of his political friends, even if he ceased to be in the ministry. This of course aroused great opposition. The king saw his chance, and when the bill came to the Lords, declared he should regard any peer who voted for it as his personal enemy. The measure was defeated, and the king sent an under-officer to tell North and Fox that they were dismissed. He chose as his new Prime Minister William Pitt, now twenty-four years of age.

While still a youth in appearance, William Pitt, as a political leader and debater in the House of Commons, had no equal. As a war minister and orator he was inferior to his father; in all else he was his superior. Besides the small party called the "King's Friends," and those few members who remained true to his father's principles, William Pitt had no adherents in the Commons. In fact, almost all his companions in the ministry were members of the House of Peers. Alone, therefore, he faced the combined oratory of Fox, Burke, Sheridan, and Lord North. But the lack of principle

William Pitt, Prime Minister (1783-1801).

shown by Fox and North in making their coalition had disgusted a great many people. One by one their adherents went over to the side of Pitt and the king, till the majority against him was reduced to one. Then Parliament was dissolved. In the general election which followed, one hundred and sixty of Fox's friends ("Fox's Martyrs," they were called) lost their seats. Pitt had a great majority, and it was full half a century before the Whig party recovered from the effects of this blow.

Secure now of a majority, Pitt brought in a new India Bill, establishing a Board of Control resident in England, and consisting of members of the ministry, as the supreme governing body. The business management of the Company was left to its directors. This system of "double government" lasted till 1858.

Pitt's India Bill (1784).

PITT SPEAKING IN THE HOUSE OF COMMONS; FROM HUCKEL'S PAINTING IN THE NATIONAL PORTRAIT GALLERY.

The leading feature of the first half of Pitt's long ministry was his financial policy. He was a friend and disciple of Adam Smith, and believed in international friendliness in matters of business. For centuries England and France had been injuring each other's trade as much as possible. It seemed to Pitt best that the two countries should buy of one another what each country could best produce. A commercial treaty between them was made. Pitt wished to extend the same principle by establishing freedom of trade between Ireland and England. But English manufacturers were too much afraid of Irish competition, and the scheme fell through. Pitt also thought that England should try to pay her national debt, and he planned a Sinking Fund by which this would be accomplished in time. For a while this scheme worked well; but in the great wars which soon followed, all thought of paying the debt was for a time abandoned, and the money already saved for the purpose was used to prosecute the war. Another scheme that Pitt had much at heart was a reform of the representation in the House of Commons. But the time had not yet come for this, and the plan failed. *Pitt's financial policy.*

In 1785 Warren Hastings returned home from India. While drawing up their India Bill, Fox and Burke had come across acts that seemed like extortion and tyranny on the part of Hastings. They now presented Articles of Impeachment; and as Pitt refused to interfere in the matter, Hastings was impeached. The trial began before the Peers in 1788, and continued at intervals for seven years. Hastings was finally acquitted. *Trial of Warren Hastings (1788).*

In 1788 the king again became insane. The Prince of Wales was the boon companion of Fox, who now proposed that the prince should, of his own authority, assume the title of regent, with full power. Of course this meant the overthrow of *The regency struggle (1788).*

Pitt. It happened that Pitt and the doctors regarded the king's attack as temporary. Pitt thought it would be more agreeable to the king when he re-

HEAD-DRESS OF A LADY (MRS. ABINGTON), ABOUT 1778: FROM THE "EUROPEAN MAGAZINE."

covered to find affairs as little changed as possible. He therefore proposed to limit the powers of the regent, at least until the king should become, in the opinion of the doctors, permanently insane. To this

Fox would not listen, and while the two sides were still debating, the king recovered, and Pitt was firmer than ever in his office.

In 1789 began the great social upheaval in France known as the French Revolution. At first most Englishmen sympathized with the movement. But when it became apparent that the revolutionary leaders were aiming to establish a democratic form of government, many Englishmen took alarm. At the same time societies for political reform sprang up in England. Edmund Burke became the leader of those opposed to change. He wrote a book called "Reflections on the French Revolution." In this book he enlarged on the democratic tendencies of the French Revolution, and called the Frenchmen "the ablest architects of ruin that have hitherto existed in the world." *The French Revolution.*

For four years Pitt maintained a policy of non-intervention. But in 1792 France offered aid to all nations who would overthrow their rulers. In 1793 those who sympathized with the excesses in France grew more outspoken in England. Pitt, now himself alarmed, called out the militia, and carried an Act through Parliament giving the Government control of the movements of aliens, or strangers, visiting England. France now declared war on England, although she was even then at war with nearly all western Europe. At the time, Pitt's attitude of repression and opposition was greatly applauded. But some historical writers now regard it as a very great political blunder. *France declares war against England (1793).*

During the early years of this war Pitt contented himself with hiring Austria and Prussia to fight England's battles on the land. He also helped the royalists to return to France to stir up disaffection and rebellions against the central government at Paris. Of course the English navy was not idle. As the war went on, Pitt's home policy became more and more repressive. The most insignificant publications and disturbances were treated as the beginnings of revolution. But there seems to have been no real danger, although there was much suffering among the working-people, and although the king was more than once insulted in the streets. Then followed a great scarcity of money in England. Much was sent abroad by the Government, and much was hoarded at home by careful people. At length the cash in the Bank of England was so diminished that the Government ordered it to suspend specie payments, and they were not resumed till 1819.

Pitt's policy.

Specie payments suspended (1797).

In this year, 1797, two mutinies broke out in the fleet,— one at Spithead, by the Isle of Wight, the other at the Nore, in the Thames. The sailors were soon brought to terms, and many of their demands granted. A few months later some of these very seamen won the battle of Camperdown over the Dutch and French fleet.

Mutinies in the fleet (1797).

France was now at peace with all the rest of Europe, and as she could not, owing to this disaster at Camperdown, attack England directly, she sent an army to seize Egypt, which lies on the road to England's possessions in India. The leader of this invasion was Napoleon Bonaparte. On his way to Egypt he seized the island of Malta, which up to that time had been in the hands of the Knights of Malta. All this time there was in the Mediterranean a great

Invasion of Egypt.

English fleet commanded by Admiral Nelson; but he did not find Napoleon's fleet till the French general had been on shore about two weeks. Nelson attacked it as it lay at anchor in Aboukir Bay, and captured or destroyed all but two of the French ships. The French army never left Egypt. But in 1799 Napoleon returned home, and made himself ruler of France. We must now turn to Ireland; for the French now helped the Irish against England, as formerly they had assisted the Scots. *Battle of the Nile (1798).*

The Irish Roman Catholics formed the great mass of the population of Ireland, but they were ruled over by the small minority of English and Scottish Protestants. Successive conquests had given nearly all the power to the Protestants. They regarded the Irish Catholics as a half-barbarized and degraded race, much as some of our ancestors in this country regarded the negro. An Irish Roman Catholic could not marry a Protestant. He could not serve on a grand jury, practise law, or act as a magistrate. He was not allowed to carry arms, and it was against the law for him to educate his children through Roman Catholic teachers. He was compelled to pay taxes for the support of the Established Protestant Church, which he detested. And finally he could neither sit in any Parliament nor vote for a member of any Parliament. *Ireland in the eighteenth century.*

During the American Revolution the English troops previously stationed in Ireland were sent to America, and an association of Protestant Volunteers was formed to preserve the peace in Ireland. In 1779, under the lead of Henry Grattan, the Volunteers turned against the Government, and some *The Volunteers (1779).*

modifications of the trade laws were made. In 1782 the Catholics joined the Protestants in urging their demands, and the Rockingham ministry so far yielded as to give up the right of the British Parliament to legislate for Ireland.

The ideas of equality forced on the world by the French Revolution spread to Ireland, and in 1789 a great association of Catholic and Protestant Irishmen — The United Irishmen — was formed. In 1792 and 1793 two Acts were passed, repealing the more odious laws against the Catholics, and even allowing them to vote for members of the Irish Parliament. But as no Catholic could sit in that Parliament, this last right really amounted to little. Later a bill was introduced to allow Catholics to sit in Parliament. But the king became convinced that if he assented to this he would violate his coronation oath, which obliges him to maintain the Protestant Church as established by law. The plan was abandoned.

The Society of the United Irishmen.

The Irish leaders now thought the only way to secure their rights lay in complete separation from Great Britain. To counteract them the Protestants formed a secret society, calling themselves Orangemen, in memory of William of Orange. The discontented Catholics appealed for aid to the French, and in 1796 a French fleet anchored off the Irish coast. A storm arose, and no Irish appeared, and the fleet returned to France. When the Frenchmen were gone, the Irish rose in various places. The rebellion was soon put down with much vigor and great cruelty by General Lake. The only conflict worthy the name of battle was at Vinegar Hill, in 1798. In 1799 the French decided to invade England, and also

Rebellion (1796–1798).

attack her on her weak side in Ireland. But the French and Spanish fleets were thoroughly beaten by the English, off Cape St. Vincent, and nothing came of this attempt.

Lord Cornwallis now became Lord Lieutenant, or Governor, of Ireland. He had for his secretary Lord Castlereagh, a young Irish Protestant. They soon decided that the only cure for Irish troubles was a union with England, like the union made with Scotland in the early part of the century. Pitt had already made up his mind that this would be the best policy. So Cornwallis and Castlereagh secured a majority of the Irish Parliament to vote its dissolution. In 1800 the Act of Union passed the Parliaments of Great Britain and Ireland. By this Act Ireland was to send one hundred commoners to the House of Commons of the United Kingdom; while the Irish peerage was to be represented in the House of Lords by twenty-eight Irish peers, elected for life. *The Union (1801).*

The Irish Catholics had not opposed the Union, probably because they expected Catholics would be allowed to sit in the Parliament of the United Kingdom. What promises Pitt and Cornwallis may have made is not known. But Pitt, when he found that the king would not permit any concessions to be made to the Catholics, felt obliged to resign. In fact, the Irish Catholics gained nothing by the Union. Their discontent resulted in Emmett's Rebellion in 1803. It was easily put down, and Emmett was hanged. *Emmett's Rebellion (1803).*

Pitt was followed by Addington, whose principal recommendation for office was the favor of the king. By this time Napoleon had conquered most of western Europe, while the English had been successful wherever their navy could be used to advantage. There seemed to be no way of attacking each other directly, and in 1802 peace was made at Amiens.

Peace of Amiens.

This peace, however, did not last long. Neither party trusted the other, and neither France nor England acted in perfect good faith. In addition, England furnished a refuge to Frenchmen hostile to Napoleon, and from London they attacked him in the newspapers with great violence. So in 1803 the war began anew. It lasted till 1815, and was waged by England and her allies against the ambitious designs of Napoleon, who took the title of Emperor of the French.

War renewed (1803).

Napoleon's first idea was to invade England, and he made great preparations to embark his army at Boulogne. He had control of the fleets of France, Holland, and Spain, and determined to combine them against the English fleet, and thus make the passage for his army to England secure. But now once more the English showed their great superiority on the water. Admiral Nelson caught the French and Spanish fleet off Cape Trafalgar. He hoisted at his masthead his famous signals, which read, "England expects every man to do his duty!" The allied fleet numbered thirty-three line-of-battle ships, and seven smaller vessels. Nelson had with him but twenty-seven ships. Of those forty ships of the allies only eight ever reached a friendly port. It was only on the sea, however, that the French were defeated. On the land they were everywhere victorious. The Austrians joining the English, Napoleon captured one Austrian

Trafalgar (1805).

army at Ulm, in October, and overthrew a combined army of Austrians and Russians at Austerlitz on December 2d, 1805.

Meantime William Pitt had again become Prime Minister. His health had always been poor, and these disasters to England's allies, coupled with the attacks of the Opposition at home, proved too great a burden. In January, 1806, he died. A ministry was now formed, comprising men of all parties; hence it was called the ministry of "All the Talents." Lord Grenville and Mr. Fox were its leading members. Fox was Foreign Secretary. He had always maintained that if Napoleon were treated fairly, he would act honestly in return In a short time he was undeceived; and, worn out by care and dissipation, he followed Pitt to the grave. Side by side the two are buried in Westminster Abbey.

Pitt's Second Ministry (1804-1806).

All the Talents (1806-1807).

> "The mighty chiefs sleep side by side.
> Drop upon Fox's grave the tear,
> 'T will trickle to his rival's bier;
> O'er Pitt's the mournful requiem sound,
> And Fox's shall the notes rebound."

Left to himself, Lord Grenville tried to modify the laws against the Catholics' serving in the army, and was dismissed by the king. A Tory ministry was then formed, which lasted, with some changes, till 1827. Mr. Spencer Perceval was at first the real head of this Government, though for a time he only held the office of Chancellor of the Exchequer. The two most remarkable members were Mr. George Canning and Lord Castlereagh, Secretaries for Foreign Affairs and War.

Tory ministry (1807-1827).

278 GEORGE III. [1809.

While these changes had been taking place in England, Napoleon had in turn defeated the Prussians, the Russians, and the Austrians. In fact the Czar of Russia became for a while the ally of Napoleon, who, to strengthen his position, married a daughter of the Emperor of Austria. He

Napoleon's successes

LORD NELSON: FROM THE PICTURE BY ABBOTT IN THE NATIONAL PORTRAIT GALLERY.

was now master of Europe, with the exception of Spain and England. He again turned his attention to the invasion of the latter country. During all this time the Danes had preserved a good-sized and well-manned fleet. Napoleon resolved to add these vessels to those he still controlled, and with their aid attack England. But Canning heard of Napoleon's plans, and sent an English fleet to Copenhagen which seized the Danish fleet and brought it to England. Thus once again all fears of invasion were removed.

Napoleon then conquered Spain, and tried to make his brother king of that country. But the Spaniards were a high-spirited people, and resisted this foreign domination. The English at first sent the Spaniards money and arms, and then an army to help them. But these early efforts produced little permanent result. In 1809, too, the English tried to seize Antwerp, and failed most ignominiously. This same year, however, a considerable force of soldiers was sent to Portugal, and the Peninsular War really began. The commander of the English army was Sir Arthur Wellesley. He had already done good service in Portugal, and at a still earlier day had achieved great distinction in India, where he had won, against great odds, the battles of Argaum and Assaye. In a short time he drove the French from Portugal, and, entering Spain, beat them at Talavera. For this victory he was raised to the peerage as Lord Wellington of Talavera. *The Spanish resistance. Arthur Wellesley, Duke of Wellington.*

Before long he was compelled to retire to Lisbon, near which town, at Torres Vedras, he had constructed great works to shelter his army. On his retreat he destroyed or carried away every eatable thing; and when the French reached Torres Vedras, they could not attack him, and retreated back to Spain again, to avoid being starved. Many *The Peninsular War (1809–1814).*

English writers regard this as the turning-point of the war, and say that the lesson taught by Wellington at Torres Vedras saved Europe. At all events, from this time on, Napoleon was attacked, first on this side, and then on that. We cannot follow Wellington's campaigns

THE DUKE OF WELLINGTON : FROM A BUST BY FRANCIS
IN THE NATIONAL PORTRAIT GALLERY.

in detail. For years the war went on with varying fortune. At last, in 1813, Wellington overwhelmed the French at Vittoria, and, forcing them north over the Pyrenees, compelled their surrender at Toulouse in 1814.

But on the day of this surrender Napoleon was no longer Emperor. In 1812 he quarrelled with the Czar, and invaded Russia. Of his great army a mere fraction returned to France. The Prussians and Austrians joined the Russians. Napoleon, defeated at Leipzig, retreated from Germany. The allies pressed on, while Wellington entered France from the south, and Napoleon abdicated. He was allowed to retire to the little island of Elba. Louis XVI.'s brother became king of France as Louis XVIII., and the allies held a great Congress at Vienna to undo, if possible, the work of the French Revolution and Napoleon. Lord Castlereagh and Wellington, now become Duke of Wellington, represented England at this meeting. *Napoleon's downfall.*

While all this had been going on in Europe, England had become involved in a war with the United States. As one means of injuring Napoleon, the English Government had issued a proclamation, or Order in Council, as it was called, declaring all the ports of Europe, from Brest to the Elbe, closed or blockaded to commerce. Napoleon had replied with the Berlin Decree, declaring Great Britain blockaded. Now there was some excuse for this first Order in Council, as the English were actually blockading the ports of France and Holland. But Napoleon could not keep a French fleet on the sea, and, what was still more laughable, at this very moment when he declared the commerce of England at an end, his own soldiers were wearing clothes made in England. Orders in Council and Decrees now followed in quick succession. It happened that the only neutral nation possessing any ships at that time was the United States, and these decrees ruined many American shipowners. Then, too, there was another cause of disagreement with England; for English cruisers were in the habit of stopping Amer- *War of 1812 with the United States.*

ican ships, and seizing any British seamen they found on board. As British and American seamen looked much alike, many Americans were seized, and much irritation was aroused. The war broke out in 1812, and lasted till 1814, when it was concluded by a treaty made at Ghent. The principal result of the war for America was the loss of the fishery rights the Americans enjoyed under the treaty of 1783. As for England, the war diverted resources soon to be sorely needed elsewhere.

The allies did not get on very smoothly in their discussions at Vienna, nor did Louis XVIII. win the good will of the French people. In March, 1815, Napoleon landed on the southern coast of France. All the troops sent to oppose him went over to his side, and he reached Paris without any trouble, and once more ruled France as Emperor. The allies dissolved the Congress, and determined to crush Napoleon at once, before he could consolidate his power.

Napoleon's return (1815).

The Duke of Wellington (the "Iron Duke," as his soldiers called him) took command of the English and Belgians in Belgium, while a strong Prussian army under Marshal Blücher marched to his aid. The Russians and Austrians entered France from the east. Napoleon determined to attack Wellington and Blücher before they could unite. He defeated the Prussians at Ligny, and then marched to Waterloo, and attacked Wellington on June 18th, 1815. For hours the English maintained their ground, even after the Belgians had fled. At length, in the early evening, the Prussians appeared. They attacked the French with vigor, and in a short time all was over. Napoleon fled to Paris; thence to the seaboard, where he tried to

Waterloo, June 18th, 1815.

embark for America. That plan failing, he surrendered himself to the English. To their keeping he was confided by Europe. For six years, till his death, in 1821, he lived on the island of St. Helena, strictly guarded.

The next five years were marked by great distress and suffering in England. During the war Englishmen had been obliged to rely upon England alone for food. The price of meat doubled, and that of breadstuffs increased threefold. This great rise led to undue extension of grain-raising, and to a great rise of rents. At the return of peace prices of breadstuffs fell nearly one-half. Great numbers of farmers were ruined. The demand for labor in the fields declined, and there was great suffering throughout the farming districts. The landowners were represented in Parliament, however, and a law was passed forbidding the importation of wheat till the price of English grown wheat had reached a high figure. This helped the farmers, but increased the distress of the manufacturing population. *Agricultural distress.* *Corn Law of 1815.*

During the years of war great inventions were made in the arts, and steam began to be used to drive machinery in large factories. Manufacturing by hand was still practised, and the hand-workers saw with dismay a machine set going in their neighborhood, capable of making as much in one day as all the workers of the village could make in a month. The workingmen thought the trouble was with the new inventions, and bands of them went about breaking machinery. They were called Luddites, from a crazy lad, John Ludd, who set the evil example. The working-men now fell under the influence of agitators. In 1816 a meeting was held on Spa Fields, in *Commercial depression.* *The Luddites.*

London, to bring about the seizure of London Tower, then, and now, used as a storehouse for arms. Other meetings followed, and the Government on its part adopted very severe measures to prevent disturbances.

GEORGE III. IN OLD AGE: FROM TURNER'S MEZZOTINT.

The most famous of these meetings was held at Manchester in 1819. The people assembled to listen to Mr. "Orator" Hunt, a popular speaker. The authorities of the town ordered the officers to arrest him while speaking. Some militiamen were sent to help the officers. The crowd was so great that these few men could do nothing. Now thoroughly

The Manchester Massacre (1819).

alarmed, the magistrates ordered a body of cavalry to disperse the mob. The cavalry charged with drawn sabres, striking right and left. The crowd became panic-stricken, and a terrible scene resulted. How many were killed and wounded will never be known. The meeting was held on St. Peter's Fields, and the massacre is known as the "Manchester Massacre," or "Peterloo."

The massacre, however, gave new strength to the ministry, and the Six Acts were passed, placing almost unlimited power to deal with disturbance in the hands of the Government. A few months later, in the beginning of 1820, King George III. died. Since 1810 he had been hopelessly insane, and for the last few years he had been blind also. His son, the Prince of Wales, had governed for him as Prince Regent; he now became king as George IV. The Tory ministry which had followed "All the Talents" was still in power, though Perceval had been murdered by a lunatic in 1812. Lord Liverpool succeeded him, and remained Prime Minister till his death, in 1827. Canning and Castlereagh had quarrelled in 1809, and had both resigned. In 1812, however, Castlereagh returned to office as Foreign Secretary.

<small>The Six Acts (1819).</small>

<small>The Regency (1810–1820).</small>

CHAPTER XXXV.

GEORGE IV.

1820-1830.

<small>Queen Caroline.</small>
THE Prince Regent, now become king, was the last of the "Four Georges," and the worst. He seems to have had no redeeming quality either as man or ruler. His first effort as king was to get rid of his wife, Caroline of Brunswick. His father had compelled him to marry her as a condition of paying his debts. Queen Caroline was by no means a high-minded woman, but George IV. was so detested that popular sympathy was on her side. A Bill of Pains and Penalties to divorce the queen and to deprive her of her rights was introduced into Parliament, but popular feeling was too strong, and the plan was abandoned. Queen Caroline was refused her proper place at the coronation, however, and died of a broken heart.

In 1822 Lord Castlereagh died, and George Canning again became Foreign Secretary. Castlereagh had sympathized with the despotic attempts of the European monarchs to revive the old state of things in their countries, and to resist all future attempts at revolution. Canning was liberal, and at once England's foreign policy underwent a complete change. He could not effect much on the continent of Europe, as there the military power of the kings was supreme. No sooner would a revolution break out in one state than all the neighboring kings would send their armies and put the rising down. In 1820-25 the Spanish American colonists, in common with the people of the mother-country, rebelled. The rising in Spain was put down by France. It was then decided to send over an army to crush the rebellion in the colonies. But the English fleet was supreme on the water. Canning declared that Spain might put down the rebels if she were able, but that neither France nor any other power should help her. England and the United States then joined in declaring to the world that the repressive systems then employed in the Old World should not be extended to America. This, with other declarations, forms what is called the "Monroe Doctrine." Of course England was glad to see Spanish America free, as in this way new markets would be open to her commerce; but, as far as Canning, at least, was concerned, a love of freedom was probably the leading motive for the action of the English Government.

In 1827 Lord Liverpool died, and Canning became Prime Minister. The Conservative members of the ministry, Wellington, Lord Chancellor Eldon, Robert Peel, and some others, at once resigned. They and their adherents then attacked Canning so fiercely that he was unable to bear the strain, and died. For a few months his friends continued in office, and then the Duke of Wellington became Prime Minister. Robert Peel, however, was the real leader in this ministry, which lasted till 1830.

Wellington-Peel ministry (1828-1830).

George Canning was Prime Minister for only a few months; but his ministry none the less marks the downfall of the repressive system forced on England by the excesses of the French Revolution. From 1827 dates the period of social and constitutional reform which has lasted to our own time. Curiously enough, two of the greatest reforms of this whole epoch are associated with Wellington and Peel, the leaders of the conservative Tories. In his earlier years Peel had been

CANNING: FROM STEWARDSON'S PORTRAIT.

Secretary for Ireland. He had introduced the constabulary, or rural police, and had so energetically upheld the rights of the Protestants as to earn the title of "Orange Peel." There was in Ireland a leader called Daniel O'Connell, a lawyer, a few years older than Peel. Under his guidance was formed a society called the Catholic Association. Before long the Association became in some parts of Ireland more powerful than the

English Government; and at a time when the Government could not collect the church tax, the Association collected what was called the Catholic rent, or annual contribution to carry on the agitation for Catholic relief. Canning favored the Catholic claims, and carried a bill for their relief through the House of Commons, which was thrown out by the Lords. At the same time a law was passed suppressing the Catholic Association. O'Connell obeyed the law, while carrying on the organization by other means.

In 1828 O'Connell discovered a new way of showing the Catholic power. In Ireland all freeholders, or leaseholders for a long term of years, to the extent of two pounds, or forty shillings, could vote for Members of Parliament. It so happened that the landlords in some parts of Ireland had broken up their estates into forty-shilling "freeholds," to increase their political influence. O'Connell now took advantage of this, and caused himself to be elected to Parliament for County Clare. Of course he could not take his seat; but the power of the great agitator was apparent. Thirty thousand Irish peasants assembled at Ennis. Not a disturbance of any kind occurred, and the only drunken man in the place was O'Connell's coachman, who happened to be an English Protestant. This meeting convinced both Wellington and Peel that something must be done; and in 1829 the Catholic Relief Act was passed. By it Catholics might sit in Parliament on taking an oath to support the state and not to injure the Established Church. The first Catholic to enter Parliament was the Duke of Norfolk, premier peer of England, whose family name of Howard recalls the defeat of the Armada and so much that is

Catholic Emancipation.

memorable in English history. Just before this Act was passed, a bill for the relief of Protestant Dissenters had become law, so that now all Christian subjects of the English Crown residing in the United Kingdom enjoyed equal civil rights, except in a very few trifling instances. At the same time the Irish franchise was raised from forty shillings, or two pounds, to ten pounds. Thus at the very time the Catholics were admitted to Parliament, the right to vote was taken away from the great mass of Catholics in Ireland. The next year George IV. died, and was succeeded by his brother, Duke of Clarence, as William IV.

ROYAL ARMS, FROM 1816 TO 1837: THE HANOVERIAN SCUTCHEON, SURMOUNTED BY A ROYAL CROWN.

CHAPTER XXXVI.

WILLIAM IV.

1830-1837.

WILLIAM IV. had been brought up in the navy. He resembled the bold, bluff admiral of the olden time. People called him the Sailor King, and trusted and liked him. It was fortunate that he was a popular man, with a good deal of common sense, though he had little of good breeding. England was, in fact, on the eve of a great revolution. The movement was guided wisely and well, and the nation took a very great step forward. Had an attempt been made to suppress the revolution, no one knows what might have happened. *The new king.*

There was vast discontent and misery. Manufacturing towns had doubled and trebled in population in fifteen years, yet nothing was done to help the people who increased England's material prosperity. Parliament was in the hands of landowners, who seemed to think that the factory hands might starve, provided the price of English-grown grain were maintained. It was felt that the merchants and manufacturers should be more fully represented in Parliament, and there fight for the good of their working-people and of themselves. The condition of the representation in Parliament was, to an American, almost incredible. A large and prosperous town like Birmingham sent no member *Causes of discontent.*

to the House of Commons, while a ruined mound of earth showing where Old Sarum once stood, but now without a single human inhabitant, sent two members. These were the two extremes. But places whose inhabitants could be counted on one's fingers sent two

OLD SARUM: FROM AN ENGRAVING PUBLISHED IN 1843, SHOWING MOUND. (IT IS NOW OBSCURED BY TREES FROM THIS POINT OF VIEW.)

members apiece, while great centres of commercial and manufacturing life were not represented at all. Then, again, in towns where many substantial people lived, only a very few could vote. In other places all the voters were tenants of some great landowner, and must vote as he directed, or be turned out of their farms. These last boroughs were called "pocket boroughs," and some great noblemen possessed several of them. So it came to pass that a majority of the House of Commons was returned by a few hundred persons, mostly landowners; and many of them were members of the House of Lords. And this was not all; the right to sit in Parliament was a great honor, and many a rich man was willing to pay a large sum of money to a borough which would return him to Parliament. Some boroughs habitually sold the right to represent them. The nation, awaking to the fact that the House of Commons no longer represented England, was beginning to demand a change. While public feeling was in this state, the Duke of Wellington made a speech to the effect that the English constitution was perfection itself, and should not be changed at all. He was obliged to resign, and the Whigs, after nearly fifty years' exclusion from office, took control of the government.

Earl Grey was the new Prime Minister. For nearly half a century he had advocated reform, and now at last, at the very end of his life, he was to bring it about. The new Lord Chancellor was Henry Brougham, who was even more radical in his views than Earl Grey. The leader of the House of Commons was Lord Althorp, eldest son of Earl Spencer. He was no speaker, but was so honest and upright that men of all parties respected and trusted him. To Lord John Russell, a younger son of the Duke of Bedford, who held at the time a minor office, was given the task of bringing in the reform bill. Lord John Russell proposed to disfranchise the smaller boroughs, giving the seats thus gained to the larger towns and to the counties. He also proposed to make the voting qualification more uniform. When the names of the boroughs to be disfranchised were read, the members of those boroughs broke forth into shouts of loud laughter. Lord John Russell was supported by Mr. Thomas Bab-

The Grey ministry.

ington Macaulay (afterwards Lord Macaulay) and Mr. Stanley (afterwards Lord Stanley, and, still later, Earl Derby). Mr. Macaulay's speeches best show in many respects the arguments for reform. The Government was soon defeated on a minor point, and Parliament was dissolved. The new election was marked by much rioting and disorder. It resulted in a great majority for the reformers. Led by Sir Robert Peel, the Opposition opposed the second reform bill by all means within its power. It finally passed the Commons by a great majority. But the Lords were so hostile to reform that, foreseeing the defeat of the bill, Earl Grey resigned. The Duke of Wellington and Sir Robert Peel then tried to form a ministry. But they could not hope to face the great reform majority in the Commons, and Earl Grey returned to office, but only on one condition; namely, that the king should create enough peers to turn the hostile majority in the House of Lords into a majority favorable to the measure. This was not necessary, however; for when the Duke of Wellington became convinced of the earnestness of the king, he and enough other hostile peers left the House, and allowed the third reform bill, which had meantime been passed by the Commons, to pass the Lords also.

In this way the Reform Act of 1832 — the First Reform Act — became law. The Revolution of 1688 had transferred power from the Crown to the aristocracy. The Reform Act of 1832 transferred power from the aristocracy to the middle class, as it is called in England, consisting mainly of merchants and manufacturers. It was, therefore, the first step in the process which has changed aristocratic England of 1800 to the democratic England

The First Reform Act (1832).

of to-day. The House of Lords still remains, but it was shorn of all its real power when it became clear that the king and ministry could at any moment control it by creating a sufficient number of new peers to form, in connection with the minority, a new majority.

In 1833 the first Reformed Parliament met, and for the next few years reform after reform was accomplished. For centuries there had been no system of slavery in Great Britain. Slavery in its harshest forms still continued in some of the colonies; but up to 1833 the capitalists interested in its maintenance had prevented abolition. This was now decreed; but the emancipation was to extend over several years, and the Government agreed to pay the slave-owners nearly one hundred million dollars as compensation. Sir Fowell Buxton carried the final measure through the Commons, the chief English abolitionists having been Thomas Clarkson and William Wilberforce. The latter died just before the bill abolishing slavery became law, though not before the success of his life-work was assured. *Emancipation of slaves.*

While doing so much for the laborers in the colonies, Parliament could hardly refuse to do something for the laborers at home. In fact, the condition of an English factory operative was scarcely better than that of a West India slave. In 1833 a Factory Act was passed, mainly through the persistent efforts of Lord Ashley. After this no woman could legally be employed in a factory more than twelve hours a day; no person under eighteen years of age more than twelve hours; no person under thirteen more than eight hours; and very young children could not be employed at all. In 1847 the hours of all persons under eighteen were still further reduced to ten hours. *The Factory Act.*

The Poor Laws passed towards the end of Queen Elizabeth's reign were still in force. Great abuses had grown up, till the honest, hardworking laborer was unable to compete with his pauper neighbor who received a small allowance per week from the parish in addition to his wages. This was called out-door relief. Of course it is easy enough to see that the man who received this out-door relief could work for lower wages than the man who depended on his wages alone. Yet such was the condition of affairs in the agricultural districts. This was now changed, and in the future any one applying for aid must go to the workhouse and there work. The discontinuance of out-door relief caused great hardship for a time, but in the end the honest laborer has been greatly benefited. A few years later the same system was extended to Ireland, and, as the condition of things there was different, it caused considerable suffering.

Reform of the Poor Law (1834).

In 1834 the king, without any valid reason, dismissed Lord Melbourne, who had taken Earl Grey's place at the head of the Reform Ministry; and Sir Robert Peel, with the Duke of Wellington, tried to form a ministry. In this ministry Mr. Gladstone first appears. A general election was held in 1835, and Peel issued a sort of party platform. It was called the Tamworth Manifesto, because it was addressed to the electors of Tamworth, which place Peel represented in Parliament. In this, he accepted the Reform Act as passed. But the Liberals were nevertheless successful, and Lord Melbourne again became Prime Minister. In 1837 William IV. died, and his niece Victoria became Queen.

Peel-Wellington ministry (1834–1835).

Second Melbourne ministry (1835–1841).

CHAPTER XXXVII.

VICTORIA.

QUEEN VICTORIA was a young woman of eighteen when she became queen, in 1837. She had been carefully brought up by her mother, and soon won the hearts of Englishmen by her dignity and good sense. In 1840 she married Albert of Saxe-Coburg-Gotha. But he was never crowned as king consort, and was called simply the "Prince Consort" to his death. Lord Melbourne continued Prime Minister, and for a time the change of sovereigns made little or no difference in England's policy. In fact, affairs were now in a satisfactory condition in Great Britain. But in Ireland, Canada, and Jamaica a spirit of resistance to the Government was the rule.

The Melbourne Government seems to have tried to govern Ireland fairly. Indeed, this was necessarily so, as it was obliged to rely on the votes of the Irish members of the House of Commons. An under-officer of the Government even went so far as to tell a delegation of Irish landlords that "property has its duties as well as its rights,"—a proposition which quite astonished the Irish landowners. But the landlords were so strong in the House of Peers that the ministry was able to do very little for the Irish.

In Canada there was open rebellion. The French and English colonists did not get on well together, and

QUEEN VICTORIA, AT HER ACCESSION: ENGRAVED BY THOMPSON AFTER A PORTRAIT BY LANE.

the English settlers themselves did not like being governed by England. The Canadian Constitution was suspended, and Lord Durham was sent over as High Commissioner, or dictator, as he might well have been styled. He acted so despotically that popular feeling was strongly against him, and he was obliged to return home. In the end Parliament passed an Act uniting the two Canadas, and giving the colonists control of their local affairs. In 1867 a confederation of all the British North American colonies was set on foot. The new constitution resembles in some particulars that of England, and, in more particulars, that of the United States. Canada now has almost complete control of its own internal affairs, though the direction of diplomatic relations is retained by England. It should be remembered, however, that Parliament still has the substantial control of Canada in its own hands, and by merely passing an Act can any day alter this whole arrangement. All the British North American colonies, save Newfoundland, now belong to this confederation. *Canada Act (1840).*

The trouble in Jamaica grew out of the scheme for gradual emancipation. While the planters owned their slaves it was in general good policy to treat their dependents fairly well, and thus prolong the period of their usefulness. Now, however, when the planter would lose his slaves' services at the end of a few years, he was naturally tempted to get as much work out of them as he could while they were yet his. The Jamaica planters in particular treated their slaves with great harshness. The English Government acted somewhat hastily in the matter, and these planters refused to pass any laws in their colonial assembly till their demands should be complied with. A bill to compel the Jamaica colonists to submission was introduced into the Commons. The Opposition saw the opportunity, and defeated the Government, upon which the Melbourne ministry resigned.

Sir Robert Peel and the Duke of Wellington now formed a ministry. It so happened that the ladies in attendance upon the queen were the wives, sisters, daughters, aunts, cousins, or friends of the Melbourne ministers. The Duke of Wellington said that, as he had no small-talk, and Peel had no manners, it was necessary to have some ladies about the queen to explain the plans of the Government. Sir Robert Peel accordingly wrote to her that it would be necessary to change some of the chief ladies of her household. The queen, alarmed at the prospect of having to surround herself with strangers, refused, and the Melbourne ministry returned. But they had a majority no larger than before, and were sneered at as "hiding behind the ladies-in-waiting." However, they struggled on till 1841, when there was a general election. Lord Melbourne proposed to reform some of the trade laws. He was opposed by Peel on this issue, and, when Parliament met, Peel had the majority and became Prime Minister.

The Bed-Chamber question (1839).

Two great questions occupied Sir Robert Peel's attention during his administration. The first was the ever-present trouble in Ireland, which will be best considered later. The second was the over-turning of England's long-cherished financial policy. During the wars with France the manufacturing industry in England had received a great impetus, which carried it safely over the dull period

Sir Robert Peel's ministry (1841-1846).

after Waterloo. The opening of the ports of South and Central America gave England's commerce new life. It now became evident to several men skilled in thinking on such subjects that, however it might be with other nations, the protective system was no longer suited to England. Mr. Huskisson was the leader of this new school, and he set on foot a revolution in England's commercial policy. As a member of Canning's ministry he opened the British ports to ships of such countries as would open their ports to British vessels. He also lowered the duty on several raw materials,— wool and silk, for instance; and this made it easier for British manufacturers to compete with those of other countries. It was impossible to repeal the duty on breadstuffs, but a scheme was proposed by which they might be imported when the price was high in England. The Duke of Wellington, however, would not hear of such legislation, and it accordingly fell through. But not long afterwards the Duke of Wellington himself was obliged to carry through just such a law, and this was in force in 1841. Sir Robert Peel had won, in the election of 1841, as the leader of the Protectionists. But he himself was in no sense a Protectionist. His mind worked slowly, and he had a habit of waiting to see which way the country was going before he fully decided on his course. Before long he became convinced that if England was to become a great manufacturing country, the tariff must be revised, and as many articles as possible added to the free list. In five years the duties on raw materials used in the arts were either entirely repealed or greatly reduced. The most notable instance, perhaps, was the abolition of the duty on cotton,— a product almost entirely imported from America. This duty amounted to 680,000 pounds sterling, or over three millions of dollars. A great deficit was thus created in the revenue; but this was made good by a tax on incomes of so many pence in the pound.

The Income Tax.

While Peel was thus reducing the taxes on the manufacturers' supplies, the manufacturers themselves were agitating for a repeal of the taxes on breadstuffs. The leaders in this agitation were Richard Cobden and John Bright. John Bright was one of the greatest orators of the time, and Richard Cobden had a remarkable power of explaining intricate details of trade to popular audiences; so that together they exercised an irresistible influence. A great association, called the Anti-Corn-Law League, was established. Pamphlets were distributed broadcast, and Bright and Cobden, travelling from one end of the country to the other, soon aroused a tremendous interest in the subject of free trade in grain. The working-people deserted their usual leaders, and money poured in from all sides to aid the new crusade. This demonstration was the one thing needed to hasten Peel's mental processes. The argument of the agitators was something like this. English manufacturers possessed cheaper coal and iron than any other manufacturers. Under the new laws other raw materials would be as cheap to them as to their competitors. One thing alone was dear, and that was labor. Labor was dear because the workers must have good wages wherewith to buy the high-priced English-grown grain, or starve. Now, if they could be permitted to buy cheap grain,— imported from America, for example,— they would be equally well off with much lower wages. Finally, if the English manufacturer could get labor

The Anti-Corn-Law League.

at a low rate, he could undersell all his rivals, manufacture for the world, and give steady work to all. Therefore the Corn Laws should be repealed. It so happened that at the precise moment when Peel, under the pressure of the Anti-Corn-Law League, was coming to this conclusion, an event occurred which made at least a temporary suspension of those laws a necessity. This event was the famine in Ireland.

The people of Ireland lived principally on potatoes. Grain was grown in Ireland, but it was sold to England, and the proceeds were used to pay the rent due from the farmers to their landlords; almost none of it was consumed by the Irish people. They lived on potatoes, and they did this because that was the cheapest food. In 1844–45 a disease, or blight, called the potato rot, swept over western Europe. In England and Scotland it did not matter so very much, but in Ireland in a few months the food supply of millions of men, women, and children was destroyed. It was now absolutely necessary, if the Irish, and even the English, poor were to live, that the Corn Laws should be at least suspended. Peel saw that if they were once suspended they could never be re-imposed, and he therefore proposed their total repeal. *The Irish famine (1844–1849).*

Now Peel's supporters were mainly landowners; and to many of them his conduct seemed simply treasonable. Among the younger men of the Conservative party was Benjamin Disraeli. He had begun life as an extreme Liberal, or Radical; but now he was a Conservative of an extreme type. Up to 1845 his career as a politician had not been remarkable, but he now saw that his opportunity had come. Placing himself at the head of the discontented landowners and other believers in "protection," he attacked Sir Robert in Parliament with all the venom and energy of a venomous and energetic nature. He called the Government "an organized hypocrisy," and clamored for "vengeance on

SIR ROBERT PEEL; FROM THE BUST BY NOBLE IN THE NATIONAL PORTRAIT GALLERY.

the betrayer." Another convert to the Conservative party was Lord Stanley, who, as a Liberal, had been one of the Reform ministry. In the earlier days of Peel's own ministry Lord Stanley had sat in the cabinet. He now found himself leading the attack on Peel's policy in the House of Lords. Disraeli's vengeance was not long delayed. Among other measures, Peel had brought forward a Coercion Bill for Ireland. The

Protectionists and Liberals joined hands, and, on the very day when the bill to repeal the Corn Laws passed the House of Peers, Peel resigned.

Sir Robert Peel never again held office. But during the remainder of his life he helped Lord John Russell and the Liberals carry out the policy he had begun. As a political leader and financier, no modern Englishman stands higher than he. He had also the highest element of true statesmanship,— the ability to subordinate one's former convictions to the necessities of the time. Peel left behind him a devoted band of disciples,— the Peelites, as they were called. The most notable of them was William Ewart Gladstone, who, even at that time, had a seat in the cabinet.

The famine in Ireland continued till 1849. In 1847 "soup kitchens" were opened in the worst districts, and English writers claim that after their establishment no one died from actual starvation. But with the famine came a dreadful fever; and diseases not always fatal now invariably resulted in death. "The people," to use the words of Mr. Stuart Trench, "died on the roads, and they died in the fields; they died on the mountains, and they died in the glens; they died at the relief works, and they died in their houses,— so that little streets or villages were left almost without an inhabitant; and at last some few, despairing of help in the country, crawled into the towns, and died at the doors of residents." How many died from the famine will never be known. The population of Ireland in 1841 was over eight millions. In 1851 it was but six and one half millions,— over one and a half million less. As a great many children must have been born in the intervening years, more than one

Lord John Russell's ministry (1846-1852).

and a half million men, women, and children must have perished in those years or have emigrated.

During the years following the passage of the Catholic Relief Act a party of young and enthusiastic Irishmen had been gradually supplanting O'Connell. In 1847 he died, and the party of "Young Ireland" carried on and extended the agitation he had begun. They established a paper, called the "Nation," at Dublin, and openly advocated separation from England as the only cure for Ireland's ills. Nor were they averse to armed resistance. In 1848 a rising came, and proved a complete failure. Famine and unsuccessful rebellion brought only misery to Ireland. Many landlords seized the opportunity, and turned the tenants out of their farms by the wholesale. Entire estates were cleared of their former occupants in a week. This was done, the landlords said, that a new and better class of laborers might be introduced. Thousands of Irishmen, with their families, sought a new home in America. In their emigration they were often assisted by their former landlords and by people in England, who seemed to think that partial depopulation, and not a just social organization, was the remedy for Ireland's wretchedness.

"Young Ireland."

The "clearances."

The Irish rebellion was not the only rising in Europe in 1848. In fact, there were so many rebellions in that year that it is still often mentioned as the "Year of Revolutions." In England there was no actual rebellion, but the radical reformers were very active. They were called the Chartists, because they had embodied their demands in a document called "The People's Charter." They demanded equal electoral districts, vote by ballot, annual elections, universal

The Chartists.

manhood suffrage, a repeal of the property qualification for members of the House of Commons, and the payment of members. To an American these things seem reasonable enough; but to Englishmen thirty and forty years ago they portended anarchy. The Chartists presented petition after petition,—the largest in 1848. It was to have been carried to Parliament at the head of an enormous procession; but the Government refused to allow any such body to march. One hundred and seventy thousand citizens of London enlisted as special constables, and soldiers and artillery were placed to command the principal streets and bridges. The whole demonstration turned out a complete failure. Moreover, when the Government clerks counted the names attached to the petition, they found that there were, not five millions, as the Chartists claimed, but only two millions. Worse yet, many signatures were forgeries, as "the Queen," "Duke of Wellington," "Peel," etc.; while others, like "Pugnose" and "No Cheese," were plainly written for the purpose of filling as much paper as possible. Since then, however, many of these demands of the Chartists have been granted.

The principal man in Lord John Russell's ministry was Lord Palmerston, Secretary of State for Foreign Affairs. Lord Palmerston thought he knew more about foreign affairs than any one else, and did many things without telling the queen, or even his fellow ministers. Now, it happened that the queen and her husband— both Germans by extraction—took a great interest in German politics. They felt that Lord Palmerston did not treat them with due respect, and the queen wrote to that effect to Lord John Russell. The next year, 1851, Prince Louis Napoleon, nephew of the great

Napoleon, seized the Government of France. Lord Palmerston distrusted the French people, and felt a good deal of contempt for them. In an off-hand way he told the French minister at London that Napoleon had done right. As Palmerston had not even asked the Prime Minister what he thought about it, Lord John Russell was furious, and Palmerston was dismissed. Soon after, he and his personal friends, joining the Opposition for the moment, defeated Lord John Russell on an unimportant matter, and compelled his resignation. Lord Stanley, now Earl Derby, became Prime Minister, with Mr. Disraeli as leader of the House of Commons.

<small>The dismissal of Lord Palmerston.</small>

Two other events connected with the Russell ministry deserve mention. The first is the entire repeal of the Navigation Laws, in 1849, and the opening of the first international exhibition in the Crystal Palace, in Hyde Park, London, in 1851. This last was a great success in every way. The surplus was used to found the South Kensington Museum for the advancement of art.

<small>The first Derby ministry.</small>

In November, 1852, Parliament came together, and the opponents of the Derby-Disraeli ministry were in the majority. That ministry resigned, and, the Peelites joining the Liberals, a coalition ministry was formed, with Lord Aberdeen as Prime Minister. Ever since the time of Peter the Great the Czars of Russia had cast longing eyes on Constantinople and the provinces of Turkey in Europe. Nicholas was now Czar, and he thought the time to seize Constantinople had arrived. He spoke of the Sultan of Turkey as "the sick man of Europe," and actually proposed to divide his territo-

<small>The Aberdeen ministry.</small>

<small>The Crimean War (1854-1856).</small>

ries with England. But England was jealous of Russia, and when Nicholas attempted to conquer Turkey, England and France joined forces with the Turks, and soon drove the Russians back. The war then took the form of a siege of Sebastopol,— a great fortress and naval station on the Crimea, as the peninsula reaching out into the eastern end of the Black Sea is called. During the winter of 1854-55 the English troops suffered terribly from cold and lack of suitable clothing, and even of the very necessaries of life. The English people declared that this suffering was due to the incapacity of Lord Aberdeen; and he and some others opposed to the war resigned. The ministry was reconstructed, with Lord Palmerston as Prime Minister. The war was now carried on with more vigor, and great reforms were made in the condition of the English soldiers, under the leadership of a woman, Florence Nightingale. In 1855 Sebastopol was surrendered, and early in 1856 peace was made at Paris. *Palmerston ministry (1855-1858).*

Scarcely was this war ended when a terrible rebellion occurred in India. The skill, energy, and unprincipled extortion of Clive and Warren Hastings laid a foundation upon which later governors built a splendid empire. In 1856 England ruled, either directly or through subordinate princes, nearly the whole peninsula of India. The number of English soldiers in India was small. The expedient of employing natives as soldiers, and teaching them to use European arms, had been adopted. The native soldiers in the English service were called Sepoys. *The Sepoy Mutiny (1857-1858).*

The English Government of India endeavored to rule according to modern ideas, and they found it very hard work. Indian society was founded on a mass of castes, or fixed grades, between which there was no intermingling. In trying to simplify the collection of taxes, the English, perhaps without realizing it, gave a great blow to this system. The good-will of the upper caste was thus lost, and the suspicions of all the natives were aroused. At this inopportune moment the English Government decided to equip the Sepoy regiments with the Enfield rifle, in place of the old-fashioned musket. In those days, before the epoch of the breech-loader, the rifle was loaded from the muzzle, the cartridge being covered with grease, to enable it to slip down the barrel more easily. Now, animal grease was an abomination to the native, whether Hindoo or Mohammedan. To his suspicious mind this seemed a direct blow at his religion, — especially as the end of the greased cartridge had to be torn off by the teeth before loading. The Sepoys mutinied, and in 1857–58 there were fearful massacres, especially at Meerut and Cawnpore. After a time, and largely through the efforts of Havelock and Sir Colin Campbell, the mutiny was suppressed. Its principal results were the repeal of Pitt's India Act, and the transference of the government of India to the Crown.

In 1858 an Italian, Orsini by name, attempted to murder Napoleon III., Emperor of the French. It was asserted that Orsini planned his scheme in England; and to prevent England's being made the basis of future attacks, Palmerston introduced a bill increasing the penalty incurred by those conspiring to murder, no matter where the murder should be attempted. This awakened great jealousy among the English people, who are very sensitive about anything which looks like "foreign dictation." Some went further, and declared that Palmerston was acting under direct orders from Napoleon. He was obliged to resign, and Earl Derby again became Prime Minister, with Mr. Disraeli as his right-hand man.

Second Derby-Disraeli ministry (1858-1859).

This second ministry of Earl Derby is memorable for the passage of an Act to admit Jews to Parliament. Hitherto all members of Parliament had been obliged to swear to certain things on "the true faith of a Christian." Ten times over, bills had been brought in to remove this disability. The Commons were in favor of the measure, but whenever it had come before the Peers they had rejected it. It was now agreed to let each House regulate its oaths as it pleased. The Commons immediately changed the form of its own oath, and in July, 1858, Baron Rothschild, the great banker, took his seat in the House of Commons.

Jews admitted to Parliament.

The next spring Mr. Disraeli brought forward a scheme for further reform in the representation in Parliament. Mr. Disraeli disliked any scheme of representation based on mere numbers. He thought, however, that all classes in the community should be represented, and in his Reform Bill of 1859 he tried to provide for this. He proposed, in short, to give the right of voting to doctors, lawyers, college graduates, those receiving a pension from the Government, or owning Government bonds, or having money in a savings-bank, and many other classes of persons. The Opposition laughed at these "fancy franchises," as they were termed, and defeated the bill. A general election was then held, and when Parliament assembled, Mr. Disraeli found himself in a minority in the Commons. He and Lord Derby resigned, and the Liberals again took office.

The "fancy franchises" (1859).

Lord Palmerston was again Prime Minister with Lord John Russell as Foreign Secretary. Mr. Gladstone now definitely threw in his lot with the Liberal party, and

LORD JOHN RUSSELL: FROM A PAINTING BY SIR F. GRANT, IN POSSESSION OF DOWAGER COUNTESS RUSSELL.

became Chancellor of the Exchequer, or minister of finance. Lord Palmerston was now an old man, and for the rest of his life, which ended with his ministry, he tried only to keep his party together, and to avoid all causes of excitement at home. In 1860 Lord John Russell brought in a Reform Bill; but no interest was taken in the subject,

<small>Second Palmerston ministry (1859–1862).</small>

Palmerston even staying away from the debates; so Russell withdrew the bill, and no reforms of any kind were attempted, except in the finances.

By this time free-trade doctrines had been accepted as true by the great mass of Englishmen. In 1859 a commercial treaty with France caused a large extension of English commerce. Mr. Gladstone seized the opportunity this treaty gave him to rearrange all the taxes. In 1845, 1163 articles were taxed when imported. By 1859 the number had been reduced to 419. During these years of Palmerston's second ministry Mr. Gladstone carried bills reducing the number of articles taxed at importation to forty-five; and yet all the time the revenue went on increasing. This was the more remarkable because during these years the Civil War was raging in America, and England's trade with the United States was seriously impaired. *Gladstone's financial policy.*

The most serious blow to trade, however, was the almost entire stoppage of the American cotton supply during the Civil War. Upon this cotton the working-people of Manchester, Liverpool, and other manufacturing towns depended. When the supply ceased, the mills stopped, and no more wages could be earned. Starvation stared the working-people in the face, and that through no fault of their own. Yet they recognized that the cause of the American Union was the cause of free labor the world over, and deserving of the sympathy of the working-class. But it must be remembered that this class had at that time little or nothing to do with governing England. *The Cotton Famine.*

It was far otherwise with the upper classes. Mr. Gladstone placed himself squarely on the side of the

Confederate States. So did other Liberal leaders, one of them going so far as to say that the separation of the North and South was desirable. Mr. John Bright and the Prince Consort remained throughout the friends of those struggling in the cause of union and freedom; and it required all their influence to prevent England's taking sides. The ministry was soon assailed by both belligerents. The seceding States wished belligerents' rights granted them, even if England would not go farther and recognize their independence. The Southern Confederacy was, in fact, recognized as a belligerent; that is, England determined to be neutral, and forbade either party using her ports as starting-points for hostile expeditions. The trouble was that the English law did not give the Government sufficient power to carry out this policy. Americans are apt to censure too severely Lord Palmerston and Earl Russell for their actions during the struggle. For some unexplained reason, " English society" sympathized very strongly indeed with the seceding States, and Lord Palmerston needed all his tact and energy to prevent the ministry from being forced to take the side of the South. Charles Francis Adams was the American Minister at London during these years. He had a most difficult part to play. An English-built privateer, the "Alabama," escaped before the Government could make up its mind to seize her. Other and more powerful Confederate cruisers were on the point of being launched, when Mr. Adams wrote promptly to Earl Russell that such negligence on the part of the English Government was equivalent to war. The ministry awoke, and seized the cruisers. In the end, the insufficiency of her laws to

England's policy during the Civil War.

The "Alabama."

prevent the fitting out of armed expeditions against friendly powers cost England fifteen and one-half million dollars, — this being the sum a Court of Arbitration held at Geneva awarded as damages to the United States. In 1865 Lord Palmerston died, and Lord John Russell, who had been raised to the peerage as Earl Russell, took his place as Prime Minister.

Earl Russell, with rather injudicious haste, now brought forward a Reform Bill; but his party was not yet ready to vote for such a measure. He was defeated, and resigned. Earl Derby and Mr. Disraeli for the third time took charge of the government. In February, 1868, Earl Derby resigned, and Mr. Disraeli for nearly a year was Prime Minister. *Derby-Disraeli ministry (1865-1868).*

The Liberals, though disunited, formed a majority in the Commons, and Mr. Disraeli was obliged to act very nearly as they wished. He soon brought in a Reform Bill himself; and as the people were now taking a great interest in the subject, a bill for this purpose was carried through. As finally passed, the Second Reform Act was really a Liberal measure, — more radical, in fact, than either Mr. Gladstone or Mr. Bright then wished; and it greatly extended the franchise. *The Second Reform Act (1867).*

Up to this time all inhabitants of the several towns and parishes in England had been obliged by law to pay taxes, or rates, for the support of the Established Church, whether they attended its services or not. On the motion of Mr. Gladstone, an Act abolishing compulsory taxation for religious purposes in England was passed. Then he hit upon a scheme for uniting the divisions of the Liberal party. *Compulsory Church Rates abolished.*

Ever since the time of Queen Elizabeth the English Church had been established in Ireland. Probably not one-tenth of the people of Ireland ever attended the services of the Established Church. The Catholics hated it, not merely because it was a Protestant Church, but also because it was a religion forced upon them by their conquerors; nor did the great mass of the Protestants like it much better. Most of them were Presbyterians, and were opposed to the English Episcopal Church on their own account. The continuance of this State Church of an alien minority seemed to English Liberals to be a great evil. They joined Mr. Gladstone to disestablish it, or, in other words, to separate it from the State. In the general election in 1868 the Liberals were successful. Mr. Disraeli resigned, and Mr. Gladstone became Prime Minister.

Fall of the Disraeli ministry (1868).

The first thing to be done was to redeem the promises made with regard to the Irish Church. This was now disestablished, notwithstanding the opposition of many Peers, who dreaded a change in the relation of Church and State. In place of the Irish Church an independent Episcopal Church was organized in Ireland. The passage of this measure opened the flood-gates for reform, and in the next five years one measure after another was carried.

First Gladstone ministry (1868-1874).

The most important of these was the Irish Land Act. To understand it and the reasons for its passage we must look a little more closely into the mode of holding land in Ireland. This is the more necessary, because to an American the whole land system of the United Kingdom seems more or less absurd. In all settled countries arable land has a

Irish Land Act of (1870).

value. In America it is usually divided into moderately small estates, owned by the farmers who cultivate them. It is true that many American farms are mortgaged; but even then the title to the property is in the cultivator, as long as he pays his taxes, and interest on the mortgage. In England, however, the case is quite different. There, the arable land is owned in large pieces by a small number of rich landowners. These estates are usually divided into farms, which are let, with all their improvements, to the farmers who cultivate them. The terms in each case are determined by an agreement between the owner and tenant, called a lease. Now, English farmers are usually men of some means, who can use their money and brains in another way if they fail to find a farm to their tastes. In Ireland precisely the same conditions prevailed in theory. In practice, however, the land systems of the two countries were as unlike as two things of the same kind could well be. The soil of Ireland was owned by a small number of persons, as was the case in England; but there the similarity ceased. In Ireland there were few well-to-do farmers able to make satisfactory terms with the landlords, or to engage in any other occupation. On the contrary, it was absolutely necessary for most Irishmen, if they wished to live in Ireland, to have land to cultivate; there was nothing else for them to do. Thus the landlords were able to make their own terms with their tenants. Instead of providing a farm with a system of drainage and buildings all complete, the landlord only let the land itself to his tenants. If the tenant wished a house to live in, he must build one. If he wished a barn to place his crops in, he must build that. If he thought draining would make the farm more profitable, he must make the necessary improvements himself. Then in Ireland there were few leases, and the great mass of the farmers were only tenants at will; that is, the landlords might turn them out of their farms at will, the forms of law, of course, being complied with.

MR. GLADSTONE, FROM A PHOTOGRAPH BY ELLIOTT & FRY, 1880.

This was called "eviction." Let us see how this system worked in practice. Suppose a tenant were to hire a farm and to improve the land so as to make it more profitable. The landlord may immediately raise the rent; for is not the tenant able to pay more rent? If the tenant demur, he may be evicted, and the farm let to some one else. So it was not for the interest of the

Irish farmer to improve his property, or, in fact, to appear to be in any way prosperous,— not even to buy a new coat; for if the landlord saw him with a new coat on his back, he might be tempted to raise the rent. The inevitable result of such a system was bad cultivation, and a conflict between the two classes, which went by the name of the "land-war." The Irish claimed a share in the land. They demanded fixity of tenure; that is, the right to one's holding as long as the rent was paid. They also demanded that the tenant should have the right, when he left his holding, to sell his improvements to the incoming tenant. Finally, they demanded fair rents,— the amount to be determined by a court instituted for that purpose. The first two demands were practically included under what was known as the "Ulster custom" of landholding, — the practice which prevailed in the Protestant northern province of Ulster. There the tenant enjoyed his holding as long as he paid his rent; and when he parted with it, he might sell his improvements under the name of "goodwill." Mr. Gladstone now made the custom of Ulster, which was indeed that of some other parts of Ireland also, the basis of his Land Act. By this Act no tenant, as long as he paid his rent, could be turned out of his holding, or evicted, without receiving from the landlord compensation for disturbance. Compensation for improvements was also provided, and the Ulster custom and other similar customs were legalized wherever they obtained.

The other great feature of the Act was the attempt to establish a peasant proprietary, or small farm system, in Ireland. The clauses embodying this scheme were mainly the work of Mr. John Bright; and they are hence called the "Bright Clauses." The Act as a whole, however, was a complete failure, owing to the imperfections of its details. No further attempt was made till 1880 to carry out the great principles of right and justice which gave rise to the bill. But by the Land Act of 1881 the Government conceded a portion of the demands of the Irish for the "three F's," as they were called, — fixity of tenure, free sale, and fair rents. Since that time the Irish have sought to secure "home rule," or local self-government.

<small>The "Bright Clauses."</small>

It is scarcely conceivable that before 1870 there was no scheme for free elementary education in England. Yet such was the case. Attempts had indeed been from time to time made to remedy this state of things; but the Churchmen and the Dissenters were never able to unite on any measure. In 1871, however, a bill was passed providing for free elementary education to all not able to pay for it. At the same time secondary education was much improved, and the religious tests at the universities were abolished, except for holders of some fellowships.

<small>National education.</small>

The next subject taken up was a reform of the army. Perhaps in all England there was nothing more antiquated than the army organization; and nothing more antiquated in that organization than the system of allowing officers to choose their own rank by purchasing a commission. Promotions for merit were rare, and splendid officers, deserving well of the nation, might be superseded by rich men who could buy a commission. Yet the conservative feelings of Englishmen were so strong that it was only by a doubtful constitutional expedient that this absurd practice could be abolished. The other reforms

<small>Abolition of Purchase in the Army (1871).</small>

in the army were not so strongly opposed, and its organization was in many ways very much improved.

The two greatest reforms in the direction of good government were the separation of the civil service from party politics, and the introduction of vote by ballot. Civil service reform had been begun long before, and it was now completed. But the Ballot Act was an entirely new measure as far as Englishmen were concerned. Up to this time the voting had been entirely open, and every landlord knew how his tenants voted; every manufacturer knew how his working-people — such of them as possessed the franchise — voted; and every parish priest in Ireland knew how his parishioners voted. Indeed, elections in Ireland were struggles between the landlord and the priests. The elections throughout the United Kingdom could in no sense be called free under such a system. In 1872 this was remedied by the passage of the Ballot Act, which introduced a system of secret voting. At the same time very stringent measures were taken for the prevention of bribery, which were made still more stringent in 1883. A further extension of the franchise was desirable, and this was won by the Third Reform Act in 1884. At the same time the old borough system was abandoned, and representation was based on population. Thus by the three Reform Acts, by the Acts forbidding contractors from sitting in the Commons, by the Acts against bribery, by the Acts separating the civil service from party politics, and by the Acts providing for secret voting, the whole structure of Parliament has been changed. The House of Commons no longer represents the landowning and wealthy classes alone, but the whole mass of the people of the United Kingdom.

Ballot Act (1872).

These changes, however much they promoted good government and freedom, could hardly fail to arouse strong opposition. And Mr. Gladstone's Government was weakened in another way. It so happened that, in 1870, a great war broke out between Germany and France. The Czar of Russia seized the opportunity, when France was engaged in this life-and-death struggle, to undo the work of the Crimean War, and to overthrow the Treaty of Paris of 1856. Single-handed, England could do nothing, and was forced to acquiesce in Russia's demands. This was not the fault of Mr. Gladstone or his ministry, but it no less made him unpopular. Then, too, while pursuing a policy of peace and justice in submitting the disputes between the United States and Great Britain to arbitration, the Government acquired still more unpopularity, for the decisions of the arbitrators were in every way against Great Britain. All these things, added to the desire for rest from reform, turned people against Mr. Gladstone. A general election was held in 1874. The Liberals were defeated, and Mr. Disraeli became Prime Minister.

Mr. Gladstone's foreign policy.

The Conservatives had opposed these reform measures as strongly as they could; but they were now compelled to carry them out, while taking off the edge of the most distasteful changes. But not much was done, in one way or the other, as far as the home land was concerned, and, in fact, the main interest of Mr. Disraeli's administration was in his foreign policy. This was in marked contrast with that of his predecessor. In the first place, Mr. Disraeli believed in what he called an "Imperial policy." That is to say, he thought England

Mr. Disraeli's ministry (1874–1880).

His "Imperial policy."

LORD BEACONSFIELD: FROM A PHOTOGRAPH BY J. HUGHES, 1876.

should take a leading part in the disputes of the world. Perhaps the most striking act of his time was the purchase of the Khedive of Egypt's shares in the Suez Canal. That canal formed part of England's road to

India. It was in danger of falling completely into the hands of the French, when suddenly the English Government, without any vote of Parliament, bought by telegraph the Khedive's shares, — not quite one half of the whole capital stock in the enterprise, — for about twenty million dollars.

Before long a great war broke out between Russia and Turkey, in which Russia was very successful, and *Congress of Berlin.* seemed about to absorb a large part of Turkey's possessions in Europe. Mr. Disraeli, who had been raised to the peerage in 1876 as Earl of Beaconsfield, regarded this as directly opposed to the interests of England. A great many Englishmen thought as he did, and the following song became popular: —

> "We don't want to fight,
> But, by Jingo, if we do,
> We've got the ships,
> We've got the men,
> We've got the money too."

The new policy was hence called "the Jingo policy." And it was for a time very prosperous. Lord Beaconsfield went to a general congress of the Great Powers of Europe held at Berlin, and Russia was compelled to give up most of the advantages she had gained from Turkey. In pursuance of this same "Imperial policy," perhaps, the queen was easily persuaded to take the title of Empress of India.

Now it happened that Mr. Gladstone was a man of very strong feelings and prejudices, as well as of tremendous energy. He became convinced that the *Overthrow of the Conservatives (1880).* Turks had treated the Christians living in the Turkish province of Bulgaria very cruelly; he also thought this "jingo policy" quite wrong. A general election was held in 1880, and Mr. Gladstone re-entered political life with all his old fire and success. In a series of speeches he converted a majority of the voters of Great Britain to his views. The Conservatives were defeated, and Mr. Gladstone again became Prime Minister.

In thus tracing the formation and growth of the great British Empire, the reader will notice the vast energy and persistence with which "the expansion of England," as it has been called, has been carried on. A little island off the coast of Europe has made itself the head of the most marvellous empire which the world ever saw. The British Empire has now an area of some nine million square miles of territory, scattered all over the globe; and it has one-half of the ocean commerce of the world. Its area is nearly three times that of the United States, and almost three times that of all Europe. This empire lies in all zones, bears all products, and represents almost every race, color, religion, and mode of government. The sun never sets upon the British Empire; and though this fact is now found to be true of the United States also, since the acquisition of Alaska, yet it is barely true; and there is no real comparison to be made between the two nations as to range of soil and variety of people.

The British Empire.

On the other hand, it is to be remembered that with the British Empire, as with the Roman Empire, its weakness lies in its very extent. It is not made up, as is mainly the case with the United States, of a population speaking the same language and adopting similar laws. Very many of those included in the British Empire, including the whole vast Indian popu-

Conclusion.

lations, are kept there by force of arms, and without any real sympathy or fellowship, and may at any moment prove a source of weakness rather than strength. Then there are colonies, almost purely British in origin, — as Australia, — which are so nearly independent that many persons consider it only a question of time when they shall become detached, like the United States, and when Canada itself may be independent, or join its fate with the North American Republic. It is a very important fact that, as stated by Sir Charles Dilke, there are three times as many natives of the United Kingdom in the United States as in all the British colonies put together. This fact, while sometimes a source of jealousy, promises in the end to bring this nation and England closer together than any other two great nations. At present, our commerce is chiefly with England, and it is the English influence which is most strongly felt in our social habits and, to some extent, in our literature. On the other hand, we draw our art from France, and our science from Germany, almost as completely as if England did not exist. Yet, on the whole, England is nearest to us among all nations, and it is the history of England which, next to that of our own country, needs to be studied by our people.

INDEX.

ABERDEEN, Lord, Prime Minister, 308.
Acadia, ceded to England, 227.
Act of succession, or settlement, 229.
Act of Supremacy (1534), 126.
Adams, Charles Francis, 314.
Adams, John, 264.
Addington, Mr., Prime Minister, 273.
Agincourt, battle of (1415), 82.
Aix-la-Chapelle, peace of, 237.
Alabama, 314.
Albert, Prince Consort, 297.
Alison, 1, 2.
Alfred, his government, 18.
Allen, Ethan, 255.
"All the Talents," ministry of, 277.
Althorp, Lord, 293.
Amiens, peace of, 276.
André, Major, 260, 261.
Angles, 12.
Anne, 224; portrait of, 225, 226.
Anne of Cleves, 129.
Anti-Corn Law League, 302.
Appeals to Rome, statute forbidding, 124.
Argaum, battle of, 279.
Army, abolition of purchase in the, 320.
Arnold, Benedict, 255, 256, 260, 261.
Ashley, Lord, 295.
Assaye, battle of, 279.
Attempt to arrest the Five Members, 163.
Atterbury, Bishop, exiled, 232.
Austerlitz, battle of, 277.

BACON, Francis, Lord Chancellor, impeachment of, 151.
Bacon, Roger, 16.
Balliol and Bruce, 51.
Ballot Act, 321.

Bank of England, established, 221; suspends cash payments, 272.
Bannockburn, battle of, 55.
Barebones' Parliament, 186.
Barrows, 2.
Beachy Head, battle of, 221.
Beaconsfield, Earl of, portrait of, 323; foreign policy, 324.
Bedchamber question, ?.
Bennington, battle of, 256.
Berlin, Congress of, 324; Decree, 281.
Bill of Rights, 215.
Bishops' wars, the, 164, 165.
Black Death, 62.
Blake, Admiral, and Van Tromp, 185.
Blenheim, battle of, 226.
Boroughs, rotten, 288.
Bouvines, 282.
Brueys, Adm, 122.
Brougheroke, Lord, 232.
Boston Port Act, 253.
Boston, siege of, 254; evacuated by the British, 254.
Bosworth Field, battle of, 20.
Boyne, battle of the, 207.
Braddock, General, 240.
Brandywine, battle of, 256.
Berlin declaration of, 1, 3.
Bretigny, peace of, 62.
Bribery Act against, 233.
Bright Clauses, the, 320.
Bright, John, 302, 314, 319.
Britain early victory of, 6; Roman conquest of, 7; Germanic conquest of, 12.
Bruces ?; mode of life ?; religion ?.
Brougham Lord Chancellor, 2.?
Bunker's Hill, battle of, 254.
Burgoyne, his campaign, 256, 258.

Burke, Edmund, 250, 262, 263, 267, 269; portrait of, 263; Reflections on the French Revolution, 271.
Bute, Lord, 244, 246.
Buxton, Sir Fowell, 295.

CADE, Jack, rebellion of, 83.
Cæsar, Julius, in Britain, 7.
Calais, siege of, 62.
Camden, battle near, 259.
Camden, Lord (Charles Pratt), 250, 262.
Campbell, Sir Colin, 310.
Camperdown, battle of, 272.
Canada Act, the, 299.
Canada, rebellion in, 297; Dominion of, 299.
Canning, George, 277, 279, 285, 286; Prime Minister, 287; Foreign Secretary, 286; portrait of, 288.
Caroline of Brunswick, wife of George IV., 286.
Caroline, Queen, wife of George II., 234.
Castlereagh, Lord, 275, 277, 281, 285, 286.
Catholic Association, 288; Emancipation, 289; Relief Act, 289; rent, 289.
Catholics, English, laws against, modified, 258.
Cavalier Parliament, the, 199.
Cawnpore, 310.
Cecil, Robert, Lord Salisbury, 137.
Cecil, William, Lord Burleigh, 121; his death, 137; portrait of, 138.
Cedric, 11.
Celts, or Kelts, 3.
Charles I., 153-180; married to Henrietta Maria of France, 153; his portrait, 155; governs without Parliament, 158; trial and execution of, 180.
Charles II., 196-208; recognized king by Scots, 182; overthrown at Worcester, 183; his escape, 184; king of England, 195; power of, 197; portrait of, 197.
Charles Edward, the Young Pretender, 236.
Charleston, attacked by English, 255; capture of, 259.
Charters, confirmation of the, 54; the People's, 306.

Chartists, the, 306, 307.
Chatham, Earl of, 257.
Chatham-Grafton ministry, 250.
Chaucer, 76; portrait of, 76.
Church rates, abolition of compulsory, 315.
Churchill, Lord, afterwards Duke of Marlborough, 224; deserts James II., 214. *See* Marlborough.
Civil War, England's policy during American, 313.
Clarence, Duke of, murder of, 87.
Clarendon, Earl of (Edward Hyde), 168, 196, 202; his history, 202.
Clarkson, Thomas, 295.
Clearances, the Scottish, 238; the Irish, 305.
Clinton, Sir Henry, 259, 261.
Cnut, or Canute, 19.
Coalition, 266.
Cobden, Richard, 302.
Colonies, North American, origin of, 248.
Commonwealth, the, 182-187.
Concord, conflict at, 254.
Confederation, Articles of, 255.
Constitutions of Clarendon, 36.
Continental Congress of 1774, 254.
Conventicle Act, the, 199.
Convention, the, of 1689, 214.
Copenhagen, battle of, 279.
Copyhold tenure, 67.
Corn Laws, 283, 303; repeal of the, 304.
Cornwallis, 259, 260, 261; Lord Lieutenant of Ireland, 275.
Corporation Act, the, 199.
Cotton famine, 313.
County Clare, election of, 289.
County, origin of the, 14.
Cowpens, battle of the, 259.
Cranmer, Thomas, Archbishop of Canterbury, 104; his martyrdom, 116.
Cressy, or Crécy, battle of, 60.
Crimean War, 308, 322.
Cromlech, 2.
Cromwell, Oliver, 158; his "Ironsides," 173; his portrait, 174; at Marston Moor, 175; at Newbury, 175; proposes the "New Model," 176; at Naseby, 176; his position on religion, 177; at Preston, 179; Ire-

INDEX.

land, 181; at Dunbar, 183; at Worcester, 183; expels Long Parliament, 181; Lord Protector, 187; his death, 191; his policy, 192.
Cromwell, Richard, Lord Protector, 192.
Cromwell, Thomas, 104; his fall, 109.
Culloden, battle of, 238.
Cumberland, Duke of, in Scotland, 238.
Cymry, 4.

Danes, invade England, 18, 19.
Danish fleet, seizure of, 279.
Declaration of Rights, 215.
Declaratory Act, the (1766), 250.
Derby, Earl (Lord Stanley), Prime Minister, 308; second ministry of, 311; third ministry of, 315
Derby, the Young Pretender at, 236.
Despenser, Lord, 55.
Dettingen, battle of, 236.
Disraeli, Benjamin, 303, 304, 308, 311, 315, 316, 322; becomes Earl of Beaconsfield, 324.
Dissenters, the, 200; relief of Protestant, 290.
Divine right of kings, theory of, 151.
Domesday Book, 27.
Dover, secret treaty of, 203.
Drake, Sir Francis, 131-135; his portrait, 133.
Drogheda, massacre of, 181.
Druids, the, 5.
Dunbar, battle of, 183.
Dunstan, St., 19
Du Quesne, Fort, 240.
Durham, Lord, 299.
Dutch, blockade the Thames, 202.

East India Company, the English, 140, 253, 266.
Economical reform, 258.
Edgehill, battle of, 172.
Edinburgh, founded, 12.
Edward the Confessor, 23.
Edward I., 50-54; conquers Wales, 50; conquers Scotland, 51.
Edward II., 54-56.
Edward III., 56-59; war with Scotland, 57; war with France, 57;

causes of, 59; French crown, succession to, 59.
Edward the Black Prince, 63.
Edward IV., 84-87.
Edward V., 88.
Edward VI., 111-113.
Edwin of Northumbria, 12, 16.
Egbert of Wessex, 16.
Egypt, Napoleon's invasion of, 272.
Eldon, Lord Chancellor, 287.
Eliot, Sir John, 155; his resolutions, 157; his death, 158.
Elizabeth, 119-139; her portrait, 119; foreign policy of, 128.
Elizabethan architecture, 140; literature, 142.
Emancipation of slaves, 295.
Emmett's rebellion, 275.
Empire, the British, 325.
England, 12; expansion of, 325.
English, 12; their religion, 13; institutions, 13; land system, 14; conversion to Christianity, 15.
Essex, 11
Essex, Earl of, in Ireland, 137; his execution, 139.
Ethelred "the Unready," 19.
Evesham, battle of, 48.
Exclusion Bill, the, 207.

F's, the Three, 320.
Factory Act, 295.
Fairfax, General, 176.
Falkirk, battle of, 52.
Fawkes, Guy, 147.
Five-mile Act, the, 200.
Flodden, battle of, 100.
"Forty," the, 236.
Forty-shilling freeholders in England, 85; in Ireland, 289.
Fourteenth century, importance of, 73; financial policy in, 73; clothes, 74; foreign commerce, 74; the guilds, 75; rise of English language during, 76.
Fox, Charles James, 251, 262, 264; India Bill, 266, 267, 271; death of, 277.
Fox, Henry, afterwards Lord Holland, 239, 246.
France, war with (1415), 79-80; alliance between America and, 257; war

330 INDEX.

with (1793), 271 ; war with, renewed (1803), 276.
Franchise, restricted, 85.
Franchises, the Fancy, 311.
Franklin, Benjamin, 264.
Frederick the Great of Prussia, 236, 240, 243.
French, the, in America, 240.
French and Indian War, causes of, 240.
French revolution, effect of, on England, 271.

GAELS, or Goidels, 3.
Gates, General Horatio, 256, 259.
Gaveston, execution of, 54.
General warrants, the case of, 246.
Geneva award, 315.
Geoffrey of Anjou, marries Maud, 33.
George, Elector of Hanover, 229.
George I., 229-233; portrait of, 231.
George II., 234-243; portrait of, 237.
George III., 244-284 ; his policy, 244; portrait of, 284; death of, 285.
George IV., 286-295 ; death of, 290.
Germaine, Lord George, 261 ; becomes Lord Sackville, 262.
Germanic race, 10.
Germantown, battle of, 256.
Ghent, treaty of, 282.
Gibraltar, seizure of, 226; relief of, 265.
Gladstone, W. E., 296, 305, 312, 313, 315, 316, 319, 322, 324; Prime Minister, 316, 325; portrait of, 318.
Glencoe, massacre of, 222.
Godwin, Earl of Wessex, 22.
Grafton, Duke of, Prime Minister, 250.
Grasse, Count de, 261, 265.
Grattan, Henry, 273.
Great Britain, Union of, with Ireland, 275.
Great Fire of London, 201.
Greene, General, 259.
Grenville, George, Prime Minister, 246 ; colonial policy of, 248, 249 ; dismissed from office, 249.
Grenville, Lord, Prime Minister, 277.
Grey, Earl, Prime Minister, 293, 294.
Grey, Lady Jane, 112.
Guilds, 75.
Guilford Court-house, battle of, 259.

Guinegaste, battle of, 100.
Gunpowder Plot, 146.

HABEAS CORPUS Act, 206.
Hales, Sir Edward, case of, 210.
Halidon Hill, battle of, 57.
Hampden, John, case of, 160; his death, 172.
Hampton Court Conference, 149.
Harold of Wessex, 23, 24 ; elected king, 24.
Hastings, battle of, 24.
Hastings, Warren, 267 ; trial of, 269.
Havelock, 310.
Henry I., 31.
Henry II., 35-39; effigy of, 38.
Henry III., 46-49.
Henry of Lancaster, claims the throne, 71 ; crowned king as Henry IV., 72, 77, 78.
Henry V., 78-81.
Henry VI., 82-85.
Henry VII., 95-97.
Henry VIII., 98-110; the Spanish marriage, 98 ; portrait of, 99 ; war with France and with Scotland, 100 ; and Francis I., 101 ; divorce from Katharine, 102.
Herkimer, General, 256.
High Commission, Court of, 130.
House of Commons, origin of, 53, 65 ; acts without king or peers, 180; expelled by Cromwell, 186 ; restored by the army officers, 192.
Howards, the, 102.
Howe, General, 258.
Hundred, the, 14.
Hunt, Mr. "Orator," 284.
Huskisson, Mr., 301.
Hutchinson, governor of Massachusetts, 253.

IBERIAN, 3.
Ierne, 1, 3.
Income tax, the, 302.
Independence, American Declaration of, 255.
"Independents," the, 177.
Indemnity and Oblivion, Act of (1662), 197.
Indulgence, Declaration of (1672), 204 ; (1688), 211.

Instrument of government, 186.
Invincible Armada, the, 132.
Ireland, Poynings' Law, 135; Established Church of, 135; rebellion in, 136; English settlement of, 136; Strafford in, 164; rebellion in (1641), 168; Cromwellian settlement of, 181; condition of, in eighteenth century, 273; rebellion in, 274; Union with Great Britain, 275; famine in, 303, 305; rebellion in (1848), 306; Young, 306; land system of, 316; Established Church of, disestablished, 316.
Irish Land Act (1870), 316; (1881), 320.
Irishmen, the United, 274.

JACOBITE Plot, the (1715), 230; (1721), 232; rising, the (1745), 236.
Jacobites, origin of the name, 214.
Jamaica Bill, 299.
James I., 144-152; his character, 144; portrait of, 150; his theory of "divine right," 151; persecuted the Puritans, 149.
James II., 208-215.
Jay, John, 264.
Jeffreys, Chief Justice, 208.
Jenkins's ears, 234.
Jews, admitted to Parliament, 311.
Jingo policy, 324.
Joan of Arc, 82.
John, 41-45; loses Normandy, 41; the interdict, 42; submits to the Pope, 42; his death, 44.
Jutes, 10.

KATHARINE of Arragon, 98-103.
Kent, kingdom of, 11.
Keppel, Admiral, 262.
King Arthur, 99.
King's Friends, 251.
King's Mountain, battle of, 259.

LABORERS, first statute of, 67.
Lafayette, 259, 260, 261.
La Hogue, battle of, 221.
Lake, General, 274.
Land Act, 316; second, 320.
Lanfranc, 28.
Langton, Archbishop of Canterbury, 42.

Laud, William, Archbishop of Canterbury, 159; his reactionary policy, 159.
Lee, Charles, 258.
Leipzig, battle of, 281.
Lewes, battle of, 47.
Lexington, conflict at, 254.
Liverpool, Lord, Prime Minister, 285; death of, 287.
Llewelyn, Prince of Wales, 56.
Lollards, 66.
Londonderry, Duke of, 218.
Long Parliament, the, 165-194.
Lord George Gordon riots, 258.
Lords, House of, 295.
Louis XVIII., 281, 282.
Louisburg, the capture of (1745), 239.
Luddites, 283.

MACAULAY, THOMAS BABBINGTON, Lord, 294.
Macdonald, Flora, 238.
Magna Charta, 43.
Major-Generals, the, 189.
Maintenance, 78.
Malta, seized by Napoleon, 272.
Manchester massacre, 285.
Marlborough, Duke of, 214, 224, 225.
Marston Moor, battle of, 175.
Mary I., 114-118; portrait of, 115; marries Philip II. of Spain, 114; the martyrs, 116; her death, 117.
Mary, Queen of Scots, 125; her portrait, 127; her claims to the English throne, 126; execution of, 131.
Massachusetts Government Act, 253.
Melbourne, Lord, 296, 297, 300.
Mercia, 12.
Methodists, rise of the, 234.
Middlesex, 99; elections, 251.
Milton, John, 187; portrait of, 185.
Ministry, formation of a, 230.
Monasteries, dissolution of, 106; effect of, 107.
Monk, General, 193; declares for a free Parliament, 193.
Monmouth, Duke of, 207, 208; rebellion of, 208.
Monmouth, battle of, 257.
Monroe doctrine, 287.
Mortimer, 56, 57.

Mosaic Ministry, 250.
Mutiny Bill, the, annulled, 216.

NAPOLEON, 272, 273, 275-279; abdication of, 281, 282.
Napoleon, Louis, 307, 308, 310, 311.
Naseby, battle of, 176.
Navigation Ordinance, 189.
Navigation Laws, repeal of, 308.
Nelson, Admiral, 273; death of, 276; portrait of, 278.
Newbury, battle of, 175.
Newcastle, Duke of, 236; Prime Minister, 240; coalition with Pitt, 241.
New Forest, the, 28.
New Model army, 176.
New Style, 239.
Nicholas, Czar of Russia, 308.
Nightingale, Florence, 309.
Nile, battle of the, 273.
Nore, mutiny at the, 272.
Norfolk, Duke of, 289.
Nonjurors, 218.
Norman Conquest, 23-28; effects of the, 26.
North Briton, the, 246.
North, Lord, 250; Prime Minister, 251; plan of reconciliation with America, 257, 258; fall of, 261; coalition with Fox, 266, 268.
Northmen, or Norsemen, 17.
Northumbria, 12.

OATES, TITUS, 205.
O'Connell, Daniel, 288, 289.
Orangemen, Society of, 274.
Orders in Council, 281.
Orsini, 310.
Out-door relief, 296.

PAINS AND PENALTIES, Bill of, 286.
Palmerston, Lord, 307-310, 312, 314, 315.
Paris, peace at (1763), 245; (1856), 309.
Parliament, first legal, 53; separation into two houses, 65; in the fifteenth century, 93, 94; duration of, 230; debates in, published, 251; the Short, 165; the Long, 165-194.
Peasants' revolt, 68.
Peel, Sir Robert, 287, 288, 294, 296;
Prime Minister, 300, 301; portrait of, 304; fall of, 305.
Peelites, the, 305.
Pelham, Henry, 236.
Peninsular War, 279.
Penn, Admiral, seizes Jamaica, 190.
Perceval, Spencer, Prime Minister, 277, death of, 285.
Peterloo, 285.
Petition and Advice, the, 190.
Petition of Right, 154.
Philadelphia, evacuation of, 257.
Pitt, William, afterwards Earl of Chatham, Paymaster of the Forces, 239; portrait of, 240; coalition with Newcastle, 241; resigns, 244; becomes Earl of Chatham, 250; death of, 257.
Pitt, William (the younger), 264; Prime Minister, 267; financial policy of, 268; portrait of, 268; India Bill, 268-271; repressive policy of, 272; resignation of, 275; death of, 277.
Plague, the, 199.
Plantagenets, the later, 71.
Pocket boroughs, 292.
Poitiers, battle of, 63.
Poor Law of Elizabeth, 142.
Poor Law, Reform of, 296.
Popish plot, 205.
Poynings' Law, 135.
Præmunire, statute of, 66.
Pratt, Charles, later Lord Camden, 247.
Preston, battle of, 179.
Preston Pans, battle of, 236.
Pretender, the Old, born, 212.
Pride's Purge, 179.
Printing, 91.
Protection, overthrow of, 301.
Protectionists, 301.
Protector Somerset, 111.
Protectorate, the, 188-195.
Protestation, the Great, 152.
Prynne, William, 159-162.
Puritans, the, 123-125, 131; under Elizabeth, 123; under James, 149; ideas of the, 194; emigration to New England, 125-163.
Pym, John, impeaches Strafford, 166; ideas on religion, 168; attempt to arrest, 169; seeks aid of the Scots, 172; his death, 173.

INDEX. 333

QUEBEC, attacked by Americans, 255.
Quebec Act, 254.

RALEIGH, Sir Walter, 143; portrait of, 145.
Reform Act, of 1832, causes of, 291; First, 294; Second, 315; Third, 321.
Regency, 285.
Regency question, 249, 269.
Regicides, the, 198.
Remonstrance, the Grand, 168.
Responsible government, origin of, 217.
Restoration, the, 194.
Richard I., 39; his place in history, 40.
Richard II., 68-72; his abdication, 70.
Richard III., 88-90; his character, 88.
Riot Act, 230.
Rochambeau, Marquis, 260, 261.
Rochelle, attempt to relieve, 154.
Rockingham, Marquis of, 250, 262-264, 274.
Rodney, Admiral, 265.
Roman walls, 7; roads, 8.
Romans, conquer Britain, 7; leave Britain, 9.
Roses, Wars of the, begin, 84.
Rothschild, Baron, 311.
Rump Parliament, the, 184; expelled by Cromwell, 186; restored, 192.
Russell, Lord John, introduces first Reform Bill, 293; Prime Minister, 305, 307, 308; portrait of, 312; becomes Earl Russell, 314, 315.
Rye-house plot, 207.

ST. HELENA, Napoleon at, 283.
St. Leger, 256.
Salisbury, oath of, 27.
Saratoga, surrender at, 256.
Saxons, 11.
Scotland, united with England, 227.
Scottish Kirk, the, 163.
Scottish national covenant, 164.
Schuyler, Philip, 256.
Sebastopol, siege of, 309.
Sedgemoor, battle of, 208.
Self-denying Ordinance, 176.
Senlac, or Hastings, battle of, 24.
Sepoy mutiny, 309.
Septennial Act, 230.
Settlement, Act of, 229.

Seven Bishops, the, 211; acquittal of, 212.
Seymour, Jane, 108.
Shelburne, Lord, 250, 262, 264, 266.
Sheridan, 267.
Shield-money, or scutage, 36.
Ship-money, 160.
Simon of Montfort, 47; his Parliament, 48.
Simnel, Lambert, 95.
Six Acts, 285.
Six Articles, Act of the, 108.
Slaves, emancipation of, 295.
Sluys, battle of, 60.
Sophia, Electress of Hanover, 229.
South-Sea bubble, 230.
Spain, war with (1739), 236; resistance of, to Napoleon, 279; rising in, in 1820, 287.
Specie payments, suspended, 272.
Spithead, mutiny at, 272.
Stamp Act, the, passed, 249; repealed, 250.
Stanley, Lord, 304.
Stanley, Mr., 294.
Stanwix, Fort, 256.
Star Chamber, court of, 96.
Stephen, 33, 34.
Steuben, General, 256.
Stonehenge, 5.
Strafford, Thomas Wentworth, Earl of, 164-167; impeachment of, 166; attainder and execution of, 167.
Stuart kings, 143.
Stuart, Lady Arabella, 146.
Stuart rising, the (1745), 236.
Succession, Act of, 229.
Suez Canal, 323.
Sussex, 11.
Swend, the Dane, 19.

TALAVERA, battle of, 279.
Tamworth Manifesto, 296.
Tarleton, Colonel, 259.
Tax, the income, 302.
Tea Party, the Boston, 253.
Test Act, 204.
Teutonic race, 10.
Thomas Becket, 36, 37.
"Thorough," government of, 164.
Thurlow, Lord Chancellor, 262.

INDEX.

Tories, origin of the name, 207.
Torres Vedras, lines of, 279.
Town meeting, 14.
Townshend, Charles, Chancellor of the Exchequer, 250; introduces bills to tax colonial imports, 250.
Townshend duties, the, 250.
Township, the, 14.
Toulouse, surrender of French at, 280.
Trafalgar, battle of, 276.
Treaty at Versailles and Paris, 265.
Trenton, surprise of British outposts at, 255.
Troyes, treaty of, 80.

ULM, capitulation of, 277.
Ulster custom, 319.
Uniformity, Act of, 123.
Union with Ireland, Act of, 275.
United Irishmen, society of, 274.
United Kingdom of Great Britain, 227.
United States, independence of, acknowledged, 264; treaty with, 264; war with, 281.
Utrecht, treaty of, 226.

VALLEY FORGE, camp at, 256.
Vane, Sir Henry, introduces the Navigation Ordinance, 189; executed, 198.
Victoria, 297-326; portrait of, 296.
Vienna, Congress at, 282.
Vikings, 17.
Villeinage, abolition of, 92.
Villiers, Duke of Buckingham, 151-153; his murder, 156.
Vinegar Hill, battle of, 274.
Vittoria, battle of, 280.
Volunteers, the Protestant, 273.
Voting, Australian system, 329.

WALLACE, Sir William, 52.
Walpole, Sir Robert, Prime Minister, 232-236; First Lord of the Treasury,
232; cabinet, 232; his policy, 233, portrait of, 235.
War of 1812, 282.
Warbeck, Perkin, 96.
Warwick, the king-maker, 86.
Washington, George, 240; commander-in-chief, 254, 261.
Wat Tyler, 68.
Wat Tyrrel, 31.
Waterloo, campaign of, 282.
Wedmore, 18.
Wellesley, Arthur, Duke of Wellington, 279.
Wellington, Duke of, 279-282, 287-289, 293, 294, 296, 300, 301, 307; portrait, 280.
Welsh bards, 51.
Wessex, 11.
Whigs, origin of the name, 207.
White Plains, battle of, 255.
White Ship, the story of the, 32.
Wilberforce, William, 295.
Wilkes, John, 246, 251.
William of Normandy, 24; claim to England, 25; crowned William I., 25; his death, 29.
William II., 30.
William of Orange, marries Mary of England, 204; lands at Torbay, 213.
William III. and Mary II., 215-224; portraits of, 218, 219; foreign policy of, 220-224.
William IV., 291-296.
Witenagemot, 15.
Wolsey, Cardinal, 100-104; his fall, 103.
Worcester, battle of, 183.
Wycliffe, John, 66.

YORK, James, Duke of, 202, 204, 205; bill to exclude from the succession, 207; crowned King James II., 208.
York and Lancaster kings, 81.
Yorktown, capture of, 261.

Epochs of American History.

Edited by ALBERT BUSHNELL HART, Ph.D.,
Assistant Professor of History in Harvard University.

MESSRS. LONGMANS, GREEN, & CO. take pleasure in announcing the completion of their series published, in three volumes, under the general title of EPOCHS OF AMERICAN HISTORY. Each volume contains specially prepared maps, working bibliographies, and full index. The maps in the three volumes have also been republished separately under the title EPOCH MAPS ILLUSTRATING AMERICAN HISTORY. The series is issued under the editorship of Dr. Albert Bushnell Hart, Assistant Professor of History in Harvard University, as follows:

I. **The Colonies, 1492-1750.** By REUBEN GOLD THWAITES, Secretary of the State Historical Society of Wisconsin; editor of the Wisconsin Historical Collections; author of "Historic Waterways," "The Story of Wisconsin," etc. With four colored maps, pp. xviii, 301. Cloth, $1.25.

II. **The Formation of the Union, 1750-1829.** By ALBERT BUSHNELL HART, A.B., Ph.D., Assistant Professor of History in Harvard University; member of the Massachusetts Historical Society; author of "Introduction to the Study of Federal Government," "Practical Essays on American Government," etc. With five colored maps, pp. xx, 278. Cloth, $1.25.

III. **Division and Reunion, 1829-1889.** By WOODROW WILSON, Ph.D., LL.D., Professor of Jurisprudence and Political Economy in Princeton University; author of "Congressional Government," "The State—Elements of Historical and Practical Politics," etc. With five colored maps, pp. xix, 326. Cloth, $1.25.

Epoch Maps, illustrating American History. By ALBERT BUSHNELL HART, A.B., Ph.D. Fourteen colored maps. Second edition. Limp, oblong, 50 cents *net*.

LONGMANS, GREEN, & CO., PUBLISHERS,
15 EAST 16th STREET, NEW YORK.

A STUDENT'S HISTORY OF ENGLAND, from the Earliest Times to 1885.

By SAMUEL RAWSON GARDINER, M.A., LL.D., Fellow of All Souls College, Oxford, etc.; Author of "The History of England from the Accession of James I. to 1642," etc. Illustrated under the superintendence of Mr. W. H. ST. JOHN HOPE, Assistant Secretary of the Society of Antiquaries, and with the assistance in the choice of Portraits of Mr. GEORGE SCHARF, C.B., F.S.A., who is recognized as the highest authority on the subject. In one Volume, with 378 Illustrations and full Index. Crown 8vo, cloth, plain, $3.00.

The book is also published in three Volumes (each with Index and Table of Contents) as follows:

VOLUME I.—B.C. 55–A.D. 1509. 410 pp. With 173 Illustrations and Index. Crown 8vo, $1.20.
VOLUME II.—A.D. 1509–1689. 332 pp. With 96 Illustrations and Index. Crown 8vo, $1.20.
VOLUME III.—A.D. 1689–1885. 374 pp. With 109 Illustrations and Index. Crown 8vo, $1.20.

*** Gardiner's "Student's History of England," through Part IX. (to 1789), is recommended by **HARVARD UNIVERSITY** as indicating the requirements for admission in this subject; and the **ENTIRE work is made the basis for English history study in the University.**

YALE UNIVERSITY.

"Gardiner's 'Student's History of England' seems to me an admirable short history."—Prof. C. H. SMITH, New Haven, Conn.

TRINITY COLLEGE, HARTFORD.

"It is, in my opinion, by far the best advanced school history of England that I have ever seen. It is clear, concise, and scientific, and, at the same time, attractive and interesting. The illustrations are very good and a valuable addition to the book, as they are not mere pretty pictures, but of real historical and archæological interest."—Prof. HENRY FERGUSON.

"A unique feature consists of the very numerous illustrations. They throw light on almost every phase of English life in all ages. . . . Never, perhaps, in such a treatise has pictorial illustration been used with so good effect. The alert teacher will find here ample material for useful lessons by leading the pupil to draw the proper inferences and make the proper interpretations and comparisons. . . . The style is compact, vigorous, and interesting. There is no lack of precision; and, in the selection of the details, the hand of the scholar thoroughly conversant with the source and with the results of recent criticism is plainly revealed."—*The Nation*, N. Y.

". . . It is illustrated by pictures of real value; and when accompanied by the companion 'Atlas of English History' is all that need be desired for its special purpose."—*The Churchman*, N. Y.

*** *A prospectus and specimen pages of Gardiner's "Student's History of England" will be sent free on application to the publishers.*

LONGMANS, GREEN, & CO., 15 East Sixteenth Street, New York

AN ATLAS OF ENGLISH HISTORY. Edited by Samuel Rawson Gardiner, M.A., LL.D.

66 colored Maps, 22 Plans of Battles, etc., and full Index. Fcap., 4to, $1.50.

A Companion Atlas to Gardiner's "Student's History of England."

HARVARD UNIVERSITY.

"For S. R. Gardiner's Atlas I have nothing but praise. The maps contain precisely the information a student most desires. They are well executed, and the Index leaves little to be desired."
—Prof. Edward Channing, Cambridge, Mass.

TRINITY COLLEGE.

"It is a very real pleasure to be able to express one's opinion about a work as well conceived, as carefully prepared, and beautifully executed, as this is. It will be of the greatest use to students of English history, and I shall be glad to recommend it most earnestly."—Prof. Henry Ferguson, Hartford, Conn.

SMITH COLLEGE.

". . . It seems to me admirable and comprehensive, yet free from that confusion which comes from over-crowding maps with names. I am sure that all teachers and students, not only of English but also of European history, will find the atlas of the greatest value. I shall cordially recommend it to my own classes."—Prof. Eleanor L. Lord, Northampton, Mass.

DARTMOUTH COLLEGE.

"Gardiner's 'Atlas of English History' is altogether the best volume of the sort."—Prof. Charles F. Richardson, Hanover, N. H.

UNIVERSITY OF MICHIGAN.

". . . It has already been recommended to our classes in English history."—Prof. Richard Hudson, Ann Arbor, Mich.

AMHERST COLLEGE.

"I am very much pleased with the copy of Gardiner's 'Atlas of English History.'"—Prof. Anson D. Morse, Amherst, Mass.

BOWDOIN COLLEGE.

"It is *excellent*—a thoroughly satisfactory piece of work—and remarkably cheap for what it contains."—Prof. D. Collin Wells, Brunswick, Me.

UNIVERSITY OF VIRGINIA.

"I am delighted with it and have recommended it to my class in English history."—Prof. Richard H. Dabney, Virginia.

"They form an almost ideal series for their purpose, thus making it possible to trace the whole course of political change and development, from Roman times down through England, and almost the whole of Europe. . . . For school and general student use these are far and away the most convenient and useful mediæval and modern history series of low priced maps we can name."—*The Independent.*

LONGMANS, GREEN, & CO., 15 East Sixteenth Street, New York.

A HISTORY OF GREECE from the Earliest Times to the Death of Alexander the Great.

By C. W. C. OMAN, M.A., F.S.A., etc. *Revised and Enlarged.* With 12 Maps and Plans, Side Notes, and Full Index. 12mo. $1.50.

* *This book appears in the Harvard, and other college Catalogues, as indicating the requirements for admission to college in Greek History.*

UNIVERSITY OF MICHIGAN.

" The best single volume of the History of Greece published."
—Prof. RICHARD HUDSON, Ann Arbor.

VASSAR COLLEGE.

" It seems to me a most admirable book—by far the best school history of Greece in existence."—Prof. HERBERT E. MILLS, Poughkeepsie.

BREARLEY SCHOOL, NEW YORK.

" Very good, pleasing and readable. The early chapters excel all other school histories I know. The geography and ethnology are well done."
—JAMES G. CROSWELL, New York.

EMORY AND HENRY COLLEGE.

" I have given Oman's Greece a running examination, and find it fresh and accurate, well arranged and well printed. It is what I wanted, just about the size and grade. So I have directed our bookseller to order copies for immediate use in my class."—Prof. GEORGE W. MILES, Emory, Va.

" This is the best school history of Greece which has appeared for many a day. While the style is never heavy, nothing of importance has been omitted. The book is, moreover, not a mere summary of larger histories; it gives proof of independent judgment, and it passes beyond earlier books in finding room for the most recent information derived from archæological discoveries."—*English Historical Review.*

" It possesses what no other of them has, so far as we know, freshness and liveliness, in spite of its brevity. This is due to the author's unerring skill in making the right selection, and choosing for notice the point which holds in it the life of the history—a great, and among the people who make school books, a rare merit."—*The Independent*, New York.

" It compares in scope and extent with the Students' Smith. . . . The style is fresh and remarkably interesting, considering the unavoidable condensation of matter. . . . It is full of those minute facts and touches which give life to a narrative. The young student will read it with ease and will rise from it with clearer ideas on some topics than can be obtained from the respectable manual we have mentioned."—*The Nation*, N. Y.

" It is composed of so clear and attractive a style, and it has been so carefully conformed to the latest discoveries in archæology, that it deserves the attention of readers on both sides of the Atlantic.—*Literary World*, Boston.

* *For other books treating on Greek History, see Longmans, Green, & Co's Catalogue of Educational Works.*

LONGMANS, GREEN, & CO., 15 East Sixteenth Street, New York.

A HANDBOOK IN OUTLINE OF THE POLITICAL HISTORY OF ENGLAND TO 1887. Chronologically arranged.

By A. H. DYKE ACLAND, M.P., Honorary Fellow of Balliol College, Oxford, and CYRIL RANSOME, M.A., Professor of Modern Literature and History, Yorkshire College, Victoria University. Third Edition, Revised, with Index. Crown 8vo. 333 pages. $2.00.

This is a college class-book for students engaged in the study of English Political History. It is used at Harvard and in other universities and colleges.

A PRIMER OF THE ENGLISH CONSTITUTION AND GOVERNMENT, for the Use of Colleges, Schools, and Private Students.

By SHELDON AMOS, M.A. Crown 8vo. 262 pages. $1.75.

ESSAYS INTRODUCTORY TO THE STUDY OF ENGLISH CONSTITUTIONAL HISTORY.

By Resident Members of the University of Oxford. Edited by HENRY OFFLEY WAKEMAN, M.A., Fellow of All Souls College, and Tutor of Keble College, and ARTHUR HASSALL, M.A., Student and Tutor of Christ Church. Crown 8vo. $2.25.

THE ELEMENTS OF ENGLISH CONSTITUTIONAL HISTORY from the Earliest Times to the Present Day.

By F. C. MONTAGUE, M.A., Professor of History, University College, London, late Fellow of Oriel College, Oxford. 12mo. 254 pages. $1.25.

"This book is designed to give such an account of the growth of English institutions as may be intelligible to those who are beginning to read history. So far as the writer knows there is no other book which aims precisely at this object."
—*Extract from Preface.*

A SHORT HISTORY OF ENGLAND, FROM THE EARLIEST TIMES TO THE PRESENT DAY. With Tables, Plans, Maps, Index, etc.

By CYRIL RANSOME, M.A., Professor of Modern Literature and History, Yorkshire College, Victoria University. Crown 8vo. 518 pages. $1.50.

*** *For other text-books on the History of England, see Longmans, Green, & Co.'s Catalogue of Educational Works.*

LONGMANS, GREEN, & CO., 15 East Sixteenth Street, New York.

YOUNG FOLKS'
HISTORY OF THE UNITED STATES.

BY

THOMAS WENTWORTH HIGGINSON.

With Maps and Illustrations, an Appendix covering a List of Books for Consultation, Constitution of the United States, Chronological Table, Index, and a Series of Questions. 12mo, price, $1.00 *net*.

The distinctive character of the book is that it sets before the mind of the student a clear idea of what the people of the United States have been from their first settlement on this continent to the present day. Names and dates are not considered by the author to be of importance, save in so far as they serve to make fully definite the thread of connected incident.

Again, less than the usual space is devoted to the events of war, and more to the affairs of peace. In this manner, two of the main objections to a condensed school history of the United States are obviated, and the mind of the youthful student, instead of being burdened with dry chronological tables, lists of names, and statistics of battles and sieges, gains a clear and philosophical view of the causes which have produced our American civilization.

The author does not consider it beneath the dignity of history to enliven his narrative with illustrative traits and incidents taken from the daily life of the people.

The book is a history of the *people themselves* in their normal state of peace, their development into an independent nation, their progress in all the arts of life, their struggles with nature in reclaiming the wilderness as a habitation for man, and their striving toward a higher and nobler form of social and political constitution—these points are on every page of the history made salient, consummate literary skill being added to profound original research.

LONGMANS, GREEN, & CO., Publishers,

15 EAST SIXTEENTH STREET, NEW YORK.

SUPPLEMENTARY READING.

YOUNG FOLKS'
BOOK OF AMERICAN EXPLORERS.

BY

THOMAS WENTWORTH HIGGINSON.

12mo. With Illustrations. Price, $1.20 *net.*

The work may also be had in 8 parts, each complete in itself, with illustrations. Paper, price, 15 cents *net*, each part.

1. THE LEGENDS OF THE NORTHMEN.
   COLUMBUS AND HIS COMPANIONS.
2. CABOT AND VERRAZZANO.
   THE STRANGE VOYAGE OF CABEZA DE VACA.
3. THE FRENCH IN CANADA.
   ADVENTURES OF DE SOTO.
4. THE FRENCH IN FLORIDA.
   SIR HUMPHREY GILBERT.
5. THE LOST COLONIES OF VIRGINIA.
   UNSUCCESSFUL NEW ENGLAND SETTLEMENTS.
6. CAPTAIN JOHN SMITH.
   CHAMPLAIN ON THE WAR-PATH.
7. HENRY HUDSON AND THE NEW NETHERLANDS.
8. THE PILGRIMS AT PLYMOUTH.
   THE MASSACHUSETTS BAY COLONY.

BY THE SAME AUTHOR:

HINTS ON WRITING AND SPEECHMAKING. 18mo, cloth, 50 cents.

SHORT STUDIES OF AMERICAN AUTHORS. 12mo, boards, 30 cents *net.*

LONGMANS, GREEN, & CO., Publishers,
15 EAST SIXTEENTH STREET, NEW YORK.

Thomas W. Higginson's Works.

THE NEW WORLD AND THE NEW BOOK. 12mo, $1.50.
"It may be said of this address and the following brief essays that one and all are devoted to creating in this country a modest and reasonable national self-respect. They are full of grace, sense, and scholarship, the delightful literary workmanship always so marked features in this author's work."—*Providence Journal.*

TRAVELLERS AND OUTLAWS. EPISODES IN AMERICAN HISTORY. 12mo, $1.50.
Apart from their historical value these sketches have all the delightful qualities of Colonel Higginson's literary style.

OUT-DOOR PAPERS. 16mo, $1.50.
"The chapters on 'Water Lilies,' 'The Life of Birds,' and 'The Procession of Flowers' are charming specimens of a poetic faculty in description, combined with a scientific observation and analysis of nature."—*London Patriot.*

MALBONE: AN OLDPORT ROMANCE. 16mo, $1.50.
"As a 'romance' it seems to us the most brilliant that has appeared in this country since Hawthorne (whom the author in some points has the happiness to resemble) laid down the most fascinating pen ever held by an American author."—JOHN G. SAXE.

ARMY LIFE IN A BLACK REGIMENT. 16mo, $1.50.
"His narratives of his works and adventures, in 'The Atlantic Monthly,' attracted general attention by their graphic humor and their picturesque and poetical descriptions."—*London Spectator.*

ATLANTIC ESSAYS. 16mo, $1.50.
"A book which will most assuredly help to raise the standard of American literature. Mr. Higginson's own style is, after Hawthorne's, the best which America has yet produced."—*Westminster Review.*

OLDPORT DAYS. With 10 heliotype illustrations. 16mo, $1.50.
"Mr. Higginson's 'Oldport Days' have an indescribable charm. The grace and refinement of his style are exquisite. His stories are pleasant; his pictures of children and his talk about them are almost pathetic in their tenderness; but in his descriptions of nature he is without a rival."—*Boston Daily Advertiser.*

COMMON SENSE ABOUT WOMEN. 16mo, $1.50.
"A thoroughly good and practical book, from the pen and heart of Thomas Wentworth Higginson. If one of its short chapters could be read aloud every day during the year in the millions of homes in the land, its power for good could scarcely be over-estimated."—*Chicago Inter-Ocean.*

YOUNG FOLKS' HISTORY OF THE UNITED STATES. Square 16mo. With maps and over 100 illustrations. $1.00 *net.*
"This book is for American youth what Dickens's 'History of England' is for the children of our cousins beyond the sea. Like it, it is so clear and charmingly written that it is scarcely fair to call it a 'Young Folks' History'; for we are sure that the old as well as the young will read it. Members of the C. L. S. C. may take it, instead of the book required, if they so desire."—J. H. VINCENT, D.D., *President Chautauqua Literary and Scientific Circle.*

YOUNG FOLKS' BOOK OF AMERICAN EXPLORERS.
Illustrated. 16mo, $1.20 *net.*

SHORT STUDIES OF AMERICAN AUTHORS. 12mo, boards, 30 cents *net.*

WENDELL PHILLIPS. Contributed to "The Nation" by T. W. HIGGINSON. Quarto, paper, 25 cents.

THE MONARCH OF DREAMS. Cloth, 50 cents.

HINTS ON WRITING AND SPEECH-MAKING. Cloth, 50 cents.

Sold by all booksellers, or sent by mail, post-paid, on receipt of price.

LONGMANS, GREEN, AND CO., Publishers, New York.

www.ingramcontent.com/pod-product-compliance
Lightning Source LLC
Chambersburg PA
CBHW030408230426
43664CB00007BB/794